THE PHILOSOPHY OF PAUL RICOEUR

An Anthology of His Work

THE PHILOSOPHY OF

Paul Ricoeur

An Anthology of His Work

Edited by Charles E. Reagan & David Stewart

BEACON PRESS : BOSTON

Copyright © 1978 by Charles E. Reagan and David Stewart

Beacon Press books are published under the auspices
of the Unitarian Universalist Association

Simultaneous publication in casebound and paperback editions

Published simultaneously in Canada by
Fitzhenry & Whiteside Limited, Toronto

Printed in the United States of America

(hardcover)   9   8   7   6   5   4   3   2   1
(paperback)   9   8   7   6   5   4   3   2   1

The article by Paul Ricoeur, "Philosophy of Will and Action,"
reprinted from *Phenomenology of Will and Action*, edited by
Erwin W. Straus and Richard M. Griffith, by permission of
Duquesne University Press © 1967, by Duquesne University.

Library of Congress Cataloging in Publication Data

Ricoeur, Paul.
   The philosophy of Paul Ricoeur.
   Bibliography: p.
   Includes index.
   1. Philosophy—Collected works.   I. Reagan,
Charles E.   II. Stewart, David, 1938-
B2430.R552E5 1978   194   77-15602
ISBN 0-8070-1516-4
ISBN 0-8070-1517-2 (pbk.)

Contents

Editors' Preface   vii

I   **Philosophy of the Will**   **1**

1. The Unity of the Voluntary and the Involuntary as a Limiting Idea   3

2. The Antinomy of Human Reality and the Problem of Philosophical Anthropology   20

3. The Hermeneutics of Symbols and Philosophical Reflection   36

II   **Existential Phenomenology**   **59**

4. Philosophy of Will and Action   61

5. Existential Phenomenology   75

6. From Existentialism to the Philosophy of Language   86

III   **Language and Hermeneutics**   **95**

7. Existence and Hermeneutics   97

8. Structure, Word, Event   109

9. Creativity in Language   120

10. Metaphor and the Main Problem of
Hermeneutics   134

11. Explanation and Understanding   149

IV   **Freud and Psychoanalysis**   **167**

12. A Philosophical Interpretation of Freud   169

13. The Question of Proof in Freud's Psychoanalytic
Writings   184

V   **Religion and Faith**   **211**

14. The Critique of Religion   213

15. The Language of Faith   223

16. Listening to the Parables of Jesus   239

Notes   247

Selected Bibliography   255

Index   257

Editor ' Preface

This anthology presents both a topical and a chronological view of the work of Paul Ricoeur. Included are selections which give the central themes of Ricoeur's early phenomenology of the will as well as his most recent study on Freud and on the Explanation/Understanding debate. The anthology also represents Ricoeur's enormously wide philosophical interests, from psychoanalysis, linguistics, and the philosophy of language to writings on religious language and biblical exegesis.

We were led to edit this collection by our desire to have something suitable to recommend to our colleagues who wanted to sample some of Ricoeur's work and by the need for an inexpensive text which would allow our students to read widely in his philosophy. We hope that the present book will fulfill both of these concerns.

As one of our criteria of selection, we preferred longer, but of course, fewer essays. Ricoeur's typical style is a dialectic which requires him to describe two apparently irreconcilable positions and then to find a way of mediating them. This cannot be shown in short snippets. Secondly, because his work is so difficult to excerpt, we have chosen Ricoeur's own precis of his major works. These selections stand on their own even while giving the essence of the main arguments of his longer books. In addition, we have chosen articles where Ricoeur makes a substantial contribution to the understanding of a current philosophical debate, such as essays on structuralism, philosophy of language, psychoanalysis, and religion.

We are especially pleased to be able to include Ricoeur's recent article, "Explanation and Understanding," which was translated into English expressly for this volume. We would also like to mention "The

Question of Proof in Freud's Psychoanalytic Writings,'' which represents Ricoeur's current thought on Freud.

Finally, we acknowledge our gratitude to Paul Ricoeur, our teacher and our friend, for allowing us to reprint some of his work, especially for the two articles mentioned above. We thank David Pellauer for his advice and assistance. Thanks also to Luna Carne-Ross, Beacon Press's managing editor, for her kindness, encouragement, and help.

PART I   Philosophy
of the Will

I. PHILOSOPHY OF THE WILL

The selections in this section are Ricoeur's summaries of the three parts thus far published of his Philosophie de la volonté. *"The Unity of the Voluntary and the Involuntary as a Limiting Idea" presents the argument for the reciprocity of freedom and necessity which Ricoeur developed in* Freedom and Nature. *"The Antinomy of Human Reality and the Problem of Philosophical Anthropology" takes up again the problem of man's finitude, "the intimate disproportion of man with himself," which is the fundamental theme of* Fallible Man. *Finally, "The Hermeneutics of Symbols and Philosophical Reflection" is both a summary of* The Symbolism of Evil *and a hint of possible directions Ricoeur will follow in the last part of his philosophy of the will.*

SOURCES

"The Unity of the Voluntary and the Involuntary as a Limiting Idea" first appeared in the *Bulletin de la Société française de Philosophie* 45 (1951): 1–29, and is used by permission. The translation is by Daniel O'Connor and is used with his permission; it appeared in *Readings in Existential Phenomenology*, edited by Nathaniel Lawrence and Daniel O'Connor (New York: Prentice-Hall, 1976).

"The Antinomy of Human Reality and the Problem of Philosophical Anthropology," *Il Pensiero* 5 (1960):273–90. The translation is by Daniel O'Connor, *Readings in Existential Phenomenology*. Used by permission of *Il Pensiero* and Daniel O'Connor.

"The Hermeneutics of Symbols and Philosophical Reflection," translated by Denis Savage, *International Philosophical Quarterly* 2 (1962):191–218. Used by permission.

CHAPTER 1

The Unity of the Voluntary and the

Involuntary as a Limiting Idea

In the particular case of the phenomenology of the will it seems to me
that the study of the articulations between the voluntary and the involuntary moments of consciousness is constantly oriented by the ideal
of the unity of the human person. It is very striking that it should be
precisely the great dualisms of history which have most prized this
unity, as if dualism were the philosophical test one had to pass through
in order to conquer the true meaning of unity. Thus Plato strives to
overcome the ascetic dualism of the *Phaedo* in a higher ontological
unity, as one sees in the *Timaeus* and the *Philebus*. Thus also, Descartes strives to overcome the methodological dualism of the *Second
Meditation* in the concrete and practical unity of the person described
in the *Sixth Meditation* and in the *Treatise on the Passions*. Once again,
Kant wishes to overcome the opposition between practical reason and
sensibility in the *summum bonum* at the end of the *Critique of Practical Reason*. The great philosophies seem then to be caught up in a
rhythmic cycle in which a defeat by dualism gives way to a victory over
dualism.

   Without making any preliminary claims about the ontological meaning of this double movement, the phenomenology of the voluntary and
the involuntary encounters it again in its own fashion under the title
of exigence and regulation. In return, the description of the reciprocity
between the voluntary and the involuntary and the functions in which
this reciprocity is expressed allow the clarification under a new light
of this unity and duality of man. The purpose of this essay is, then,
to show how the study of the reciprocity of the voluntary and the involuntary can revitalize the classical problem of the relations between

"freedom" and "nature," by proposing between them a "practical mediation."

I

The dualism which phenomenology encounters on its own terrain and from which it must ceaselessly rescue itself proceeds from those very attitudes of consciousness following out its own life. It is therefore not yet an ontological dualism, but, if one can put it that way, preliminary to any ontology, preontological. As a matter of fact, the concrete life of consciousness undergoes the pull of two opposing requirements.

On the one hand, an objective thought is elaborated, i.e., a thought which posits objects valid for all in a world not tied to any particular perspective, hence a thought which passes over itself as consciousness in order that there should be objects. This objective thought, however, has as its first effect the treatment of the life of the body and the whole range of involuntary life as a part of this objective world. In this manner is born, legitimately, a scientific biology and psychology. And it is necessary to say that, to the extent that my bodily and involuntary life is for me confused, enigmatic, and sometimes even foreign, there is every invitation to relegate it thus to the realm of things.

On the other hand, consciousness, recoiling from its objects, tends to identify its own life, recognized in all its concrete thickness, with self-consciousness and to exile itself thus in its capacity for reflection. One must say, however, that this tendency, too, is inscribed in the very structure of consciousness; we see it clearly in the Cartesian *cogito;* the philosophy of Descartes shows well enough how these two movements are interdependent, namely, the consolidation of an objective world not tied to any consciousness, and its polar opposite, the reduction of consciousness to self-consciousness.

To understand the reciprocity of the voluntary and the involuntary is to battle at every level against the dualism which issues from such postures of consciousness and consequently to replace these postures by a more fundamental one: on the one hand, we must pass beyond self-consciousness and see consciousness as adhering to its body, to all its involuntary life and, through them, to a world of action; passing beyond, on the other hand, the objectification of this involuntary life, we must recover all this life in consciousness, under the form of motives of the will, of organs and of situation for the will. In short, we must reintegrate consciousness in the body and the body in consciousness.

II

Let us begin by following the first direction, that of a second reflection on the reflective aspects of willing.

5 The Unity of the Voluntary and the Involuntary

The three aspects which description reveals as complementary—to decide, to move, to consent—can be arranged indifferently in any order if one considers them only from a descriptive point of view; but they appear in a progressive order if one considers them from the point of view of a "practical mediation." A decision still maintains a certain distance from action, which alone actually incorporates the will into things. (It makes little difference that no delay separates decision from action; the vague intention which runs through a "guided automatism" can be recognized as voluntary after a blow only because I can resume it as the virtual project of a delayed action.)

1. We begin then with an analysis of decision. For reflection, decision culminates in the determination of self by oneself: I make up my own mind (*Je me décide*), it is I *who* determine myself and myself *whom* I determine. The pronominal form of speaking underlines very well this relation at once active and reflective of the self on itself. Furthermore, this reflective judgment is by no means artificial; it suffices that I shoulder the responsibility for my acts or that I accuse myself of them in order that this reflected imputation of myself should stand out in my consciousness. Indeed, if I go to the bottom of this reflective movement, I discover my possibility of being myself which continually precedes and repeats itself in the agony of the "could-be." We must orient our analysis in a direction counter to this reflective separation which is itself symmetrical with the objectifying of my body. In fact, the reflective imputation of myself is a complication of a prereflective imputation, hidden at the heart of my projects. A decision runs toward the future and it is in this intentional aim, in the "willed" object or project that the discreet reference to myself is hidden. I determine *myself* to the extent that I determine myself *to*. . . . In fact, decision specifies in outline a future action as my own action, as an action lying within my power. I project myself into the action to be done, I designate myself—if I may use the expression—in the accusative case as an aspect of the project; I involve myself in the very design of the action to be done; and this imputed self is not yet a true "Ego," but the veiled presence of my powers, themselves unrealized and projected, apprehended in the shape of the action, which will occur. So, before any reflective judgment—of the type "it is I who . . ." there is a pre-predicative consciousness of self which is enough to hold the intention of my projects in readiness for reflection. It will suffice that I assume an attitude toward these projects in order to privilege the relation of the self to itself implied in the volitive intention. We are thus led to subordinate the reflective moment of the will to its intentional moment: in willing I am first turned out toward a "something to be done," specified in outline as a practical meaning, having a categorical modality different from that of wish or desire, and a future temporal dimension different

from that of anticipation. In this sense the first possibility opened up by willing is not my own "could-be" but the incidental possibility that I open in the world by projecting an action; it is the "can-be-done" aimed at the world itself, that world which always remains on the horizon of my choice as the field of operation for my freedom.

But in its turn the project musters my existence in a given moment only because it takes root in some way in my involuntary life. There is no decision without a motive: I decide this because. . . . There is an original bond between an initiative and a pursuit of lawfulness; there is, as Jean Nogué says, a dialectic of impetus and rest which is very difficult to respect. This bond supposes, to be sure, that I no longer confuse motive and cause. The motive is precisely that which inclines the will by depicting for it a good (at least a good for me, here and now); it is therefore purely reciprocal to a will which receives it, invokes it, and bases itself upon it. Thus, motivation expresses very clearly in this first moment of my decision one of the hinges of the voluntary and the involuntary. By contrast, a cause—as opposed to a motive—pertains to the objective sphere and is related to the naturalistic explanation of things. Here for the first time we touch upon "practical mediation": motive and project are, in fact, strictly reciprocal in this sense that the developing of my choice and the maturing of my reasons are one and the same thing. For example, for a hesitating consciousness there is a wavering motivation which accompanies a wavering project, and I fulfill my designs in fulfilling my reasons.

Within the will there is inscribed a particular receptivity which one has no right to confuse with a simple passivity. And, anticipating a bit of what follows, one can say already that it is by this receptivity that the artificial opposition between value and freedom can be overcome, because I encounter values only in a process of motivation, and because there is no motive outside of the reciprocal relation with an emerging decision. On the one side, I have to say that it is of the essence of a volition to try to find supporting reasons; but in its turn this special receptivity by which any value appears to me is inseparable from a consciousness which gropes toward a choice. If it is thus of the essence of a volition that it legitimate itself in motives which make values emerge for me here and now, it is, reciprocally, of the essence of these values that they emerge only as possible motives for a decision which fulfills their meaning by grounding itself on them.

When we have seen, presently, how my involuntary life transcends itself precisely in an affective representation of values, we will have observed in some fashion both sides of this "practical mediation."

2. The study of voluntary motion, as I announced it a moment ago, marks from the point of view of practical mediation an advance beyond

decision, since it annuls this distance from things, this species of unreality from the design or project. We should say that "to decide" has the meaning of "to designate in outline" what I am to do; and that "to act" is "to realize it in full," fleshing it out in movement, carrying out my project. There is then between action and intention an identity of meaning which permits me to say: that is what I willed, or else: I did not will that; the difference is not in the meaning, but in some way in the emptiness and the fullness of that meaning; and gestures are by that token beyond discourse. Or, more exactly, the only thing I can say about my acting is precisely the intention which my acting comes to carry out; but the gesture as such is no longer a *logos,* or more exactly, no longer a *lectón,* but the present state of the act, the very advance of my existence on the bodily front.

Let us attempt to apply to the lived experience of "action" this same probing below the most deliberate kind of experience, which is a product of reflection. In fact, this second voluntary moment normally rises to the level of consciousness only under the deliberate repetition of effort. What we are trying to recover is in some sense that voluntary movement which is animating the bodily spontaneity without any effort. But this is difficult because the whole psychology of will tends to center around the moment of effort in which the will is known in its opposition to bodily resistance, in the same way that, a moment ago, the prereflective imputation of the self tended to culminate in a deliberate affirmation or determination of the self by itself.

And here, too, it will turn out that effort is the complication of a nonreflective willing which goes directly to the things themselves. In fact, the complete intention of acting is not the body, but through it a project in the world. (We will come back in a moment to the meaning of "through it.") I do not, for example, "move my arm," I "write a letter." I would say that what has been acted out as such, the *pragma,* is the action passively performed against the background of the world. In order to analyze correctly this intentional structure of an action, it would be necessary to say: "I do my-writing-on-the-paper" emphasizing the *sui generis* character of the auxiliary verb "to do"; but what remains outside the scope of the auxiliary is the entire intentional correlate of the doing. There is an analysis of the structure of this *pragma* for which the excellent analyses of Tolman and certain of the Behaviorists are quite usable; following them one can recover in the complement of acting, in this *pragma,* all the practical articulations of signals, means, ways, tools. Acting would then appear stretched between the "I" as willing and the world as field of action, it being well understood here that, before any reflexivity of the effort upon itself, the "I" is at this stage only the will's act of going beyond itself into the features of the world construed as a field of labor and, moreover, a field already being worked; my task always stands out as a figure on the ground of a world of action which appears to me not as a spectacle, but truly as a tangled practical complex, constantly requiring me to adopt a posture for myself and my body.

But, in this practical relation to work in process of accomplishment and to the world as theatre of action, the body is "passed through"; this means that the body is not the object of acting, it is not *what* I do, but the organ of what I do. This noninstrumental relation of the organ to the acting can be detected in habitual movements performed with dexterity and grace. In order to see this, attention must be shifted from the *pragma,* from the work in process of accomplishment, to the organ which I use. Such an upsurge of the body in my field of attention is exactly reciprocal to and contemporary with the upsurge of effort in the center of my consciousness. We see thus how the body normally reveals its mediating function only by its intractability. This is the moment when the movement, complicated by the awareness of a resistance, is reflected in the effort. But at the same time we have a paradoxical situation from the descriptive point of view, since action has its full sense only when the will forgets itself by reason of its intentional involvements in its work, only when the mediating function of the body effaces itself, gets ahead of itself, in some way transcends itself in the work passively accomplished. Thus reflection, which ought to bring into clear consciousness the whole structure of the relation "act-organ-work," is already in the process of transforming the situation and disrupting the practical mediation. As soon as I notice the organ of acting and as soon as the acting reflects itself in effort, I have already relapsed into a nascent dualism; consciousness already begins to take stock of itself in effort, and the body having been reduced to the pole of resistance, is construed as an objective being. This is why one can only practice here a sort of reflection on reflection which gives some inkling of the original bond between the acting will, the moved body, and the world acted upon.

3.   At this point the analysis must be reopened, for an experience, even one of action, i.e., the experience of a voluntary force which has begun to deploy itself in the body, has as its constant counterpart a background of invincible nature, necessity. Let us go straight to the most subtle forms of necessity, not those which are external as when I collide with a piece of furniture I am not able to move, but rather those which are involved in the very exercise of will: this means primarily the partiality of my motives, the partiality of my action. This partiality, which constitutes each individual's character, far from merely occurring in a scale of values, is rather the unique perspective from which all value appears; far from being changeable, character is always the original formula of my effectiveness.

The unconscious, in its turn, is always the background of my biography which I cannot put on the same level as transparent consciousness and which, moreover, I cannot reach without the mediation of a third person who must interpret it for me before I can reintegrate it into my field of consciousness.

Finally, to be living—that is to say, to be organized, to grow according to a sort of vital "impetus," irrepressible and irreversible, to be born and descended from a particular set of forebears—all that constitutes a vital fundamental situation which is the background of every decision and of every action, as the condition and even the limitation of the *cogito.*

It is precisely in the face of the necessity both outside and inside myself that my consciousness tends to recoil upon itself, to make a circle with itself, in order to expel outside, into an empirical subject which it is supposed to constitute, these limitations of character, unconsciousness, and life-situation. By this act of expulsion, reflection tends to posit itself as a universal constituting ego, which is supposed to transcend the limitations of the empirical subject.

Thus emerges the moment of implicit refusal in reflection, the refusal of the human condition. One sees the point of this refusal in the threefold wish of absolute consciousness: the wish to be total, that is, without the finite perspective associated with a particular character; the wish to be transparent in the perfect correspondence of self-consciousness with intentional consciousness; the wish to be self-sufficient, without the necessity for being dependent on the nutritive and healing wisdom of the body which always precedes the will.

At bottom, the desire of reflective consciousness is that it should be immune from any passion of the soul; it wishes to regard itself as pure act. It seems to me that self-sufficiency is the supreme desire of reflecting consciousness.

The third moment of willing acquires hereby its meaning: it is a revival of that tendency of consciousness to posit itself as a constituted empirical subject and a revival of the refusal of the human condition harbored in that desire. If consent were possible, the unity of man would be achieved; that is why consent is the culminating point of this second reflection oriented toward the coincidence of will and its concrete condition. If consent were possible, it would be this endurance with respect to the involuntary self, not the theoretical representation of objective necessity, but rather the active adoption of the necessity which I am, something like a "fact" which would end in that which is, something like a movement which ends in the immovable. Thus, by joining itself to the necessity of its nature, freedom would convert it into itself.

A further consideration will assure us, later on, that this limit can never be attained.

We must now consider the second movement of thought, by which I attempt to recapture the meaning of my involuntary life as my own, before the interpretation of that involuntary life as a realm of objects, correlative to a scientific consciousness.

I cannot insist here on the methodological difficulties of the enterprise. I will simply recall a few points, and first the one that dominates everything: the reconciliation of the voluntary and the involuntary presupposes that they confront each other in the same universe of discourse. I cannot therefore treat the will in a style of subjectivity and the involuntary in a style of empirical objectivity; a homogeneous treatment of the problem requires that I reconquer in all its fullness the experience of "I think," by integrating in it the meanings "I need to...," "I am in the habit of...," "I can," "I live," and in a general fashion all my existence as body.

I want to add to this first remark three others which respond to three possible difficulties. Are we then to go back simply to the testimony of private and incomparable experience? By no means: "My body" is also body in the second person; to the extent that introspection can remain the prisoner of a sort of naturalness of consciousness, just so far can, in return, comprehension of the other in his body become, if I may use the expression, denaturalized. By *subjectivity* I mean the subject function of an intentional consciousness, such that I understand it as applying to me and to others; thanks to this mutual elaboration of knowledge of self and other, I arrive at true concepts of subjectivity, valid for man, my fellow. And that is why the phenomenology of the lived body is a phenomenology of intersubjectivity.

One will still object that the return to the subject—be it you or me—marks a relapse in comparison with the victories of scientific psychology: what I know has more value than what I feel. Let it be well understood that there is no intention of dismissing empirical knowledge of the voluntary; on the contrary, such knowledge ought to help, momentarily, the diagnosis of self and other in the integral experience of the *cogito.* There would be no sense indeed in trying to relate an organic breakdown, say an alimentary one, objectively known, to a voluntary attitude; only the lived need can enter into a voluntary synthesis; by contrast, scientific knowledge of this need is the index of intentional functions to be thematized on the phenomenological plan. That is why the phenomenology of each epoch is in tension with the contemporaneous state of scientific psychology. By recognizing that a good phenomenology is always implied in a good psychology (as one sees in Tolman's behaviorism and particularly in Gestalt psychology), one is in a position to retain their descriptions before they relapse into a naturalistic explanation.

11 The Unity of the Voluntary and the Involuntary

Finally, it will be objected that I do not have access to my purely involuntary life, that I have lost the naïveté of felt experience, that I could not know what a given desire was unless I had begun to take up some attitude toward it. This objection should be faced in its radical form: There is no phenomenology of the purely involuntary, but only of the reciprocity of the voluntary and the involuntary; I apprehend the involuntary as the other pole of my life, affecting my will; in this sense I never grasp the multiplicity of the involuntary except in relation to the one will.

It is this last remark on method which will provide me henceforward with the guiding thread in the labyrinth of involuntary life. Each moment of voluntary life we described a moment ago—to decide, to act, to consent—reveals a reciprocal aspect of involuntary life and furnishes thus a principle of order in the treatment of the involuntary functions. We are thus led to decipher the involuntary-for-the-voluntary, that is in its relations to motivation and to motion, and as incoercible condition.

I would like to give some examples of this investigation of non-objectivated aspects of the involuntary, by placing myself at the point of view of the progressing practical mediation.

1. I said a moment ago that every decision admits of a receptive moment: I decide this because. . . . We gave the name *motivation* to this relation of the will to an intentional stream which inclines it. Resuming the analysis in reverse, we shall see, in the example of desire, how the body in some way nourishes motivation, and we shall see by which aspects desire is included in the field of motivation. (It should be well understood, desire is not the whole of the involuntary; nevertheless it would be possible to show—though I cannot undertake the task here—that the most abstract values pass through the whole breadth of the affective [scale] in order to solicit the will; for this reason I think that desire has an exemplary value for all motivation.)

Consider a man who undertakes a hunger strike or a man who explores the two poles or the deserts and takes no notice of cold or thirst in order to pursue his life-project. The sacrifice which he makes of his needs shows that he was able to weigh them against other values, and thus they lend themselves to an evaluation. We come thus to a crossroad and must take our bearings. The least need, such as hunger, pertains to the *cogito* in the sense that the opaque affectivity—the specified want, the oriented drive which is hunger, not knowing itself—finds in the representation of the absent thing and of the way to attain it a form, which is here an image-making form. What I am calling imagination, a sort of crossroads of formless affectivity and voluntary attitudes, is not yet the realm of fancy, an element of our cultural life (I mean the contradiction which we can oppose to the existing world), but a manner of anticipating an absent reality on the background of the world. By its militant and investigating character, this kind of imagination can mediate between need and will.

But that is not all: desire is not just the image-making anticipation of perceptive contours and qualities, of bread for example, but rather the image-making anticipation of pleasure itself. There is, of course, a difficulty; it is not easy to isolate this dimension of image-making affectivity; I apprehend the goodness of bread through a sensed affect, which is in some way the affective effigy or representative, the *analogon* of future pleasure. Yes, we are dealing here with an affective imagination which is already a kind of prereflective apprehension of value. We are still short of the reflected judgment of value (of the form: that is good); we are, however, already beyond the simple impression of a lack and even beyond the simple representation of an absent thing, the pure affect surpasses itself in becoming flesh—"the fullness," as Husserl says, of a mute evaluation: by means of the anticipated pleasure I believe in the goodness of bread, without yet affirming it, without judging it.

The same analysis could be made with other vital values: with sorrow, with the easy and the difficult, and even with all nonvital values, to the extent that they appear in affects, where they are delineated in image-making anticipations related to desire or to fear.

Whatever is the case with other examples, that of the most elementary need well illustrates the convergence of our two lines of analysis: on the one hand the will, in its least reflective and most receptive movements, is open to the suggestions of the involuntary; and, on the other hand, human affectivity, inasmuch as it is an established lack and the anticipation of satisfaction is, on its side, transfigured by an evaluative intention which raises our body to the level of a field of motivation. It is thus that the two aspects of our life can be put in balance with honor and friendship, as if, in this evaluation which has not yet crossed the threshold of discourse, of *logos,* our body had transcended itself to become the body of a man, the body of a self that wills.

2. We are going to consider now the second dimension of the involuntary, the one suggested by the analysis of action.

To be sure, the bodily involuntary is also something other than this kind of affective anticipation of good and of evil, something other than this image-making evaluation. Just as the project specifies in outline what is to be done, so the body too, in the example we considered a moment ago, negates itself in a sense by desire; it negates itself by participating in this nascent evaluation.

But the point is precisely that desire is still another thing: it is also nascent action. And it is here that desire rejoins, in some fashion, from below, the organic realization of the will in the act; it is thus the same reality that we read right side up or upside down. Indeed, we said a moment ago that action terminates in the things themselves "through" the body. The analysis of the involuntary has just added its own meaning to this mediation of the body; the phenomenology of the involuntary becomes the phenomenology of the power which the body offers to voluntary action.

I will say nothing here of those first rough outlines of motor activity which, from the beginning of life, give us a grip on things and an unreflective use of our body before all informed knowledge of it, and even before all apprenticeship of movement; and I will also say nothing of the reasons that permit us to distinguish this native know-how from reflexes. But I would like to insist on two properly human forms of involuntary action which, to my mind, illustrate well the fecundity of the method employed here and at the same time the general intentions of this study of the reciprocity of the voluntary and the involuntary: I am thinking of emotion and habit.

Indeed, it is striking to see that these two functions, emotion and habit, are understood by each other, by their contrast: the one is a nascent irregularity, the other affects my will by the power of what is acquired. Habit is "contracted," emotion "takes one by surprise": habit, being old, has prestige; emotion, being new, has power; habit is the fruit of what has endured, emotion is the irruption of the moment. But this contrast can be understood only if one knows how to recognize in each the properly human, involuntary aspect. That is why, taking emotion first, it is important not to be misled by the lessons of pathology, which draws the whole psychology of emotion from the side of sterile irregularities; instead one should try to surprise forms of emotion in which the irregularity is in a nascent state; Descartes saw this very clearly in his *Treatise on the Passions:* he does not draw emotion from a shock, but from a surprise; he describes it not as a crisis but as an incentive to act according to the lively representations which engender surprise. Only in this way is emotion intelligible: when it unhinges action by a spontaneity perilous for self-mastery; but if the will ought always to guard its integrity against this spontaneity, it is also through emotion that it moves its body, according to the famous formula: "The will moves by desire."

It seems to me, then, that one ought to interpret great emotional upheavals by starting from the emotion of surprise; this follows the trend of deterioration from a meaningful disorder to an incoherent disorder.

A psychology of emotion which begins with the latter necessarily lacks the involuntary meaning of emotion; and it is precisely because it obliterates this involuntary meaning that a naturalistic explanation can make itself appear inevitable. On the contrary, it is possible to pass in reverse from one to the other; for the incoherent disorder still has a meaning as waste product; it is typical of the *fragile* order of man: but it is still a disorder of *man.*

Habit requires an analysis of the same type: here also we must reject the primacy of automatisms just as we rejected that of shock-emotion, that is, if we would understand anything about habit, or the power of habitual gestures, knowledge, or tastes which we have contracted. It is the still pliant habit which has meaning; it is only this kind of habit which can illustrate the original bond between will and power. An automatism, in this respect, is not a return to a primitive stage, a simpler stage, but a degradation possible only to human habits. (It is a degradation whose threat is expressed in the very notions of "habit forming" and "breaking a habit.")

Our description ought then to show new aspects of the involuntary which correspond to the inciting power of emotion; the two most remarkable concern first, the coordination of an action both in its elements and in relation to regulating signals for the action and secondly, the facility which it offers to the activation of movement. The involuntary aspect of coordination and the involuntary aspect of facilitation exemplify very well what a power is. Our body offers itself to us as a moving totality of powers, of motor and affective structures, more or less flexible, more or less general, in the fashion of rules, transposable methods whose spontaneity is offered in some way to our will. It suffices to look at our familiar gestures in order to see how our body goes ahead on its own, trying out or inventing movements, either responding to our expectations or eluding them. In short, the body is a practical spontaneity, by turns emotive and habitual, which mediates our volitions. One must go still further: our acquisitions of knowledge themselves constitute a kind of body—a psychical body, if I may use the expression: through rules of grammar and calculation, through social and moral understanding, we think new objects and thus we activate our knowledge just as we activate our bodily powers. In both cases, the empty intention of the project finds in the naturalization of the will the instrument of its efficacy. According to the admirable intuition of Ravaisson in his little book *Habit,* the will operates through *frustrated* volitions just as through lively desires.

Thus, for the second time, we notice the converging movement of two lines of analysis: just as we have seen the will descend into bodily spontaneity and pass through it toward a task, so also, in the reverse sense, the meaning of the body is to make itself a human body, to the extent that it surmounts its presence to itself, its self-enclosure; and this it does in its powers, thus opening itself for practical use toward the world in accordance with the voluntary intentions of a man.

3. The two attempts which I have just made to recover the meaning of the body as motivating and as acting, condition the third step of this phenomenology of the involuntary, namely, rediscovering the stamp of subjectivity in necessity: my character, my unconscious, my life. I say that the previous attempt conditions the new step, for it is precisely in the exercise of my powers that I take unawares the provisions of nature which they are breaking away from. It is truly necessary that I understand my character as being mine, that I admit the partiality of my choices and motivation, the limited style of my efforts and my concrete action; I will not succeed in opposing it to my real self; it is not to be posited outside as an object, it is truly the constituted partiality of the concrete constituting self which I am; for this reason I describe this style as the limited mode of being of the voluntary and the involuntary.

And thus we cannot make of the style a function comparable to habit, to emotion, or to need; it is rather the very finitude of all these functions. This is not the place to show how the science of character—one that elaborates character as a definite empirical object which would be at one and the same time a class of properties, a possible type, and an analytic formula—acquires its full meaning only when it will permit a diagnosis of character which I am. This character is neither a class, a type, nor a formula, but rather the primordial narrowness of my existence. It is thus by a critique of the empirically constituted object—character—that I recover the vanishing meaning of character in the first person, the original character which I am. The unconscious of the psychoanalysts calls for a similar critique, but a critique which will retain the essentials of the psychoanalytic discoveries and also rediscover the stamp of subjectivity in the unconscious by liberating it from a naturalistic naïveté. I will even say that this critique is decisive for our research, for the considerable importance of psychoanalysis from the viewpoint of philosophy is to take us back to the fundamental fact that the impressions, the dispositions left in consciousness by lived experience, like stratifications of past consciousness, can be thus forbidden entry into my consciousness now, such that they simulate a second, psychologically autonomous, nature.

A moment ago our reflection on habit led us to something similar: the spontaneity of our acquired knowledge in some way sedimented in consciousness already simulates the independence of a second nature; psychoanalysis opens up a still more impressive situation, when the disrelated affective dispositions become inaccessible to me. Consciousness never reflects anything but the form of its actual thoughts; it never wholly penetrates a certain affective matter which gives it indefinite possibilities for self-questioning, for giving meaning, and yet for doubting all the meaning which it has built up on its own affects. If then we reject the Freudian mythology, it nevertheless remains true that reflective consciousness always remains inadequate to its own potentialities, which constitute a genuine first personal nature within me. The unconscious would allow us to sketch out a dialectic of definite form and indefinite content, just as a moment ago the idea of personality instigated an analogous dialectic of unlimited drive and limited style.

But nature's highest claim on me is my life-situation, which can hardly be revealed except by the mute consciousness of being alive, by a consciousness which modulates on the tonalities of well-being and discomfiture, on the feelings of growth and aging, and which loses its own traces in the dim memories of childhood. The consciousness of being alive can be clarified only through the biological sciences. But, in return, these sciences make us attentive to the most extreme moment of the involuntary, namely, the necessity which comes from living in a particular place, being born on a particular day. In this case, to exist no longer signifies an action but a state. I must be in a life-situation to be responsible for my life. More deeply, I should say that existence is both willed and endured. My act of existing and my state of existing are fused in the "I am." And it is only in this sense that I can say that the *cogito* as an act envelops the fact of existing; in this sense, I can say *cogito ergo sum;* but here *ergo* no longer designates an implication emerging from the realm of logic: it is the practical mediation itself, the pact, the connivance, which binds the consenting will to its situation, to the absolute involuntary element reasserted in its subjectivity.

IV

We have thus arrived at the point where our plan of recovering the unity of the voluntary and the involuntary seems about to succeed. But here, too, we encounter the point where the failure of the enterprise becomes most manifest and where all our analysis will be frustrated. This failure appears as soon as one tries to go beyond the plan of a simple articulation of meanings—meanings of will and desire, of acting and being able to act, of consenting and of personality-type—as soon as one tries to get closer to the concrete life of consciousness, to the existential development of an individual.

It would seem then that we have surmounted one form of dualism only to give rise to another more subtle and radical one. We have been totally opposed to the dualism of method, the dualism which opposes a reflective consciousness, caught up in a circular relation with itself, to an objectified involuntary life, leveled down to the status of a thing. We have called it a dualism of understanding because it is instigated by the very method by which consciousness interprets its own life and because it expresses the two directions of thought, the reflective direction which tends to a positing of the *cogito* by itself, and the direction of objectification which tends to absorb the body and all subjective life into the system of objects elaborated at the level of scientific consciousness.

But this dualism of understanding is motivated on a more radical plan: it is motivated by a duality of existence which routs a monism as well as any dualism. That is why we will speak of a "dramatic" or "polemical" *duality*. We will begin to recognize its peculiar status by rising from its most manifest aspects to its most dissimulated aspects; and consequently, by running through in reverse the three moments of the phenomenology of the voluntary and the involuntary. It is through a recognition of the failure of unity that the notion of a limiting idea will acquire all its meaning.

1.   Consent to necessity is never achieved. Who can accept himself without qualification, concretely, daily? It is here that suffering acquires its philosophical significance, as the impossibility of coincidence with oneself; it introduces into the self a specific negativity, in the sense that necessity is now lived not only as affecting, but as wounding: I am not at home in my own nature. That is why, in return, freedom remains the possibility of not accepting myself, of saying no to what is negating; consequently, the active denial of freedom arouses the diffuse negativity of my condition. And I do not understand by suffering only physical pain and interpersonal sorrows but also, at all levels of the involuntary, the sadness of aging, of being "overstretched" by time, of being misshapen, finished. With suffering, the mode of the failure of unity is the scandal.

Consent can therefore take responsibility for necessity only by the detour of a metaphysics of creation, which is not our subject here. Instead we shall recognize the existential split in the unity of the person at two other levels of the phenomenology of the voluntary and the involuntary, at the level of acting, then at the level of deciding.

2.   We have tried to understand the passage from will to power in its indivisibility. And certainly action is intelligible only insofar as it is one, apart from the dualism of thought and movement. But another sort of duality makes an interior division of this unity. In fact, voluntary motion is always a nascent effort, in the same measure that the spontaneity of the body is always a nascent resistance. Maine de Biran was fond of repeating, *Homo simplex in vitalitate, duplex in humanitate.* The voluntary life is a debate with the body. This concrete dialectic is expressed through the contrast between emotion and habit which we mentioned a moment ago. Incessantly, the will plays off one against the other; in some cases it profits from the surprise of emotion in order to rouse itself from the sleep of habit—and the whole *Treatise on the*

Passions of Descartes rests on this intuition of the synthesis of will and emotion in "generosity"—in other cases, the will works with the complicity of the pacifying function par excellence, habit—that is why, having said that will moves by desire, it is necessary to add that effort is a willed habit. Thus spontaneity is by turns organ and obstacle. In a sense, voluntary movement would be perfectly intelligible if the body effaced itself completely in its function as organ; but then there would be neither consciousness of movement nor consciousness of power. It is the unexpectedness of emotion which makes us attentive to the habits of the body and the acquired order of habit which makes us attentive to the disorder produced by emotion.

Thus the place of resistance in voluntary life appears in all its fullness; it is not solely external or muscular resistance, but the functional resistance of spontaneity which escapes me; therefore, the hold on my body is always to some degree a regained one. We are thus led to recognize that the unity of effort and spontaneity remains a limiting idea. Here the failure of unity is no longer a scandal for us, but rather a conflict.

3. Finally, our regressive movement leads us to the threshold of the voluntary act: indeed if we relocate the decision in time in order to understand its advance, if we witness the birth and development of a decision instead of considering its movements abstractly, the abstract relations which we considered at the outset between project, imputation, and motivation take on a certain life; one sees consciousness oscillate between hesitation and choice; once again, what we called a moment ago the existential split will emerge. This split is manifested in a descriptive and rather paradoxical situation, namely, that the occurrence of a choice can always be read in two different fashions; it is in one sense attention which fixes upon a group of motives: I make up my mind because I yield to this or that reason; but in another sense it is the upsurge of a new act: the final meaning of my reasons is that I so decide. But this double reading is inscribed in the very structure of a decision which, on the one hand, is an invention of the project and, on the other hand, a reception of values, an activity and a receptivity.

And this is no doubt why there have always been two philosophies of freedom: according to one, a choice is only the cessation of deliberation, the coming to rest of attention; M. Laporte has interpreted the philosophies of St. Thomas, Descartes, and Malebranche in this sense; according to the other, choice is an upsurge, an irruption of existence. Of course, one can always reconcile them theoretically by saying that abstractly it is the same thing to fix upon the reasons for a course of action and to choose it; but in the concrete life of consciousness these two readings do not correspond to the same situations; there are choices which tend toward a simple obedience to reasons not questioned at the moment of choice, and other choices which, in confusion of motives, tend toward a risk, even the throw of the dice. Pushing these two alternatives to an extreme, we would have on the one hand, the scruple in which the choice cannot emerge from a fruitless evaluation, on the other hand, the gratuitous act which is, strictly speaking, a choice without value. But these two possibilities always lie before me, and they reveal the tension inherent in a choice. For unity of these two it would be necessary for choice to satisfy at once both lawfulness and inventiveness, value and boldness of existing. A fine cleavage runs through our freedom precisely because it is active and receptive, because it is a human freedom and not a creative "fiat." And that is why I would say that the synthesis of lawfulness and inventiveness remains a limiting idea.

What are these limiting ideas? The sketch of an answer to this question may serve for a conclusion. We can see here an illustration of the regulative idea of Kant, that is the a priori requirement of unifying any field of inquiry whatever. But Kant puts this requirement solely with respect to the foundations of scientific knowledge. We should recover a similiar function for the regulative idea with respect to the originating phenomenological field. I will say then that there is a human ideal— a meaning for human unity which is the idea of a motivated, incarnate, contingent freedom.

I leave entirely to one side the relation of this limit to the idea of a creative freedom of which it is at once the image and the counterpart. I have only attempted here to consider the relation of this limiting idea of an achieved unity for man to the experience of the dramatic duality. The limiting idea is the guiding thread; it is this which makes the scandal, the conflict, and the tension only categories of the duality. But, on the other hand, we have no other access to the meaning of a unified person than the deciphering of the relations between the voluntary and the involuntary; it should be considered as the intentional unity toward which is aimed the experience of a dramatic duality.

In sum, I will say that what I understand about man is the synthesis of inventiveness and lawfulness, an agile will and a docile body, consent and necessity. In brief, what I understand is the unity; it is upon this background, on this horizon of unity that I see the dramatic duality of man. It would be necessary then to see how this unity is illustrated in stories and myths, as for example in the innocent, the dancer, the Orpheus of Rilke. But that would be another story.

CHAPTER 2

The Antinomy of Human Reality

and the Problem of Philosophical Anthropology

Philosophical anthropology has become an urgent task of contemporary thought because all the major problems of that thought converge on it and its absence is deeply felt. The sciences of man are dispersed into separate disciplines and literally do not know what they are talking about. The revival of ontology, for its part, raises the same question in its own way: who is this being for whom being is in question? Finally, the very "modernity" of man indicates the vacuum which this meditation must fill: if man can lose himself or find himself in labor, in pleasures, in politics, or in culture—what is man?

1. FROM PATHOS TO LOGIC

There can be no question of resolving the problem of philosophical anthropology in a few pages nor even of posing it in its full scope. But it is perhaps possible to choose a problem which is both specific enough and yet revelatory of the problem of philosophical anthropology as such.

The problem is the one I have placed at the center of my book on *Fallible Man:* the problem of the intimate disproportion of man with himself or the antinomical structure of man, suspended between a pole of infinitude and a pole of finitude. This problem is the modern form of the Platonic problem of the "intermediary," the *metaxú*, which is developed in Book IV of *The Republic* in relation to *thumos*. It is the same problem which turns up in Kant as the problem of "the third term" in relation to the transcendental imagination.

Why pose the problem of man as a being of the mean? For its value as an approach to one of the greatest difficulties of philosophy, the problem of evil. As Kant remarks in his "Essay on Radical Evil," there is something mysterious and perhaps inscrutable (*unerforschbar*) about the origin of evil. It might be necessary to say that to understand the problem would be to suppress it; but if evil is impenetrable as an event, perhaps there could be a preliminary understanding which could make clear its possibility. In other words, perhaps we can understand in what sense man is fallible. But fallibility is implied in the disproportion which makes man a fragile being. Disproportion, need for an intermediary, fragility, fallibility, make up a progression full of meaning. So Descartes at the beginning of his *Fourth Meditation* attests that man is "like a mean between being and nothingness" and he concludes: "if I consider myself as somehow participating in nothingness or nonbeing, that is, insofar as I am not myself the supreme being, I find myself exposed to an infinity of defects such that I should not be astonished if I go wrong."

What is the interest of reason in this problem? Two interests, one of doctrine, one of method.

The interest of doctrine: by using the problem of disproportion and an intermediary, a reformulation of the notion of finitude becomes possible. To put it in a formula, I doubt that the central concept of philosophical anthropology is finitude, it is rather the triad finitude-infinitude-intermediary. One should not begin therefore with the simple, for example, perception, but with the couple, perception and word; not with the limited but with the antinomy of limit and the unlimited. From this vantage point it becomes possible to detect something of the originally dialectical structure of human reality which is infinite position, negation of finitude, limitation (we thus rediscover something of the dialectic of the *Philebus:* "limit," "unlimited," "mixture," "cause," and also something of the Kantian progression of the categories of quality: "position," "negation," "limitation"). Hence the problem of the disproportion and the intermediary (*metaxú,* "third term") receives a considerable philosophical importance.

But the interest is also one of method, for philosophical anthropology finds itself confronted with a *prephilosophical* comprehension, based on pathos and myth, of the theme of the disproportion of man understood as a being in a milieu, fragile and fallible. Before the philosophy of the *mixture* there is what I have called the pathos of *misery;* this allows us to detect the birth of philosophy *in* nonphilosophy, *in* prephilosophy. The pathos of misery is the nonphilosophical origin, the poetical matrix, of philosophical anthropology. The choice of this perspective allows us to understand how philosophy always has a presupposition, even though it be in the search for the point of departure. The problem is in effect to *reduce* this presupposition, but in such a way that one preserves it and understands it. This will be a search for the starting point, even though philosophy is not an absolute beginning; before it, there is already a complete language, that of myth, of symbol which has already said *enigmatically* everything that the philosopher can ever say rationally "in clear terms," everything which the philosopher can ever bring into the *lumen naturale.*

I will give some examples of this prephilosophical richness: the Platonic myth of the soul as a composite, then the beautiful Pascalian rhetoric of the finite and the infinite, finally the reflection of Kierkegaard in the *Sickness unto Death.*

From one to the other of these three examples there is also a certain progress toward a kind of reflection which I wish subsequently to advance.

Plato's meditation on the soul as intermediary is still immersed in symbols: for example the composition of the soul is compared with that of the city; the representation is deliberately "mythical" for there is no direct, rigorous, dialectical language with which to describe the instability of the soul oscillating between corruptible things and incorruptible ideas; it is "perplexed and it searches": *aporei kai zetei;* it asserts opinions and is wrong; it is not seeing but sighting and that not through contact but through tendency. This strange reality which is no longer that of things and not yet that of ideas is given over to myth.

Moreover, the myth is an indivisible unity comprising a myth of finitude and a myth of guilt; the myth is a great nebula in which reflection will have to decide between the original limitation and the supervening catastrophe. The myth of the "composite soul" in the *Symposium* recounts the birth of *Eros* starting from a principle of abundance, *Poros,* and a womb of need, *Penia.* Is this original poverty an evil principle? One would think so, if one were to put the myth of the *Symposium* alongside that of the *Phaedrus* which seems to be a myth of "downfall": the fall of souls into an earthly body seems to place at the origin of man an evil of existing which is indistinguishable from his incarnation, from his sensory and historical existence. And yet, even in the *Phaedrus,* it is possible to distinguish a myth of the fall properly speaking (the fall into an earthly body) and a preliminary myth of a composite soul: all the souls in the heavenly procession drive a winged chariot; the composite soul before any fall already conceals an original mischance (*syntychia*), the balky horse; the fragility seems to be anterior to the downfall.

Thus the theme of the intermediary soul remains bound up with the symbolic and mythical expression of the "composite soul" and, on the other hand, it remains derivative from the confusion, the primitive indivision between an original limitation and moral evil.

From the standpoint of the rigor of thought, the Pascalian theme of "misery" is located at a higher level: it is no longer mythical, it is eloquent and this eloquence is dependent more on a rhetoric of persuasion than on a logic of conviction.

The celebrated fragment on the two infinities comes to mind. "What is man in the infinite?" In contrast to Plato, who uses the symbolism of a composite soul, Pascal has recourse to a scheme borrowed from the cosmological sensitivity of a century in the process of discovering the magnitude of the universe. The initial symbol is that of the spatial disproportion. Man is "intermediate," in the literal sense, between the very large and the very small. But the spatial symbol is surpassed in the direction of a properly existential scheme: "limited as we are in every way, this state which holds the mean between two extremes is found in all our powers." Little by little the infinitely large which embraces me delineates the "end" which eludes me and the infinitely small which I embrace delineates the "origin" or even "the nothing from which I was made." It is here that our misery becomes clear: "Let us then take our measure; we are something and we are not everything; our mode of being deprives us of the knowledge of first principles which are born of the nothing; and the smallness of our mode of being conceals from us a view of the infinite." Concealing our own intermediary position is the summit of human error: "We sail within a vast domain, always drifting about in uncertainty, driven from one extremity to the other . . . ; nothing can fix the finite between the two infinites which enclose it and flee from it."

Thus by underlining the important differences in the symbols—the Pythagorean symbol of the unlimited and Plato's symbol of the limit, the symbol of the infinitely large and the infinitely small in Pascal— the myth of the "composite soul" and the rhetoric of "misery" orient reflection toward the same theme: that of an unstable "composition" between two extremes which stretch and distend man.

But it is perhaps Kierkegaard who approaches nearest to the initial intuition of our research: in *Sickness unto Death* consciousness (the self) is defined in a roundabout way as "a relation which relates itself to itself (freedom) by relating itself to another (God)"; but that which renders the relation to an absolute other unstable is just the relation to the self which is, says Kierkegaard, "a conscious synthesis of finitude and infinitude." For Kierkegaard, infinitude is the imaginary purveyor of unlimited possibilities; finitude is the achieved realization of life in the family, the profession, the state. Despair, from which sin is born and which is sin, is to betray the finite in a fantastical existence without duties or obligations, or to betray the infinite in a submissive, trivial, philistine existence.

In Kierkegaard too this intuition of an unstable composite stands out—this same duality in man which we evoked at the outset; but the discourse of Kierkegaard is still rhetoric, confession, an appeal from man to man.

2. THE TRANSCENDENTAL SYNTHESIS

How can we pass from myth, from rhetoric and indirect appeal, to philosophical discourse, and why this resistance of the *mythos* to *logos?*

A first philosophical stage will be the one we will call the "transcendental" stage: here we make free use of the Kantian analysis of the "intermediary function" par excellence, the transcendental imagination, and we will try to say why this analysis is necessary and why it is insufficient.

The analysis is necessary because—in spite of the reproach of subjectivism leveled at Kant—the "transcendental imagination" reveals the fundamental unity of understanding and sensibility only in its projection onto the "thing" or "object." Therein lies the force of the Kantian analysis: the unity of man is only intentional, that is to say, the unity is projected outwards into the structure of objectivity which it makes possible; but how is man for himself this "intermediary"? A reflection in the transcendental manner is pulled up short here: it remains purely objective; in the sense that the unity of the self remains merely intended, that is to say, represented in a relation to an opposite. That is why one must pass beyond this level and not remain there.

The point of departure for a transcendental approach to man as an intermediary and to the "intermediate" function of imagination is the split which *reflection* introduces between sensibility and understanding. As soon as reflection intervenes it splits up man; it is one thing to *receive* the presence of things—another to determine their meaning; to receive is to open oneself intuitively to the very existence of things; to think is to relate, to put in order. Every advance in reflection is also an advance in the split: on the side of sensibility, for example, which has been characterized as dependent on what it allows to appear, and as suffering under a limitation of incurable perspectivism. The thing presents itself in aspects, unilaterally; one can perceive only from a definite point of view, starting from the zero point, my body, the original "here" which determines the places of things in the world. On the other hand, the intellectual determination of things, which has been characterized as a work of relating, is shot through with a signifying intention which cuts across every point of view and reveals the points of view as points of view; language is the privileged place of this cutting across, just as the glance is the place of each perspective; and, in language, the word goes beyond the simple function of denominating by adding the existential significance, the positing of existence and, with it, the intention or the pretense of truth, what might be called the "vehemence of affirmation." The disproportion between the word which expresses both being and truth and the glance bound to a particular appearance and perspective is the ultimate manifestation of the split between understanding and sensibility, noted in reflection. It is the new form of the Cartesian dialectic of the infinite and the finite; one no longer between two human faculties, will and understanding, but cutting across every faculty which is both finite and transcendent, both a point of view and the intention of truth, good and being.

The problem of the intermediate third term therefore arises: but this third term is not given *in itself* but in the thing, upon the thing; this means that, for a purely transcendental reflection, man carries out his proper synthesis only intentionally.

The thing is an already achieved unity of speech and point of view; it is the objectivity of the synthesis. Objectivity, in fact, is nothing other than the indivisible unity of an appearance and an articulation; the thing shows itself *and* can be articulated. Each of the aspects refers to the other; to articulate the thing is to determine its appearance; to appear is to be capable of being articulated, universalized in a communicable and convincing discourse.

So true is this, that it is by starting from the synthesis of the *thing* and *upon* the thing that reflection has been able to discern first the inadequacy of perception—what might be called the "incoherence of silhouettes"—and then the transcendence of meaning over this flux of silhouettes; it is the thing which refers reflexively to man as point of view and to man as power of speech.

The objectivity of the object is not at all *within* consciousness; it is rather in front of it, as that to which it is related; that is why it can serve as a guiding thread when searching for the synthesis to which it refers *within* man. Furthermore, it does not prejudge the *real* unity of man *for* himself, for it is entirely intentional. Man makes himself intermediate by projecting himself into the mode of being of a thing; he makes himself a "mean" between the infinite and the finite by outlining this ontological dimension of things, namely, that things are a synthesis of meaning and presence. In this sense one can say that a thing is a thing only if it conforms to this synthetic constitution, if it can appear *and* be articulated, if it can affect me in my finitude *and* lend itself to the discourse of every rational being.

Let us go back now, by a reflexive return upon ourselves, to the function which makes possible this synthesis *upon* the thing, the function which makes the objectivity of the object possible by projecting it in advance. If I constitute myself a synthesis of speech and perspective by *opening up* a space for appearance and discourse, before any particular appearance and before any particular discourse, what is this power of opening *in* me and *for* me?

I am reconstituting here the problem which Kant faced under the name: transcendental imagination. I would like to demonstrate its importance for a philosophical anthropology which rests on the polarity infinite-finite.

The unity of meaning and presence is expressed in Kantian terms as follows: the categories of the understanding are applied to the phenomena and intuitions are subjected to rules. This occasions Kant's celebrated formulation of the problem: "Obviously there must be some third thing, which is homogeneous on the one hand with the category, and on the other hand with the appearance, and which thus makes the application of the former to the latter possible. This mediating representation must be pure, that is, void of all empirical content, and yet at the same time, while it must in one respect be *intellectual*, it must in another be sensible. Such a representation is the *transcendental schema*" (A138, Smith trans., 181).

For us, the interesting thing in the theory of the transcendental imagination is that the third term does not have the character of being *for-itself:* it is wholly exhausted in the task of bringing about objectivity; for itself the imaginative synthesis is *obscure.* The schema is "an art hidden in the depths of the human soul." While the objectivity of the object becomes most clear and manifest, the transcendental imagination, which is properly called the *lumen naturale,* and is the polar opposite of the object—remains an enigma. The first thing one notices in man is the two poles: thinking, sensing; in the thing one first notices their synthesis. I understand what is meant by receiving, being affected; I understand what is meant by intellectual determination. But as Kant says, "The two powers cannot exchange their functions, understanding cannot intuit anything, nor can the senses think anything"; their common root, which constitutes precisely the humanity of man, is "unknown to us," moreover the movement of the object toward the transcendental imagination is "never painful." There is something like a blind spot at the center of a luminous vision, "a function of the soul, blind but indispensable," as Kant repeats.

Not only is everything that goes by the name transcendental imagination obscure—(calling it the transcendence of finitude, or the openness of human being is only baptizing the difficulty)—but the crepuscular gleam of reflection is wholly borrowed from the synthesis in the object. There is no intelligibility *proper* to the mediating term. That is the point one can make about time, which is the *medium,* the *metaxú,* par excellence; at first sight we grasp, with time, the instrument of the subjective synthesis of activity and sensibility. Time is in effect a surmounted paradox; on one side, by its *distention,* it is the form of all diversity, the style of incoherence (in Kantian language, pure succession); on the other side, it is intellectually determinable, since all the categories are rooted in it under the form of schemata.

Are we not touching here on the intimate and unified structure of human reality? This transcendental marvel, Time, dispersed and ordered, is ultimately even more enigmatic than the transcendental imagination of which it is the hidden soul. All that one can say of the function of Time as "intermediary" is that it carries out two tasks: letting all diversity appear and letting itself be determined by categorial thought. The notion of a radical genesis of the rules of intellect and intuition starting from the "common root" of imagination and Time remains a pious promise. To put the same point in other words: if one calls this synthesis of understanding and sensibility in the transcendental imagination "consciousness," this consciousness is not yet self-consciousness; the unity of consciousness—what Kant is talking about when he says: "it is clear that the unity which necessarily constitutes the object can be nothing other than the formal unity of consciousness in the synthesis of various representations"—this multiple unity is wholly intentional; it expends all its energies "upon" the object, it exhausts itself in founding the unity of meaning and presence "in" the object.

The transcendental unity of consciousness remains therefore very much short of the unity which a person could constitute in himself and for himself; it must also be said that the unity of the I think is no-one; the "I" of the I think is not a person, a particular person: it is merely the form of the world, that is to say the projection of objectivity, insofar as it is a synthesis of the sayable and the perceptible. In short, the I of the I think is only the project of the object.

It would be a mistake to conclude from this reflection on the transcendental synthesis that a philosophy of "formal" style is useless; it should be regarded instead as the first stage of anthropology, necessary but not sufficient. A reflection on the "intermediary" role of imagination in the constitution of man in his intimate unity outlines the empty framework within which we must now trace the figure of concrete man. But if one should try to cut out this stage of reflection one would blunder into a fantastic ontology of the "mixture" between being and nothingness. If man is a "mixture" of being and nothingness, it is because he first carries out "mediations" among things; his "intermediary" place between being and nothingness proceeds from his same function as "mediator" of the infinite and the finite among things. In this way the myth of the "mixture" is transposed into philosophical discourse.

By saving philosophically the myth of the "mixture" in a theory of "synthesis," a reflection in the transcendental style also saves the rhetoric of "misery" which has always accompanied the myths of "mixture" like a shadow. Actually, the synthesis which is considered in transcendental philosophy is merely intentional and merely formal. Merely intentional, since it is exhausted in the unity of the object; merely formal, since it is anterior to all content. It is in this sense that transcendental philosophy allows us to begin, but not to continue, a philosophical anthropology worthy of the name.

There is a surplus in the myth of the "mixture" and the rhetoric of "misery" that a merely transcendental reflection in the Kantian style does not succeed in bringing to the level of reason.

3. FROM THE TRANSCENDENTAL TO THE PRACTICAL

I will present two examples of what a philosophical anthropology might be, which would preserve both the precomprehension of pathos *and* the rigor of the transcendental method: (1) an example in the practical dimension; (2) an example in the affective dimension.

I propose to call the form which the disproportion of man at the level of *praxis* assumes the antinomy of *character* and *happiness*.

What is *character*? If we want to avoid making it what characterology makes of it: a congealed portrait, arrested, enclosed within a formula—we must say that character is a generalization of the notion of perspective; or better, we should say that the notion of perspective is substracted from that of character, that it is in reality an abstraction. It is supposed that man has only things as his correlative opposite; perspective is his point of view on the thing as such. In this role perspective does not constitute a limitation in all respects, but solely a limitation on perception. But we have in perspective and perception a model for approaching the limitation which is character. How can we generalize the notion of perspective?

One can say that there is a perspective of *desire;* this perspective is bound to its own intention; all desire is a lack of . . . , an impetus toward. . . . In this sense, it has a certain *clarity*; but if it is clear by reason of being a desire for some particular thing, it is confused when taken as a mode of feeling or finding *oneself* to be well or ill. In desire my body is not an openness to the world, traversed by all the intentions which it serves as an organ; it is an obscure reflection on itself, a mute presence to itself, an inexpressible singularity incommensurable with any point of view. It is here that egoism as a vice finds an occasion and something like a temptation; it makes of difference a preference, but this preference is rooted in a feeling innocent of difference, what the Stoics called a "feeling and affection for the self." This attachment to its own constitution is thus the one ground base for all affective intentions, which are multiple and diverse by reason of their objects.

A further step toward the idea of character is supplied by a reflection on the "I can" which is tied not now to an *obscure* aspect, as in desire, but to the aspect of *inertia* in all habits. Husserl has noted that the *ego* is constituted in its habits. (This point is very important: there is a considerable philosophy of habit since Hume.) Ravaisson has seen the philosophical significance of habit: habit represents the *constituted* side of the ego; all habits are learned; once learned, they protect an acquired form, and this form affects the *I can* and gives it a *practical perspective* on the world. This is the ego as "habituality" (Buytendijk).

One might continue to build up the notion of character: the acquired form of my evaluations, the sedimented world of values which I do not question, my "personal idea of happiness and honor" (Bergson).

Character is the totality of these diverse aspects of finitude (which Descartes had reduced to understanding); we have just enumerated them: perspective, an affective immediacy of the living person to himself or an original affection for oneself, preservation, and inertia. What character adds to the aspects is the consideration of a totality, the finite totality of my existence.

What then is meant by the finitude of character? Far from being a thing, it is the limited openness of our field of motivation considered in its entirety. Openness, for I have access to all the values of all men throughout all cultures; my field of motivation is open to the human as such (nothing human is foreign to me); but the humanity of man is accessible to me only according to the existential angle of my character, from this angle there is an everyman. Everyman is man, but man comes to be in an everyman. Character is thus not a destiny which governs my life from without, but the inimitable manner in which I exercise my freedom as man; it is never glimpsed in itself, just as the origin of perception never becomes an object of perception. It is involved in the humanity of my own existence, as the origin zero of my field of motivation. I only discern it by allusion in the feeling of difference which makes me other than every other.

But hardly have I pronounced these words: other than every other, than the most important polarity, the one to which this whole analysis has been tending, is discovered: perspective, desire, the power of rooting oneself in a finite and singular mode of being, in a character which is their ontological place—all of these can only be thought dialectically, by relation to a series of opposite terms which culminates in a certain infinite: happiness.

One can accede by degrees to this embrace of happiness: a reflection on desirability reveals the bipolar constitution of desire; on the one side it is anchored in the affection for self, on the other it opens onto an infinite horizon: happiness, beatitude.

As Stephan Strasser has well demonstrated, happiness designates the presence to human activity, considered as a totality, of the end which will fulfill it. Not the achievement of an isolated act: that would still be only a feeling of "result," an awareness of triumph. But the achievement which corresponds to what we called, a moment ago, the total field of motivation, what Plato called "the entire soul" and Bergson "our personal idea of happiness and honor." Thus I can think character and happiness only conjointly, as a constitutive antinomy of human reality. Character is the perspectival orientation of the total field of motivation; happiness is the end toward which all my motivation is oriented. Zero point and horizon. In this way one can generalize the analysis of perception with its "point of view" and its "horizon" of the world; but while the polarity of point of view and world remains restricted to the consideration of the "thing," the polarity of character and happiness concerns "the entire soul." On one side, character is attained by allusion; on the other, happiness is not included within any one experience: allusion is made to it also in certain privileged experiences which designate its direction; in those precious instants when we are not attending to our limits, our particular character, but instead to a disengagement from the horizon, to the promise hinted at by the event. The feeling of the "immense" thus responds dialectically to the feeling of the "circumscribed."

At the end of this analysis we discover the *polarity* which causes the fragility of man and, as we can already see, his fallibility. Indeed, there is no given "mediation," no immediate mediation (if the expression may be allowed) between happiness and character.

On the "theoretical" level, the only mediation is external; it is the *thing:* the unity of understanding and sensibility, which Kant called the transcendental imagination, is only a condition for the possibility of the synthesis in the object; the unity of happiness and character is a *task:* and this task is what we call the idea of the person.

The synthesis of understanding and sensibility is not "for itself" because it is the project of an object; the synthesis of happiness and character has *to become for itself,* since it is the project of the person.

Kant is once again a good guide, for he has clearly seen that the person is a task rather than a reality; but this task is precisely the reconciliation of happiness and a character.

Is it not obvious, however, that the concept of the person, far from cancelling out the tension between happiness and character, between the infinite and the finite, rather presupposes it? Indeed, I do not see the person, but I ought *to treat* the other and myself as a person. I am not a person by immanent right, I ought to *respect* the person "in" the other and "in" myself.

Respect plays, on the ethical or practical level, the role played by the transcendental imagination on the level of knowledge or theory. The transcendental imagination reconciles understanding and sensibility only by making possible the synthesis of the object. Just so respect reconciles the finitude of desire and the infinitude of reason and happiness only by making possible the very idea of man which serves as the ideal mediator between practical reason and sensibility.

So we will have to say about *respect*—respect for the moral law and respect for the person, inseparable in Kant—what we have already said about imagination: "it remains an art hidden in the depths of the human soul whose real modes of activity nature is hardly likely ever to allow us to discover, and to have open to our gaze" (B180, Smith, 183). For here too it is in a polar opposite that the fact is noticed: the humanity of men who respond to the objectivity of objects in the world. Respect is what makes possible the practical representation of man taken as a person rich in value and meaning. But I do not coincide with this practical representation, I ought to *treat* myself and others *as* an end; in itself, respect remains the fragile bond between morality and sensibility. One can speak of it only in paradoxes: it is reason which is made a psychological motive power, it is sensibility which lets itself be influenced by reason. In order to say this, Kant ought to coin the surprising expression, an a priori motive power. So, it is in a *feeling* that the synthesis of the rational and the sensible is accomplished, in the feeling of being "injured" by the duty which requires the sacrifices of my sensibility and of being "elevated" to the level of a rational being. But I cannot reflect this feeling without shattering it anew and without representing my personality under the sign of a twofold appurtenance, one to the sensible order, the other to the intelligible order. Into this twofold appurtenance is written the possibility of discord and something like the existential "split" which is the fragility of man.

4. AFFECTIVE FRAGILITY

The remaining task is to find the place of *feeling* in an anthropology of finitude. Feeling is the most intimate point of the person, the place where the disproportion is concentrated, the point of culmination or intensity in human fallibility.

What gives this philosophical significance to feeling? And why look for the ultimate evidence of human fragility in feeling?

Because of the most general function of feeling in the constitution of the person; feeling, as W. Stern has seen, is the inverse of the function of "objectification" which consists in detaching and placing at a distance from oneself the objects which, according to the apt expressions, "do not touch us" and "leave us cold." The function of feeling is to "reincorporate" into the vital depths what has been thus "removed" from the depths of life. This function of inclusion and absorption confers on feeling the property which W. Stern has appropriately called its "proximity to the person."

If this is the case, it is legitimate to end this reflection on human fragility in a philosophy of feeling. All the synthesis and mediations we have considered have been syntheses "upon" the object; even the synthesis of the idea of the person was a synthesis projected in a task and in this sense still an objective synthesis. If feeling is in fact the way I was sketching it a moment ago, a movement of interiorization, it is in feeling that the kind of synthesis which is projected in the object or in the idea of man ought to be in some way reflected, it is in feeling also that we should find the primary outburst of that "disproportion" which we have been referring to by its extreme terms, character and happiness.

This does not curtail the risk of falling into some sort of emotionalism or affectivism; I accord no primacy to affectivity over knowledge and the function of objectification. For philosophical anthropology, knowledge and feeling (objectification and interiorization) are contemporary; they are born together and grow together. Man conquers the "depth" of feeling as the counterpart of the "rigor" of knowledge. If then we respect this correlation between feeling and knowledge, more exactly between the "inclusion" of feeling in the person and the "removal" of the object from the depths of the world, the risk of foundering in a "philosophy of feeling" is slight; it is even slighter since we have begun with the synthesis in the object and in the idea of the other and have interrupted feeling on its return journey to itself.

What new form of fragility does feeling reveal? Here we go back to Plato's priceless idea of *thumos,* the mediating function par excellence; feeling is the privileged region of the medium, the zone of transition from simple vitality to pure spirituality; *von Bios über Pathos zu Logos,* says Stephan Strasser in a remarkable book entitled *Das Gemüt.* Still better, we could echo Plato by saying: *von Bios über Thumos zu Logos.*

As Plato has clearly seen, *thumos* is ambiguous: it struggles now with reason, for which it supplies energy and courage, now with desire, for which it supplies the power of enterprise, irritation, and anger. A modern philosophy of feeling should return to this intuition of Plato; but how?

For orientation in this life of *thumos* I propose to adopt the guiding thread that Kant gave in his *Anthropology from a Pragmatic Point of View,* when he distinguished three kinds of passion: passions for possession (*Habsucht*), for power (*Herrschsucht*), and for honor (*Ehrsucht*). Not that we could begin with these contingent passions, as with a *fact,* even an *aberrant* fact. Rather these passions invite us to discern, in their transparence, certain authentic demands which belong to the primordial constitution of man; the fragile image of a human self is constituted through these demands—through a *Suchen* more primitive than the *Sucht* of *Habsucht, Herrschsucht,* and *Ehrsucht.* What is more, these demands refer in their turn to a transcendental structure which comes to them from certain "objects" (in the sense that Hegel speaks of "objective spirit") designated by the words "possession," "power," and "honor"; the latter dominate the fundamental thematic of an economy, a politics, and a culture.

If then we know how to detach in reflection the demands which are central to the constitution of self from the man of successive objective spheres which are their expression in the world, the psychological theory of feeling will not get bogged down in an arbitrary "psychology of passions" but will receive a transcendental a priori structure quite comparable to that which Kant has given to respect. We are dealing in fact with a priori *feelings,* regulated by "intentional objects," which call attention to a theory of objectivity of a higher rank, related to *self-consciousness* in the way that the thing or the natural world in general are related to *consciousness.*

These three demands—possession, power, honor—or if one prefers, appropriation, domination, and fame, constitute the *thumos* of man midway between the life of the body and the life of the spirit; we thus arrive at our question: if it is indeed in these three demands that a "self" different from things and men is constituted, a felt self, a lived self, in what does the fragility of this *thumos*, this "self," consist?

It seems to me that this fragility best appears when one examines how these demands can be satisfied, what are their modes of termination, achievement, and accomplishment. In this way one gets the clearest impression of their unstable function between the vital and the spiritual. Vital demands terminate in pleasure and the cessation of pain, spiritual demands in happiness. Where do the demands of possession, domination, and fame terminate?

We are immediately struck by the fact that the self is never guaranteed, and that the demand in which it searches for itself is in a certain sense without end. While pleasure is a species of provisional repose, as Aristotle has so well demonstrated in his analysis, and while happiness is the enduring repose par excellence or at least the movement toward repose, *thumos* is restless. The French word *"coeur"* (heart), as magnificent in its own way as the Greek *"thumos"* and the German *"Gemüt"*— refers preeminently to that within me which is restless. Between the finitude of pleasure which rounds off a clearly delimited act and is the seal of its repose and the infinitude of happiness, *thumos* drifts along, an undefined power; and already there is a threatening nuance attached to an endless pursuit. When will I have *enough*? When will my authority be *sufficiently* established? When will I be *sufficiently* appreciated? Where do we find in all this that "enough," that "sufficiently"?

As one can see, *thumos* locates the trouble in the structure of acts at the vital level, which are characterized by a cycle: need, starting on the way, development, completion in pleasure or pain. The affective regulation will be complete if the process terminates without remainder, if all tensions are resolved. Human action, taken as it develops under the three fundamental demands of the self, no longer presents a cyclical structure closed and finite; it is in principle a perpetual movement. As a result the end-means, goal-instrument structure undergoes a kind of stretching or distention: no action is terminated, all actions become intermediary, and human life is in danger of forgetting or of losing its goal by reason of the indeterminate character of the threefold demand where the self searches for itself; and the strange thing sometimes happens that the more our action becomes precise and even technical, the more its goals become remote and elusive. The reducing of actions to techniques and the postponement of the self's goals contribute to the feeling of insecurity and emptiness which often pervades human action.

By introducing an indefinite demand between the vital and the spiritual, *thumos* is involved in a double system of exchange with the one and the other. It is in these exchanges between vital tensions and demands of the "self" on the one hand, and between those demands and the desire for happiness on the other, that the life of the person is "mediated"; and it is in this "mediation" of *thumos* that the instability of this life appears.

Let us first consider the relations between the vital and the human: it is certain that all our instincts are recast and, as it were, transmuted by the triple demand which makes us men; that is particularly clear in the case of sexuality. Sexuality becomes human to the extent that it is traversed, recovered, and, as it were, cooled off by the properly human demand. That is why one easily finds in sexuality a note of possession, a note of domination, and also a search for mutual recognition.

But on the other hand these demands aspire to the promise of *totality* in which we have recognized the desire of happiness. So, man invests all his energy, all his heart, in "passion" because an object of desire has become *everything* for him: in this "everything" we find the mark of the desire for happiness. Life does not desire "everything"; the word "everything" has meaning not for life but for spirit. It is spirit which wills the "whole," which thinks the "whole," and does not rest except in the "whole."

In this way, the twofold influence of pleasure and happiness, finite fulfillment, and infinite fulfillment, is exerted through human *thumos;* and it is in the indefinite demand for possession, domination, and esteem by others that the drama of the infinite and the finite is played out.

We can now give a name to the specific fragility of human feeling: it is *conflict. Conflict* is inscribed in the very disproportion of happiness and pleasure and in the fragility of the human heart. Freud is, in this sense, the first psychologist to have understood the central and essential significance of conflict in human anthropology, but he has failed to understand its origin. By placing the origin of repressive forces in a "superego" which is derivative and interiorized, he has referred to society for the proximate cause of conflict with the pleasure principle; our whole analysis tends on the contrary to seek the first origin of "conflicts" in the very intimacy of human *thumos,* apportioned between the vital and the spiritual and polarized by the principle of pleasure and the principle of happiness.

We are thus led to place the "conflict" at the center of philosophical anthropology; we have arrived here at the term of an analysis which has developed from the most abstract to the most concrete level, from the transcendental imagination and its art hidden in the depths of the human soul, to the *thumos* with its internal tensions, its conflicts, its fragility. Our analysis taken as a whole constitutes an exegesis of the idea of the "intermediary" received from the mixture and from the rhetoric of human misery.

At the end of this movement, we can say this: (1) The situation of man between being and nothingness, to speak with Descartes, is the situation of a being who is himself a *mediation* between being and nothingness, between the infinite and the finite. (2) This *mediation* is projected in the synthesis of the object, which is at once discourse and existence, meaning and appearance. (3) The mediation is translated into *action* in the practical synthesis of the person who is at once end and existence, value and presence. (4) This mediation is reflected internally in the feeling of a disproportion of self to itself, of a noncoincidence or an interior "difference" which attests to the original fragility of human reality.

Thus the project of the theoretical synthesis, praxis and feeling, respond, on the level of philosophical meditation, to the themes of pathos which instructed us at outset: the myth of the "mixture," the rhetoric of "misery," existential anxiety over not being able to be a self.

The initial pathos, *reduced* by transcendental reflection, is recovered in a theory of praxis and feeling. But the preunderstanding of pathos is inexhaustible. That is why philosophical anthropology is never completed. Above all it is never done with its task of recovering the irrationality of its nonphilosophical source in the rigor of reflection. Its misfortune is not to be able to save both the depth of pathos and the coherence of logos.

CHAPTER 3

The Hermeneutics of Symbols and

Philosophical Reflection

The aim of this essay is to sketch out a general theory of symbol by investigating one precise symbol, or rather a determined complex of symbols: the symbolism of evil.[1]

The essay is organized about the following preoccupation: How can thought that has once entered into the immense problematic of symbolism and into the *revealing* power of symbol develop along the line of rationality and rigor that has been proper to philosophy from its origins? In brief, how can philosophic reflection be *articulated* upon the hermeneutics of symbols?

I shall first say a few words about the question itself. A meditation on symbols occurs at a certain moment of reflection; it answers to a certain situation of philosophy and perhaps even of modern culture. This recourse to the archaic, the nocturnal, and the oneirotic, which is also an approach to the birthplace of language, represents an attempt to avoid the difficulties in the problem of a starting point in philosophy. We are all too familiar with the harassing backward flight of thought in search of the "first truth," and still more radically, of inquiry after a radical starting point that might not be a first truth at all.

Perhaps one must have experienced the deception that accompanies the idea of a presuppositionless philosophy to enter sympathetically into the problematic we are going to evoke. In contrast to philosophies concerned with starting points, a meditation on symbols starts from the fullness of language and of meaning already there; it begins from within language which has already taken place and in which everything in a certain sense has already been said; it wants to be thought, not presuppositionless, but in and with all its presuppositions. Its first problem is not how to get started, but, from the midst of speech, to recollect itself.

However, to oppose the problematic of symbol to the Cartesian and Husserlian search for a starting point is to tie this meditation too narrowly to a precise stage of philosophical discourse. Perhaps we should take a larger view: if we raise the problem of symbol *now*, at *this* period of history, we do so in connection with certain traits of our "modernity" and as a rejoinder to this modernity. The historical moment of the philosophy of symbol is both the moment of forgetting and the moment of restoring: forgetting hierophanies, forgetting the signs of the Sacred, losing hold of man himself as belonging to the Sacred. This forgetting is the counterpart of the imposing task of nourishing men and satisfying their needs through a technical control of nature. The dim recognition of this forgetting is what bestirs us to restore the integrity of language. In the very age in which our language is becoming more precise, more univocal, more technical, better suited to those integral formalizations that are called precisely "symbolic" logic (we shall return to this surprisingly equivocal use of the word "symbol") —it is in this age of discourse that we wish to recharge language, start again from the *fullness* of language. But this too is a gift from "modernity." For we moderns are men of philology, of exegesis, of the phenomenology of religion, of the psychoanalysis of language. The same age develops the possibility of emptying language and the possibility of filling it anew. It is therefore no yearning for a sunken Atlantis that urges us on, but the hope of a re-creation of language. Beyond the wastelands of critical thought, we seek to be challenged anew.

"Symbol invites thought." (*Le symbole donne à penser.*) This maxim that I find so appealing says two things. The symbol invites: I do not posit the meaning, the symbol gives it; but what it gives is something for thought, something to think about. First the giving, then the positing; the phrase suggests, therefore, both that all has already been said in enigma and yet that it is necessary ever to begin and re-begin everything in the dimension of thought. It is this articulation of thought left to itself in the realm of symbols and of thought positing and thinking that I would like to intercept and understand.

I. THE ORDER OF SYMBOL

Of what value is the example of the symbolism of evil for an investigation of such a wide range? It is an excellent touchstone in several respects.

1. It is quite noteworthy that before all theology and all speculation, even before any mythical elaboration, we should still encounter sym-

bols. These elementary symbols are the unique language of the domain of experience that we shall briefly call the experience of "avowal," or self-confession (*l'aveu*). In fact there is no direct, nonsymbolic language of evil undergone, suffered, or committed; whether man admits his responsibility or claims to be the prey of an evil which takes hold of him, he does so first and foremost in a symbolism whose articulations can be traced out thanks to various rituals of "confession" that the history of religion has interpreted for us.

Whether we are dealing with the stain image in the magical conception of evil as blemish, or with deviation images of the crooked path, of transgression, of wandering, in the more ethical conception of sin, or with the weight image of a burden in the more interiorized experience of guilt—in all these cases the symbol of evil is constituted by starting from something which has a first-level meaning and is borrowed from the experience of nature—man's contact and orientation in space. I have used the term "primary symbols" for this elementary language to distinguish it from mythical symbols; mythical symbols are more articulated; they leave room for the dimension of narrative with its fabled characters, places, and times, and tell the Beginning and End of the experience of which the primary symbols are the avowal.

The primary symbols clearly point out the intentional structure of symbol. Symbol is a sign in this, that like every sign it intends something beyond and stands for this something. But not every sign is a symbol. Symbol conceals in its intention a double intentionality. There is, first, the literal intentionality, which, like any meaningful intentionality, implies the triumph of the conventional over the natural sign: this is the stain, the deviation, the weight—words which do not resemble the thing signified. But upon this first intentionality is built a second intentionality which, through the material stain, the deviation in space, the experience of burden, points to a certain situation of man in the Sacred; this situation, aimed at through the first meaning, is precisely stained, sinful, guilty being. The literal and obvious meaning, therefore, points beyond itself to something which is *like* a stain, *like* a deviation, *like* a burden. Thus, in distinction to technical signs, which are perfectly transparent and say what they mean only by positing the signified, symbolic signs are opaque: the first, literal, patent meaning analogously intends a second meaning which is not given otherwise than in the first. This opaqueness is the symbol's very profundity, an inexhaustible depth.

But let us rightly understand the analogous bond between the literal and the symbolic meaning. Analogy is a nonconclusive reasoning that proceeds through a fourth proportional term (A is to B as C is to D). But in symbol I cannot objectivize the analogous relation that binds the second meaning to the first. By living in the first meaning I am drawn by it beyond itself: the symbolic meaning is constituted in and through the literal meaning, which brings about the analogy by giving the analogue. Unlike a comparison that we *look at* from the outside, symbol is the very movement of the primary meaning that makes us share in the latent meaning and thereby assimilates us to the symbolized, without our being able intellectually to dominate the similarity. This is the sense in which symbol "gives"; it gives because it is a primary intentionality that gives the second meaning.

2. The second advantage of this investigation of the primary symbols of avowal is that it brings directly to light a dynamics, a life of symbols. Semantics opens to us the fact that there are veritable linguistic revolutions, oriented in a definite direction; a certain experience blazes its own trail by means of these verbal stages. The trajectory of the experience of fault is thus laid out by a succession of symbolic sketches. Hence we are not delivered over to a doubtful introspection of the sentiment of fault; in place of the short and, to my mind, suspect way of introspective psychology, there must be substituted the long and more sure way of reflection upon the dynamics of the great cultural symbols.[2]

The dynamics of the primary symbols, marked off by the three constellations of stain, sin, and guilt, has a double meaning. The very equivocation is most revealing of the dynamics of symbol in general. On the one hand, it is a movement of incontestable interiorization; on the other it is a movement of impoverishment of symbolic richness; that is why, let it be said in passing, one must not let himself be misled by a "historicist" and "progressivist" interpretation of the evolution of consciousness in these symbols. What is gain from one point of view is loss from the other. In this progression, each "step" maintains itself only by taking up the symbolic charge of the preceding; so we shall not be surprised that stain, the most archaic symbol, survives as the essential in the third step. Though submerged in fear, the experience of the impure already achieves speech, thanks to the extraordinary richness of the stain theme.

From the beginning stain is more than a spot; it points to an affection of the person as a whole as regards his situation in relation to the Sacred. Whatever it is that affects the penitent cannot be removed by a physical washing. Through interchangeable gestures (covering with earth, spitting, throwing at a distance), the rites of purification intend an integrity that can be spoken of in none but a symbolic language. This is why it is the magic conception of stain, however archaic and obsolete it be, that has transmitted to us the symbolism of the pure and the impure with all its richness of harmonics. At the center of this symbolism stands the schema of "exteriority," of investiture by evil,

which is perhaps the inscrutable depths of the "mystery of iniquity."
Evil is evil only insofar as I posit it, but at the very heart of freedom's
positing of evil is revealed a power of seduction by "evil already there"
which the ancient "stain" had from the start already affirmed in the
symbolic mode.

But an archaic symbol survives only through the revolutions of experience and of language which submerge it. The iconoclast movement
does not proceed first from reflection but from symbolism itself; a
symbol is first of all a destroyer of a prior symbol. Thus we see the
symbolism of sin take shape about images which are the inverse of stain
images; in place of exterior contact, it is now deviation (from the target, the straight path, the limit not to be crossed, and so on) which
serves as guiding schema. This switch in themes is the expression of an
overturning of fundamental motifs. A new category of religious experience is born: that of "before God," of which the Jewish *berit,* the Alliance, is the witness. An infinite exigency of perfection comes to light,
which keeps remodeling the terse limited commandments of the old
codes. To this infinite exigency is coupled an infinite menace that
revolutionizes the old fear of the taboos and makes one dread the encounter of God in his Anger.

What becomes then of the initial symbol? On the one hand, evil
is no longer a thing, but a broken relationship, hence a nothing; this
nothing is expressed in the images of the breathiness, the emptiness,
the vaporousness and vanity of the idol. The very Anger of God is like
the nothingness of his absence. But at the same time a new positivity
of evil arises, no longer an exterior "something," but a real enslaving
power. The symbol of captivity, which transforms a historical event
(the Egyptian captivity, then the Babylonian captivity) into a schema
of existence, represents the highest expression achieved by the penitential experience of Israel. Because of this new positivity of evil, the first
symbolism, that of stain, was able to be taken up again: the schema of
exteriority is recovered, but at an ethical and no longer at a magical
level.

The same movement of breaking with and taking up again can be
observed in the transition from sin symbols to guilt symbols. On the
one hand the purely subjective experience of fault tends to be substituted for the realist and, if we may so express it, ontological affirmation of sin. Whereas sin is real even when it is not known, guilt is measured by man's awareness of it in becoming the author of his own fault.
In this way the weight and burden image is substituted for the image
of separation, deviation, wandering; in the depth of his consciousness,
"before God" is being replaced by "before myself"; man is guilty when
he feels guilty. To this new revolution we incontestably owe a finer and
more measured sense of responsibility which from being collective be-

comes individual, gradual instead of total. We have entered the world of reasonable indictment, the indictment of the judge and the scrupulous conscience. But the ancient stain symbol is not, for all that, lost, for hell is displaced from the exterior toward the interior. Crushed by the law which it shall never satisfy, consciousness recognizes itself captive in its injustice, and even worse in the lie of its pretention to justice proper. At this extreme point of involution the stain symbol has become that of servile liberty, servile will, of which Luther and Spinoza speak in terms so different, but borrowed from the same symbolism.

3. I have deliberately carried to this point the exegesis of the primary symbols of fault, as well as the general theory of symbol which depends on this exegesis, without relying on the mythical structure that usually surcharges these symbols. It was necessary to bracket the second degree symbols both to make clear the structure of the first degree symbols, and to bring out the specificity of myth itself. These great narratives which, as was said, put into play space, time, and characters woven into story form, have in fact an irreducible function. It is a threefold one. First, they place the whole of mankind and its drama under the sign of an exemplary man, an *Anthropos*, an Adam, who symbolically stands for the concrete universal of human experience. Secondly, they give to this history an élan, an allure, an orientation, by unfolding it between a beginning and an end; they thus introduce a historical tension into human experience, starting from the double horizon of a genesis and of an apocalypse. Finally, and more fundamentally, they explore the cleavage in human reality represented by the passage or leap from innocence to guilt; they recount how man, originally good, has become what he is in the present. That is why myth can exercise its symbolic function only through the specific means of narrative: what it wants to say is already drama.

But at the same time myth can take root only in a multiplicity of narratives and leaves us before an endless diversity of symbolic systems, similar to the multiple tongues of an unfixable Sacred. In the particular case of the symbolism of evil, the difficulty of an exegesis of myths appears from the start under a double form. On the one hand, the infinite multiplicity of the myths must be overcome by imposing upon them a typology that permits thought to become orientated within their endless variety, while not doing violence to the specificity of the mythical figures brought to the light of language by diverse civilizations; on the other hand, the difficulty is to move from a static classification of myths to a dynamics of them. For it is the understanding of the oppositions and secret affinities among diverse myths that prepares the philosophic assimilation of myth. The world of myths, even more than that of the primary symbols, is not a serene and amicable world;

myths have never stopped battling one another; every myth is iconoclast toward others, in the same way that every symbol left to itself
tends to thicken, to solidify in an idolatry. It is necessary, therefore, to
share in this battle, in this dynamics, by which symbolism is subject to
being itself surpassed.

This dynamics is animated by a deep-seated opposition: on one side
are the myths that take the origin of evil back to a catastrophe or primordial conflict prior to man; on the other, the myths that take the
origin back to man.

To the first group belongs the drama of creation, illustrated by the
Babylonian poem of creation, *Enuma Elish,* that tells of the primordial
combat whence proceed the birth of the most recent gods, the foundation of the cosmos, and the creation of man. To this same group belong
the tragic myths which show the hero subject to a fatal destiny. According to the tragic schema, man falls into fault as he falls into existence;
and the god who tempts and misleads him stands for the primordial
lack of distinction between good and evil. With the Zeus of *Prometheus
Bound,* this god has attained the terrifying stature that no thought can
sustain. The orphic myth of the soul in exile in an evil body should also
be placed in this first group; for this exile is necessarily prior to every
positing of evil by a free and responsible man. The orphic myth is a
situational myth which clearly seems to have been later projected into
an origin myth; the roots of the latter reach back to the theomachy
which is close to the cosmogonic and tragic myths.

Over against this triple myth stands the biblical narrative of Adam's
fall. This alone is the anthropological myth proper. In it can be seen the
mythical expression of the whole penitential experience of Israel. It is
man who is accused by the prophet; it is man who in the confession
of sins discovers himself to be the author of evil and who discerns, beyond his evil acts told off in time, an evil constitution more original
than any individual decision. The myth recounts the arising of this evil
constitution in an irrational event that unexpectedly takes place in a
good creation. It compresses the origin of evil into a symbolic instant
that is the end of innocence and the beginning of malediction. Through
the chronicle of the first man is unveiled the meaning of the history of
every man.

The world of myths is thus polarized between two tendencies: one
takes evil back beyond the human; the other concentrates it in an evil
choice from which stems the pain of being man. So again we come
across, at a higher level of elaboration, the polarity of the primary
symbols, stretched between a schema of exteriority, which is dominant in the magical conception of evil as stain, and a schema of interi-
ority, which only fully triumphs with the painful experience of the
guilty and scrupulous conscience.

But that is not yet what is most remarkable. The conflict is not only between two groups of myths, it is repeated within the Adam myth itself. This myth has in fact two faces. Not only is it the narrative of the instant of the fall, such as we have just presented it. But at the same time it is the narrative of the temptation, which is spread out over a duration, a lapse of time, and puts into action a number of characters: the God who interdicts, the object of the temptation, the woman who is seduced, and finally and above all the serpent who seduces. The same myth that concentrates the event of the fall in one man, one act, one instant, likewise disperses it over several characters and several episodes. The qualitative leap from innocence to fault is, in this second aspect, a gradual and indiscernible passage. The myth of the caesura is thus at the same time the myth of the transition; the myth of evil choice is the myth of temptation, of intoxication, of imperceptible slipping into evil. The woman, figure of fragility, is the polar counterpart of the man, figure of evil decision.

The conflict of the myths is thus included in a single myth. That is why the Adam myth, which at first reading might be looked upon as the net result of an energetic demythologizing of all the other myths concerned with the origin of evil, introduces into the narrative the highly mythical figure of the serpent. The serpent, at the very heart of the Adam myth, stands for evil's other face which the other myths tried to recount: evil already there, pre-given evil, evil that attracts and seduces man. The serpent signifies that man does not begin evil. He finds it. For him, to begin is to continue. Beyond the projection of our own covetousness, the serpent stands for the tradition of an evil more ancient than man himself. The serpent is the *Other* of human evil.

From this can be understood why there is a dynamics of myths. The schema of exteriority which finds projection in the body-tomb of the orphics, the wicked god of Prometheus, the primordial combat of the drama of creation—this schema, doubtless, is invincible. That is why, dispelled by the anthropological myth, it rises again within it and takes refuge in the figure of the serpent. The figure of Adam is much more than the paradigm of all present evil. Adam, as primordial man, is prior to every man; in his own fashion he is once again the figure of evil prior to every actual evil. Adam is older than every man, and the serpent older than Adam. Thus the tragic myth is at the same time reaffirmed and destroyed by the Adam myth. This is undoubtedly why tragedy lives on after its double destruction by Greek philosophy and Christianity; if theology cannot be thought, if it is, in the proper sense of the term, unavowable, still, what it wants to say—and cannot say—continues to be pointed to in the basic spectacle of the tragic hero, innocent and guilty.

It is this war of the myths that invites us to attempt the passage

from a simple exegesis to a philosophy of myths through the mediation
of symbols.

II. FROM SYMBOLISM TO REFLECTIVE THOUGHT

Accordingly, the task is now to think starting from the symbolic,
and according to the genius of the symbolic. And it *is* a matter of
thinking. For my part, I do not in the least abandon the tradition of
rationality that has animated philosophy since the Greeks. It is not a
question of giving in to some kind of imaginative intuition, but rather
of thinking, that is to say, of elaborating concepts that comprehend
and make one comprehend, concepts woven together, if not in a closed
system, at least in a *systematic* order. But at the same time it is a question of transmitting, by means of this rational elaboration, a richness
of signification that was already there, that has already preceded rational elaboration. For such is the situation: on the one hand all has
been said *before* philosophy, by sign and by enigma. That is one of the
meanings of the phrase of Heraclitus: "The master whose oracle is at
Delphi does not speak, does not dissimulate: he signifies" (ἀλλὰ ση-
μαίνει). On the other hand, we have the task of speaking clearly, by
taking perhaps also the risk of dissimulating, by interpreting the oracle.
Philosophy begins with itself, it *is* a kind of beginning. Hence the coherent discourse of philosophies is at once hermeneutic recovery of the
enigmas which precede, envelop, and nourish this discourse and inquiry
after the beginning, and also search for order, desire for system. Happy
and rare would be the conjunction within one and the same philosophy
of both the abundance of signs and retained enigmas and the rigor of
a discourse without complacency.

The key, or at least the crux, of the difficulty lies in the relation
between hermeneutics and reflection. For every symbol gives birth to
understanding by means of an interpretation. How can this understanding be both *in* the symbol and *beyond* the symbol?

I see three stages of this *understanding,* three stages that stake out
the movement which advances from living *in* symbols toward thought
that thinks *from* symbols.

The first stage, that of a simple phenomenology, remains an understanding of symbol by symbol, by the totality of symbols. This is already a manner of intelligence, since it runs through and interconnects
the domain of symbols and gives it the consistency of a world. But it
is still a life abandoned to symbol, delivered up to symbol. The phenomenology of religion rarely goes beyond this plane; for it, to understand a symbol is to replace it in a larger homogeneous totality which,
on the very plane of symbol, forms a system. Sometimes this phenomenology lays out the multiple values of one and the same symbol to show

its inexhaustible character. In this first sense, to understand is to repeat within oneself this multiple unity, this permutation of all the values within the same theme. Sometimes phenomenology is used to understand one symbol by another; understanding is then gradually extended, according to a remote intentional analogy, to all the other symbols that have some affinity with the symbol under study. In another way, phenomenology will understand a symbol by a rite and a myth, i.e., by the other manifestations of the Sacred. It will further be shown, and this shall be the fourth way of understanding, how the same symbol unifies several levels of experience or representation: the exterior and the interior, the vital and the speculative. Thus, in multiple ways, the phenomenology of symbol brings to light an internal coherence, something like a symbolic system. On this level, to interpret is to bring out a coherence.

This is the first stage, the first level of thought that starts from symbols. But one cannot rest here; for the question of *truth* has not yet been posed. If a phenomenologist should give the name truth to internal coherence, to the systematization of the world of symbols, it is a truth without belief, truth at a distance, a reduced truth. From such truth the question has been eliminated: *Do I myself believe that? What do I personally make of these symbolic significations?* Now this question cannot be raised as long as one remains on the level of comparativism, passing from one symbol to another, without personal involvement. This stage can only be a stage, the stage of an intelligence that is horizontal and panoramic, curious but not concerned. We now have to enter into a relationship with symbols that is both emotionally intense and at the same time critical. To do so I must leave the comparatist point of view aside; I must follow the exegete and become implicated in the life of one symbol, one myth.

Beyond the horizontal intelligence of the phenomenology of the comparatist, there opens up the field of hermeneutics properly so-called: interpretation applied in each case to an individual text. It is in modern hermeneutics that are bound together the symbol's giving of meaning and the intelligent initiative of deciphering. Hermeneutics makes us share in the battle, the dynamics, by which symbolism is subject to being itself surpassed. Only by sharing in this dynamics does understanding enter the properly critical dimension of exegesis and become a hermeneutics.

But then I must quit the position, or better, the exile, of the remote and disinterested spectator, in order to appropriate in each case an individual symbolism. Then is discovered what may be called the circle of hermeneutics, which the simple amateur of myths unfailingly passes by. The circle can be stated bluntly: "You must understand in order to believe, but you must believe in order to understand."

This circle is not vicious, still less deadly; it is quite alive and stimulating. You must believe in order to understand. No interpreter in fact will ever come close to what his text says if he does not live in the *aura* of the meaning that is sought. And yet it is only in understanding that we can believe. The second immediacy, the second naïveté that we are after, is accessible only in hermeneutics; we can believe only by interpreting. This is the "modern" modality of belief in symbols; expression of modernity's distress and cure for this distress. Such is the circle: hermeneutics starts out from the comprehension of the very thing which through interpretation it is trying to understand. But thanks to this hermeneutic circle, I can today still communicate with the Sacred by explicitating the pre-comprehension which animates the interpretation. Hermeneutics, child of "modernity," is one of the ways in which this "modernity" overcomes its own forgetfulness of the Sacred. I believe that being can still speak to me, no longer indeed in the pre-critical form of immediate belief, but as the second immediacy that hermeneutics aims at. It may be that this second naïveté is the postcritical equivalent of the precritical hierophany.

But hermeneutics is not yet reflection; it is bound up with individual texts whose exegeses it rules. The third stage of the understanding of symbols, the properly philosophical stage, is that of thought starting from symbol.

However, the hermeneutic relation between philosophic *discourse* and the symbolic is threatened by two spurious substitutes. On the one hand it can be reduced to a simple allegorical tie. This is what the Stoics did with the fables of Homer and Hesiod. The philosophical meaning rises victorious from its imaginative shell; it was there all armed like Athena in the head of Zeus. The fable was but an outer wrapping; stripped off, it is rendered vain. Allegory implies that the true meaning, the philosophic meaning, preceded the fable, which was only a second disguise, a veil deliberately thrown over the truth to mislead the simple. I am convinced that we must think not *behind* the symbols, but starting from symbols, *according* to symbols, that their substance is indestructible, that they constitute the *relevant* substrate of speech which lives among men. In short, the symbol invites thought. On the other hand, a further peril lies in wait for us: that of repeating the symbol in a mimic of rationality, of rationalizing symbols as such, and thereby fixing them on the imaginative plane where they are born and take shape. This temptation of a "dogmatic mythology" is the temptation of gnosis. It is impossible to exaggerate the historic importance of this movement of thought that has covered three continents, held sway over numerous centuries, animated the speculation of so many minds eager for knowledge and salvation through knowledge. Between gnosis and the problem of evil there is a disquieting and in fact deceptive alliance. It was the gnostics who posed in all its pathetic bluntness the question: πόθεν τὰ κακά—whence comes evil?

In what does this power of misleading, inherent in gnosis, consist? First of all in this, that by its content it is structured exclusively upon the tragic theme of fall or disgrace, a theme which stems from the orphic myth and which is characterized by its schema of exteriority. For the gnostic, evil—as has been shown by Jonas, Puech, Quispel, and others—is outside. It is body, thing, world, a quasi-physical reality that invests man from the exterior. It resides in a substance that infects by contagion. By the same token—and this is the second characteristic we wish to emphasize—all the images of evil, inspired in a way by this schema of exteriority, "take" in this represented materiality—in the sense that plaster is said to take, or preserves to gel. The drama of sin and salvation fixes upon and clings to a topography: the soul comes from elsewhere, falls here, has to return over there. The existential anguish that is at the root of gnosis is immediately linked to an oriented space and time. In a stroke, everything that is image, symbol, parable— whether one speaks of wandering, fall, or captivity, etc.—is transmuted into a pretended knowing where the letter of the image becomes solidified. Thus is born a dogmatic mythology, as Puech says, inseparable from its spatial and cosmic figuration: evil is the world's very act of becoming a world.

My problem then is this: How can thought be elaborated in starting from symbol, without going back to the old allegorizing interpretation, or falling into the trap of gnosis? How can a meaning be disengaged from symbol that will put thought into motion, without presupposing a meaning already there, hidden, dissimulated, covered over, or without getting involved in the pseudo-knowing of a dogmatic mythology? I would like to try another way, the way of a creative interpretation, an interpretation that would respect the original enigma of symbols, let itself be taught by this enigma, but, with that as a start, bring out the meaning, give it form, in the full responsibility of an autonomous systematized thought. But how can thought be at once *bound* and *free*? How can one maintain both the immediacy of symbol and the mediation of thought?

It is this battle between thought and the symbolic that I wish now to explore, with the help of the problem of evil taken as a paradigm case. In effect, thought manifests itself alternately as *reflection* and as *speculation.*

Thought as reflection is essentially "demythologizing." It tends to treat myth as an allegory; its transposition of myth is at the same time an elimination not only of its etiological function but of its power to open and uncover. Reflective thought is essentially demythologizing; it interprets myth only by reducing it to allegory. The problem of evil is in this regard an exemplar: *reflection upon the symbolism of evil reaches its peak in what we shall henceforth call the ethical vision of evil.* This philosophizing interpretation of evil feeds on the richness of primary symbols and of myths, but it continues the movement of their demythologization that we have sketched out above. On the one hand, it prolongs the progressive reduction of stain and sin to personal and interior guilt; on the other, it prolongs the movement of demythologization of all the myths except the Adam myth and reduces this latter to a simple allegory of servile will.

Reflective thought, in its turn, is at battle with speculative thought. Speculative thought wants to save what an ethical vision of evil tends to eliminate. It not only wants to save it, but to show its *necessity.* And its specific peril is *gnosis.*

We shall turn first to the ethical vision of evil. This level must be attained and traversed all the way to the end; a level, however, on which we will not be able to stay for long. But it is from within it that we shall have to go beyond it. To do that it is necessary to have completely thought out a purely ethical interpretation of evil.

By "ethical interpretation of evil" I understand an interpretation in which evil as far as possible is reset within the context of freedom; in which, therefore, evil is an invention of freedom. Reciprocally, an ethical vision of evil is a vision in which freedom is revealed in its depths as power to act and power to be; the freedom that evil supposes is a freedom capable of digression, deviation, subversion, wandering. This mutual "explanation" of evil by freedom and of freedom by evil is the essence of the moral vision of the world and of evil.

How does the moral vision of the world and of evil relate to the symbolic and mythical universe? In two ways: first, it is a radical demythologization of the dualist myths, the tragic and the orphic; secondly, it is the recapture of the Adam narrative in an intelligible philosophic theme. The moral vision of the world is thought that *goes counter to* evil as substance and *along with* the fall of primordial man.

Historically the ethical vision of evil carries the stamp of two great names which are not customarily associated, but whose intimate relationship I would like to make felt: Augustine and Kant. When I say Augustine, I mean at least Augustine in his fight against Manicheism, for we shall see further on that "Augustinianism"—in the precise and narrow sense that Rottmayer gives it—stands, in opposition now not to Mani but to Pelagius, for the surpassing of the moral vision of the world and, in certain respects, for its liquidation. We shall return to this point later.

From its demythologizing side, the Augustinian interpretation of evil, prior to the struggle against Pelagius, is dominated by the following affirmation: evil has no nature; evil is not a something; it is not matter, substance, world. The reabsorption of the schema of exteriority is pushed to its furthest limits: not only does evil not have being, but one must suppress the question: *quid est malum?* (what is evil?) and put in its place the question: *unde malum faciamus?* (whence do we do evil?). Hence it will be necessary to say that evil, as regards substance and nature, is a "nothing."

This "nothing," inherited from the Platonic non-being and the Plotinian nothing, but desubstantialized, has now to be coupled with concepts inherited from another tradition of Greek philosophy, the *Nicomachean Ethics.* It was here, in fact, that was first elaborated the philosophy of the voluntary and the involuntary (*Nic. Eth.*, Book III), but Aristotle does not go all the way to a radical philosophy of *freedom.* He elaborates the concepts of "preference" (προαίρεσις), of deliberate choice, of rational desire, but not of freedom. It can be affirmed that it was St. Augustine who made evil's power of *nothing* meet head-on with freedom at work in the will, and thereby so radicalized reflection upon freedom as to make it into the originative power of saying "No" to being, the power of "defaulting" (*deficere*), of "declining" (*declinare*), of tending toward nothingness, *ad non esse.* By elaborating the concept of *defectus* as that of a consent negatively oriented, he makes nothingness surge up no longer as inert counterpole of being, but as inverse existential direction of conversion, as *aversio a Deo.*[3]

But Augustine does not dispose of the conceptual tools to give integral expression to his discovery. Thus we see him, in the *Contra Felicem*, oppose evil will and evil nature; in his commentary on Matthew 12:33 ("Either the tree is good and its fruit good, or the tree is bad and its fruit bad"), he cries out: this "either . . . or" designates a power and not a nature (*potestatem indicat, non naturam*). With that, he sums up indeed the essence of the Christian philosophy of evil, in the face of gnosis: "If there is penitence, it is because there is guilt; if there is guilt, it is because there is will; if there is will in sin, it is not a nature which constrains us."[4] But the Neoplatonic framework of his thought does not allow him to lay out and stabilize the opposition *nature-will* in a coherent conception; that would take a philosophy of action and a philosophy of contingence, in which evil would be said to surge up as an event, as a qualitative leap. Thus the movement toward nothingness, defaulting, declining, remains an impossible concept.

Moreover it is not certain that the overly negative concept of *defectus*, of *declinatio* (which becomes *corruptio* in a nature), takes account of the positive power of evil; likewise the nothing of *ad non esse* is poorly distinguished from the *ex nihilo* of the creature, which only designates his own want of being, his creaturely dependence. Augustine did not have the means of thematizing his discovery except in the language of the Neoplatonic ontology. He would have had to move all the way to the *positing* of evil as a qualitative "leap," as an event, an instant. But then Augustine would no longer be Augustine, but Kierkegaard. . . .

What is, now, the significance of Kant, and especially of his "Essay on Radical Evil" (found in his *Religion within the Limits of Reason Alone*), as regards the anti-Manichean treatises of Augustine? I propose that we try to understand them through each other. To start with, Kant elaborates the conceptual framework that is wanting to Augustine by pushing to the extreme the specificity of the "practical" concepts: *Wille, Willkür, Maxim:* will, freedom (free will or free choice), maxim of the will. This conceptualization is achieved in the *Introduction to the Metaphysics of Morals* and the *Critique of Practical Reason.* By it, Kant brings to full explicitness the opposition will-nature sketched out by Augustine in the *Contra Felicem.*

But above all Kant elaborated the principal condition of a conceptualization of evil, as radical evil, namely, formalism in morality. This relationship does not appear on a reading of the "Essay on Radical Evil" apart from its ties with the *Critique of Practical Reason.* But by his formalism Kant brings to achievement a movement already started in Plato: if "injustice" can be the figure of radical evil, it is because "justice" is not just one virtue out of many but the very form of virtue, the unifying principle which makes the soul from being several into one.[5]

Aristotle, in the *Nicomachean Ethics,* is also on the road to a formalization of good and evil: virtues are defined both by their object and by their formal character of "mean" ($\mu\varepsilon\sigma\acute{o}\tau\eta\varsigma$); evil therefore is absence of "mean," deviation, extremity in deviation. The Platonic $\dot{a}\delta\iota\kappa\acute{\iota}a$, the Aristotelian $\dot{a}\kappa\rho a\sigma\acute{\iota}a$ herald, therefore, qua imperfect formalisms, the entire formalization of the principle of morality. I am not unaware that one cannot remain in a formalism in ethics; but it is without doubt necessary to have reached it in order to surpass it.

Now, the advantage of this formalism is to construct the concept of wrong maxim as rule that the free will forges itself. Evil no longer resides in sensibility. An end is put to the confusion between evil and the affective, the passional. It is worth noting that it was the reputedly most pessimistic of ethics that accomplished the feat of disjoining evil from sensibility; this separation is the result of formalism and its bracketing of desire in the definition of the good will. Kant can say: "Natural inclinations that result from sensibility do not even have a direct relationship with evil." But neither can evil reside in the subversion of reason; a completely lawless being would no longer be bad but diabolic. It remains that evil resides in a relationship, or the subversion of a relationship. It is what happens, says Kant, when man subordinates the pure motive of respect to sensible motives, when "he reverses the moral order of motives by accepting them in his maxims."

Thus the biblical schema of deviation, opposed to the orphic schema of predilective exteriority, receives its rational equivalent in the Kantian idea of the subversion of the maxim. More precisely still, I see in Kant the complete philosophical manifestation that the supreme evil is not the gross infraction of a duty, but the malice that makes pass for virtue what is virtue's betrayal. The evil of evil is the fraudulent justification of the maxim by apparent conformity with law—it is the semblance of morality. Kant was the first, as I see it, to orientate the problem of evil in the direction of imposture or bad faith.

Here we have the extreme point of clarity attained by the ethical vision of evil: freedom is the power of deviation, of disrupting order. Freedom is not a something, but the subversion of a relation. But who does not see that at the very moment we say this, we triumph, in a way, in emptiness? The price of clarity is the loss of depth.

III. DIMMING OF REFLECTION AND RETURN TO THE TRAGIC

What is lacking in the ethical vision of evil? What is lacking, what is lost, is the darksome experience of evil which comes up in different ways in the symbolism of evil and which constitutes, properly speaking, the "tragic" aspect of evil.

At the lowest level of the symbolic, the level of primary symbols, we have seen the confession of sins acknowledge evil as evil *already* there, evil in which I am born, evil which I find in myself before the awakening of my conscience, evil which cannot be analyzed into individual culpability and actual faults. I have shown that the symbol of "captivity," of slavery, is the specific symbol of this dimension of evil as power that binds, of evil as reign.

It is this same experience of evil already there, powerful in my powerlessness, that gives rise to the whole cycle of myths other than the Adam myth, all of which start out from the schema of exteriority. But this mythic cycle is not simply excluded by the Adam myth; it is in a certain way *incorporated* in it, at a subordinate level surely, but not a negligible one. Adam is for all men the prior man and not only the exemplary man; he is the very priority of evil as regards every man; and he has himself his other, his prior, in the figure of the serpent, already there and already sly. Thus the ethical vision of evil thematizes only the symbol of actual evil, the "swerving," the "contingent deviation." Adam is the archetype, the model of this present, actual evil that we repeat and imitate each time that we begin evil; and in this sense each one begins evil each time.

But by starting evil we continue it, and that is what we have to try to express now: evil as tradition, as historical concatenation, as reign of the already there. But here we also take great risks, for by introducing the schema of "heritage" and by trying to coordinate it with that of "deviation" in a coherent concept, we again run up against gnosis, taken in the largest sense, namely: (1) dogmatic mythology; (2) reification of evil in a "nature." For it is the concept of *nature* that is here proposed in order to counterbalance that of *contingence,* which ruled the first movement of thought. We are going to try to think something like a *nature* of evil, but a nature which would not be a nature of things, but an originative nature of man, a nature of liberty, hence a contracted *habitus,* freedom's manner of having come to be.

Here again we come across Augustine and Kant, Augustine when he moves from actual sin to original sin, Kant when he goes from the wrong maxims of free will back to the *ground* of all wrong maxims. (Let me digress here for a moment to remark that I reject the usual disjunction of spheres of competence to which people are so ready to submit the work of Augustine, as if the philosophy of actual evil was the philosopher's province and that of original sin the theologian's. I, for one, do not divide philosophy and theology in this way. As *revealing*—and not as revealed—the Adam symbol belongs to a philosophical anthropology just as much as all the other symbols. Its belonging to theology is determined, not by its proper structure, but by its relation in Christology with the "event" and "coming" of the Man par excellence, the Christ Jesus. For my part, I hold that no symbol qua opening and uncovering a truth of man is foreign to philosophic reflection. Hence I do not take the concept of original sin to be a theme extraneous to philosophy, but, on the contrary, to be a theme subject to an intentional analysis, to a hermeneutics of rational symbols whose task is to reconstitute the layers of meaning which have become sedimented in the concept.)

Now what does this intentional analysis bring to the surface? It brings this: as a so-called intelligible concept, the concept of original sin is a false-knowing and should be likened, as for epistemological structure, to the concepts of gnosis: a metaempirical fall according to Valentin, an aggression of the realm of darkness according to Mani. Antignostic in its intention, original sin is a quasi-gnostic concept in its form. The task of reflection here is to break it as false-knowing, in order to get hold of its intention as rational symbol—for which there is no substitute—of evil already there.

Let us make this double movement of reflection.

We must, we said, break the concept as false-knowing; in effect "Augustinianism" in the narrow sense that we used before, lays out in an inconsistent notion both a juridical concept, that of imputation, of imputable guilt, and a biological concept, that of heredity. On the one hand, for there to be sin, fault must be a transgression of will: such was the fault of man understood as an individual having really existed at the origin of history. On the other hand, this imputable guilt must be carried *per generationem* so that each and all, we may be made guilty "in Adam." Throughout the polemic with Pelagius and the Pelagians, we see the idea of a guilt of personal character juridically meriting death and inherited by birth in the manner of a blemish take on consistency. Augustine's motivation merits a pause: it aims essentially at *rationalizing* the most mysterious of Pauline themes, that of reprobation: "I loved Jacob and I hated Esau." [6] Because God is just, the reprobation of little infants in the womb of their mother must be just, perdition must be just, and salvation operated by grace; from this derives the idea of a guilt of nature, effective as an act, punishable as a crime, though inherited as a malady.

This is an intellectually inconsistent idea, we maintained, inasmuch as it mixes two universes of discourse—that of ethics or of right, and that of biology. It is an intellectually scandalous idea, inasmuch as it returns on this side of Ezekiel and Jeremiah to the old idea of retribution and en masse inculpation of men. It is an intellectually derisory idea, inasmuch as it throws up again the eternal theodicy and project of justifying God.

And though I do not hesitate to say that Pelagius can win out a thousand times over the pseudo-concept of original sin, yet St. Augustine instills into this dogmatic mythology something essential that Pelagius wholly misunderstood. Pelagius is still right perhaps, against the mythology of original sin, and yet it is Augustine who is right, through and in spite of this Adam mythology.

What must in fact be scrutinized in the concept of original sin is not its false clarity but its obscure analogous richness. Its force lies in intentionally referring back to what is most radical in the confession of sins, namely, the fact that evil precedes my awareness, that it cannot be analyzed into individual faults, that it is my pregiven impotence. It is to my freedom that which my *birth* is to my actual consciousness, namely, always already there; birth and nature here are analogous concepts. Hence the intention of the pseudo-concept of original sin is this: to incorporate into the description of the bad will, such as this will was elaborated against Mani and Gnosis, the theme of a quasi-nature of evil. *The concept's irreplaceable function is therefore to integrate the schema of heritage with that of contingence.*

There is here something of hopelessness from the point of view of conceptual representation, and of irreplaceability from the metaphysical point of view. The quasi-nature is in the will itself; evil is a kind of involuntary at the very heart of the voluntary, no longer over against it, but in it—and there you have the servile will. In a stroke, confession is shifted to a deeper level than that of simple repentance for acts; if evil is at the radical level of "generation"—in a symbolic, not a factual, sense—conversion itself is "regeneration." Thus is constituted, by means of an absurd concept, an *antitype of regeneration;* because of this antitype, will is shown to be affected by a passive constitution implied in its actual power of deliberation and of choice.

It is this antitype of regeneration that Kant tried to elaborate as an a priori of the moral life. The philosophical interest of the "Essay on Radical Evil," which we left hanging in midair, lies in its having achieved what I a moment ago called the critique of original sin as false-knowing and in having attempted its "deduction"—in the sense in which the transcendental deduction of the categories is a justification of rules by their power to constitute a domain of objectivity. The evil of nature is thus understood as the condition of possibility of evil maxims, as the *ground.*

As such, the tendency toward evil is "intelligible." Kant says: "If the *Dasein* of this penchant can be shown (*dargetan*) by empirical proofs of conflict in time, the nature (*Beschaffenheit*) and the ground (*Grund*) of this tendency have to be acknowledged a priori, for it is a relation of freedom to law whose concept is in each case nonempirical."[7] Experience "confirms" our judgments about radical evil, but it "can never discover the root of evil in the supreme maxim of free will in relation to law, for it is a question of an intelligible action preceding all experience."[8] Thus is swept away all *naturalism* in the conception of a "natural," "innate" tendency toward evil. It can be said to be given "at birth," but birth is not its cause. It is rather a "manner of being of freedom which comes to it from freedom." The idea of a "contracted" habit of free will thus furnishes the symbol of the reconciliation of the contingence and antecedence of evil.[9]

But then, in distinction to every "gnosis" which pretends to *know* the origin, the philosopher recognizes here that he is entering upon the inscrutable and the unfathomable: "As to the rational origin of this tendency to evil, it remains impenetrable to us because it must be imputed to us, and because otherwise this supreme ground of all maxims would require in its turn the admission of an evil maxim."[10] More strongly still: "Therefore we have no intelligible reason for knowing whence moral evil could have come to us in the first place."[11] The inscrutable for us consists precisely in this, that evil, which always begins *by* freedom, is always already there *for* freedom: it is act *and* habit, arising *and* antecedence. That is why Kant expressly makes of this enigma of evil for philosophy the transposition of the mythical figure of the serpent. The serpent, I think, represents the "always already there" of evil, of this evil that is nevertheless beginning, act, determination of freedom by itself.

Thus Kant completes Augustine: first by definitively destroying the gnostic wrappings of the concept of original sin, next by attempting a transcendental deduction of the ground of wrong maxims, finally by replunging into nonknowing the search for a ground of the ground. Thought has here a kind of movement of emergence, then of replunging: emergence to the clarity of the transcendental, replunging into the darkness of nonknowing. But perhaps philosophy is responsible not only for the circumscription of its knowing, but also for the *limits* by which it restricts to nonknowing; limit is no longer here a confine, but an active and sober self-limitation. Let us say again with Kant: "as to the origin of this inclination to evil, it remains impenetrable to us, *because it must be imputed to us.*"

Having arrived at this point, we may legitimately ask ourselves why reflection reduces the symbolic richness that yet keeps nourishing it. Perhaps in order to answer this we must return to the initial situation. A symbolism that would be only a symbolism of the soul, of the subject, of the "I," is from the start iconoclastic; for it represents a split between the "psychic" function and the other functions of symbol: cosmic, nocturnal, oneirotic, poetic. A symbolism of subjectivity already marks the breaking up of the symbolic totality. A symbol starts to be destroyed when it stops playing on several registers: cosmic and existential. The separation of the "human," of the "psychic," is the beginning of forgetfulness. That is why a purely anthropological symbolism is already on the way to allegory and heralds an ethical vision of evil and of the world.

Hence we understand that the resistance of symbol to the allegorizing reduction proceeds from the nonethical face of evil. The Adam symbol is protected against all moralizing reduction by the mass of the other myths; and it is the tragic figure of the serpent at the heart of the Adam symbol that protects it against all moralizing reduction. That is why the myths of evil have to be taken all together; it is their very dialectic that is instructive. Therefore, just as the figure of the serpent, at the center of the Adam myth, counters the demythologization of the Babylonian myths, so too original sin marks, within the ethical vision of the world, the resistance of the tragic to the ethical. But is it really the tragic that resists? We should rather say that it is an aspect irreducible to the ethical and complementary to every ethical, which has found a privileged expression in the tragic. For tragic anthropology is inseparable, as we have seen, from tragic theology; and this latter is at bottom unutterable.

Nor can philosophy reaffirm the tragic as such without committing suicide. The function of the tragic is to question self-assurance, self-certitude, one's critical pretensions, we might even say the presumption of the moral conscience that is laden with the entire weight of evil. Much pride is concealed, perhaps, in this humility. It is then that the tragic symbols speak in the silence of the humiliated ethical. They speak of a "mystery of iniquity" that man cannot entirely handle, that freedom cannot give reasons for, seeing that it already finds it within itself. Of this symbol there is no allegorical reduction. But, it will be objected, the tragic symbols speak of a *divine* mystery of evil. Perhaps it is necessary also to envelop in darkness the divine which the ethical vision has reduced to the moralizing function of judge. Against the juridicalism of accusation and justification, the God of Job speaks "from the depth of the tempest."

In its lowest reaches symbolism is never purely and simply symbolism of subjectivity, of the separated human subject, of interiorized self-awareness, of man split from being, but symbol of the union of man with being. One must, then, come to this point where he sees evil as the adventure of being, as part of the history of being.

IV. SPECULATIVE THOUGHT AND ITS FAILURE

Is every possibility of thought, therefore, extinguished with the non-knowing of the origin of the ground of evil maxims? Does the battle between reflective rigor and symbolic richness cease with the return of the impenetrable symbol of the fall? I do not think so. For there remains a hiatus between the understanding that we can have of man's essential nature, and the avowal of evil's unfathomable contingence. Can one leave side by side the necessity of fallibility and the contingence of evil?

It may seem here that we have neglected a whole dimension of the world of symbols on the mythical level, namely, that symbols of the "beginning" receive their complete meaning only from their relation to symbols of the "end": purification of stain, remission of sins, justification of the guilty. The great myths are at once myths of the beginning *and* of the end—thus the victim of Mardouk in the Babylonian myth, the reconciliation in the tragic and by the tragic, salvation through knowledge of the exiled soul, finally the biblical redemption characterized by the figures of the end: the king of the last times, the suffering servant, the Son of Man, the second Adam, type of the man to come. What is noteworthy in these symbolic representations is that the meaning proceeds from the end to the beginning, from the future to the past. So the question becomes: What does this chain of symbols, this retrograde movement of meaning, *give us to think about?*

Does it not invite us to move from the contingency of evil to a certain "necessity" of evil? This is the greatest task, but also the most perilous one for a philosophy nourished by symbols. It is the most perilous task: as we have said above, thought advances between the two chasms of allegory and gnosis. Reflective thought moves along the first chasm, speculative thought along the second. Yet it is the greatest task, for the movement which in symbolic thought goes from the beginning of evil to its end seems indeed to suppose the idea that all this finally has a meaning, that a meaningful figure imperiously takes form through the contingency of evil—in short, that evil belongs to a certain totality of the real. A certain necessity . . . a certain totality . . . but not just any necessity, not just any totality. The schemata of necessity that we can test have to satisfy a very strange demand; the necessity appears only afterwards, viewed from the end, and "in spite of" the contingency of evil.

St. Paul, it seems, invites such an inquiry when he confronts the two figures, that of the first Adam and that of the second Adam, the type of the old man and the type of the man to come. He does not limit himself to comparing and opposing them: "Just as the fault of one brought condemnation upon all men, so too the work of justice of one procures for all a justification that gives life" (Rom. 5:18): just as . . . so too. . . . From one to the other there is a movement, a progress, a rise in value: "If by the fault of one the multitude is dead, how much more (πολλῷ μᾶλλον) the grace of God and the gift conferred by the grace of a single man, Jesus Christ, are shed in profusion upon the multitude" (verse 15); "where sin was multiplied, grace was superabundant" (20). This "how much more," this "superabundance," outline a great task for thought.

But it must be admitted that no great philosophy of the *totality* is capable of giving an account of this inclusion of the contingency of evil in a meaningful design. For *either* the thought of necessity leaves contingency aside, *or* it so includes it that it entirely eliminates the "leap" of evil which posits itself and the "tragic" of evil which always precedes itself. . . .

CONCLUDING PERSPECTIVES

Three formulas present themselves to my mind, which express three connections between the experience of evil and the experience of a reconciliation. First, reconciliation is looked for in spite of evil. This "in spite of" constitutes a veritable category of hope, the category of contradiction. However, of that there is no proof, but only signs; the milieu, the locus of this category is a history, not a logic; an eschatology, not a system. Next, this "in spite of" is a "thanks to"; out of evil, the Principle of things brings good. The final contradiction is at the same time hidden teaching: *etiam peccata*, says St. Augustine as an inscription to Claudel's *Satin Slipper*, if I may put it that way. "Still the worst is never sure," replies Claudel in a litotes; but there is no absolute knowing, nor any "in spite of," nor any "thanks to." The third category of this meaningful history is the "how much more" (πολλῷ μᾶλλον). This law of superabundance englobes in its turn the "thanks to" and the "in spite of." That is the miracle of the *Logos;* from Him proceeds the retrograde movement of the true; from wonder is born the necessity that retroactively places evil in the light of being. What in the old theodicy was only the expedient of false-knowing becomes the intelligence of hope. The necessity that we are seeking is the highest rational symbol that this intelligence of hope can engender.

II. EXISTENTIAL PHENOMENOLOGY

The selections in this section represent Ricoeur's more "existential" writings. The first article, "Philosophy of Will and Action," gives a brief phenomenology of volition, then applies it to a "psychopathology of the will." Ricoeur works out a confrontation between the eidetic description of willing and the Freudian concept of the unconscious. The second essay, "Existential Phenomenology," addresses itself to the question of the apparent paradox of a pure eidetic science which would be somehow "existential." Ricoeur argues that this is not a contradiction and shows how the paradox can be overcome. In the third selection, "From Existentialism to the Philosophy of Language," Ricoeur describes an autobiographical intellectual journey, tracing the development of his philosophy from its most Husserlian stage to his more recent concern with symbols, language, and hermeneutics.

SOURCES

"Philosophy of Will and Action," in *Phenomenology of Will and Action*, edited by E. W. Straus and R. M. Griffith (Pittsburgh: Duquesne University Press, 1967), pp. 8–25. Used by permission.

"Existential Phenomenology," in *Husserl: An Analysis of His Phenomenology*, translated by Edward G. Ballard and Lester E. Embree (Evanston: Northwestern University Press, 1967), pp. 202–12. Used by permission.

"From Existentialism to Philosophy of Language." *Criterion* 10 (Spring, 1971): 14–18. Used by permission.

and finds it in what he calls προαίρεσις which we translate by the word *"preference."* Now, what is preference? The concept of preference is reached through a twofold difference: the opposition between preference and desire; and the opposition between preference and wish. Both oppositions are now looked upon as commonplace distinctions, but they were literally created by Aristotle by a kind of semantic decision. (The Greek word βούλεσθαι means, indifferently, to will, to wish, or to desire.) The first opposition between choice and desire is based on the structure of "election," of rational consultation; in the word of Aristotle, to pre-fer means to pre-deliberate: προαίρεσις means προβού-λευμα. Our entire rationalistic philosophy of will is based on these distinctions and identifications both at the level of reflection and at the level of semantic analysis. The second distinction—between will and wish—is no less interesting, since for a Greek it was difficult to elaborate; it relies on the famous axiom: Deliberation concerns means, not ends; wishing concerns ends, inasmuch as these lie outside of our control; willing concerns means, inasmuch as they depend upon us. The analysis here is based on a sort of practical logic: "We deliberate not about ends, but about means to an end. No physician deliberates whether he will cure, no orator whether he will persuade, no statesman whether he will produce a good constitution; nor in fact any man in any other function about his particular end; but having set before themselves a certain end, they consider how and by what means it may be accomplished." As may be seen, this kind of practical logic finds its limitations in the examples themselves, borrowed from the human crafts and professions and from a consideration of political discussion; we may even say that this model of political deliberation taken from the Greek *agora* has both inspired and misled our entire philosophy of deliberation and imposed an official and artificial pattern on will. That is why we may say that Aristotle has opened the field and at the same time limited the scope of our philosophy of the will.

I want to emphasize further two other great moments in the birth of our philosophy of choice: Augustine and Descartes. To the first we owe a radical discovery, the link between will and nothingness. The circumstances of this discovery deserve to be recalled: Augustine is faced with the problem of evil and with the attempt to solve it in the gnostic manner, that is, through a cosmic drama in which man would no longer be responsible. By rooting the origin of evil in human freedom, Augustine radically changes the nature and the scope of human will; within this will he discerns an awful power: the power of separation, the power of negating what is true and good, of denying being itself. Whereas the Aristotelian will was limited to the choice of means, with Augustine the human will is the power of saying "no." Man can freely choose the good, the true, being, because he can negate all these things. Thus far, then, we have two philosophical approaches to the concept of choice, that of relative preference, and that of absolute choice.

This gives us the background for understanding Descartes' problem; as you know, the Cartesian analysis of will is linked to the problem of error; we may look upon it as a transformation of the Augustinian problem of sin. Once again will is the power of the alternative between *yes* and *no;* in that sense it is a kind of absolute; even divine freedom has no greater extension; it simply consists in the power of doing something or not doing it, in the power of affirmation and negation; in itself this power has no degrees; there are only degrees of clearness in our motives and reason, not in this power of contraries.

The Cartesian analysis does not suffer from the Aristotelian limitation, since it has got rid of the distinction between means and ends, but it does suffer from another kind of limitation; in order to isolate the moment of choice, Descartes had to separate will and understanding, and to inquire into the relationship between these two powers or faculties; but the question of how the will acts on the understanding and the understanding on the will could only be a misleading question; one of the tasks of the phenomenology of will is to draw the analysis out of this dead end.

However, we are now in a position to face a new dimension of this act of choice. We do so with Kant. Instead of introducing a new description, Kant leads the previous description to a kind of critical point by means of his famous *antinomy* between free causality and natural causality. The problem is thus transferred from the sphere of rational psychology to that of cosmology; at the same time there is revealed the antinomic structure of a philosophy of will, and it is seen that the Aristotelian, Augustinian, and Cartesian descriptions led to a sort of breaking-point. This antinomic structure was discernible only when the concept of nature itself had been completely elaborated according to Galilean and Newtonian physics.

Now that nature is considered as a regular succession of phenomena, there is no longer any place within nature for an absolute power of choosing. The idea of an absolute beginning can no longer be a cosmological idea.

We may say that thought which has not reached this level of antinomy can never be a critical philosophy of will. Now what does antinomy imply for our inquiry? First of all, it implies that there is no longer a unifying system under which we could relate both natural laws and the responsibility of an ethical subject. The question of a free choice is now linked to a crisis within reason itself, and it is this question alone which has the awful power to reveal the antinomic structure of reason.

This, too, will be a grave question for a phenomenology, namely, whether it is able to go beyond the antinomy of free and natural causality.

But the philosophy of will has a second root, which is, so to speak, the counterpart of the first. We called the first question the question of the human act: it led us to the concepts of preference and free choice and to the Kantian free causality. The second question, on the contrary, concerns the link between will and *life*—life meaning either the spontaneity of desire or the bodily structures supporting organized motion and action. We will call this second question the question of *motivation.* The problem is as old as the first one; we find its first formulation in Plato's *Phaedo;* Socrates, explaining why he remained in jail and didn't flee, states:

> . . . is it because the movements of my body brought me and keep me here? No! Rather it is because, "the Athenians have thought fit to condemn me, and accordingly I have thought it better and more right to remain here and undergo my sentence; for I am in-clined to think that these muscles and bones of mine would have gone off long ago to Megara or Boeotia—by the dog, they would, if they had been moved only by their own idea of what was best, and if I had not chosen the better and nobler part, instead of playing truant and running away, of enduring any punishment which the state inflicts" (*Phaedo,* 98e–99a).

The problem of motivation is here already clearly formulated; it is a kind of causality, but something other than a natural cause; in Plato's words, the natural cause is that "without which" ($\alpha \nu \epsilon \upsilon$ $o\upsilon$) we could not act; the motivational process is that "through which" ($\delta \iota \grave{\alpha}$ $\acute{o}$) we act; the problem of motivation is raised and will no longer be forgotten; even if it, too, is overshadowed by a narrow concept of deliberation.

I do not wish to tell the story of this concept of motivation; I pre-fer to focus attention on the *one* philosopher who gave the concept its full strength. I mean Leibniz. His philosophy is truly the birthplace of the modern concept of motivation; from then on this concept has had two connotations. On the one hand, these derive from the logi-cal principles known as the principle of sufficient reason—which Leib-niz opposes to mere logical and mechanical necessity; as applied to the sphere of psychical life, this principle means that motivation implies inclination without compulsion; a motive is a "reason why" and not a cause which infallibly produces its effect. The same distinction can be found among modern epistemologists trained in the school of linguistic analysis; but it remains at the level of semantics and lacks reference to a specific mode of intelligibility. The second aspect of the concept of motivation is equally important; it results from the concatenation of all the events within the individual unity called the monad; this philosophy of individual being, irreducible to a logic of genus and species, affords a theoretical framework for any kind of relation between a whole and its parts, wherein the law of the whole finds a differential expression in each particular event. Motivation, in the psychological sense, is one of these relations. Under this second aspect, the concept of motivation is connected up with that of totality; this connection is overlooked in the other tradition, running from Aristotle to Descartes and culminating in the existentialist theory of radical choice; it is better preserved in the contemporary psychologies of personality; but these psychologies fail to elaborate adequate concepts required by their field of experience; with Leibniz we do have such concepts.

Let us pause here. We have followed two distinct lines of thought; the first, that of the philosophy of act, finds its fulfillment in the Kantian antinomy between free cause and natural cause; the second, that of the philosophy of motivation, finds its fulfillment in the Leibnizian conception of the monad. These two lines are often blended: there is a concept of motivation in Aristotle, Descartes, and Kant; on the other hand motivation, in spite of its link with the concept of totality, begets a new antinomy within causality itself. To distinguish between motive and cause is to reinstate the Kantian distinction between physical and free causality. Thus each of these two problematic approaches implies the other. For this reason we may say that the fundamental problem for phenomenology will be to describe and understand the deep connection between these two classical approaches to the philosophy of will, that of choice and that of motivation.

On this occasion we shall reduce the philosophical problem to these two questions. But we must not lose sight of the fact that both of them receive their dignity and, if we may say so, their gravity from a third and more radical question, which constitutes the horizon of any philosophy of will and action. This question is represented by Spinoza; it can be phrased in these terms: Where is freedom? In the removal of all dependency? In the lack of determination? In the anxiety of choosing oneself? Or does it coincide with the discovery and understanding of an inner necessity, deeper than any choice and any kind of autonomy? In a word, does the highest degree of freedom consist in the surging up of an absolute power of choosing or in the love of fate?

Our inquiry will not reach the level of this question, which will remain merely its horizon. Nevertheless it is back to this ultimate question, the question of freedom and fate, that the most rigorous science of human behavior leads through a long and roundabout way.

II. THE PHENOMENOLOGY OF VOLITION

I would like first of all to indicate what the phenomenology of the will owes to Husserl. In truth, the founder of phenomenology did not constitute a phenomenology of affectivity, of volition or of action. The principal emphasis of phenomenology was laid upon what Husserl called, in his first period, "objectifying acts" or "representation." His last philosophy itself, at the time of the *Krisis,* is much more centered on the problem of perception and the "Lebenswelt"; it is more concerned with a "view" than with a theatre of action. To the end, the phenomenology of Husserl remains an analysis of the "to see"; phenomenology itself aims at seeing; its descriptions are an exercise of visions applied to vision. Nevertheless, even if a phenomenology of will and of action breaks open the de facto limits of Husserlian phenomenology, and even if, as we will see, it rather radically transforms its spirit, it remains faithful to it with regard to two essential points: the recourse to descriptive analysis and the application to volition of the thematic structure of intentionality. I would like to emphasize these two points. At a first level, at least, phenomenology is a description which proceeds by analysis; it interrogates in the following way: What is the meaning of the "to will," the "to move," of motive, of situation? Far from being, as its critics have suggested, an appeal to sentiments and emotion, phenomenology is, from beginning to end, an analysis of significations. It is not afraid to look for what it calls the "essences of the lived," that is, the structures of experience capable of being understood directly by means of a small number of well chosen examples. Its favorite technique is the method of imaginative variation. It is in varying the possible realizations of the same essential structure that the fundamental articulations can be made manifest.

I would prefer that phenomenology be accused of Platonizing; this reproach is much more worthy; but one really Platonizes only when one actualizes essences in another world. For Husserl these essences are, rather, the a priori structures of all lived experience; they are the ideal contents which language presupposes each time that we say: "I want," "I desire," "I long for," or that we understand a situation or a behavior as signifying willing, desiring, or longing. These significations can be identified and recognized in spite of the flux of consciousness and in spite of the singularity of each consciousness. Phenomenology makes a wager for the possibility of thinking and of naming, on the one hand, even with regard to the confusion of affective life. Phenomenology wagers that the lived can be understood and said. It is this search for the meaning of the lived which justifies its title of phenomenology, that is, of *logos* of *phainomena.* The second presupposition of Husserlian phenomenology is that there reigns, in every experience, the correlated structure of "intention"—"object." To tell the truth, Husserl has shown this only in the order of perception; but, if it is true that intentionality characterizes the whole psychological order in contrast to the physical order, a phenomenology of volition and of action should likewise take as a guide the noetico-noematic analysis; it also must be able to analyze "acts," "aims," and "intentions" starting with the corresponding objects, that is, it must attempt to analyze all the correlations capable of being distinguished between the "intendings" and the "aspects" of the world, of my body and of others corresponding to these affective, volitional and practical intendings.

I will retain for this intentional analysis the guidelines which our prior philosophical analysis has offered us. I will consider successively the question of choice, then that of motivation. It is in the confrontation of these two themes that we will best grasp the originality of the phenomenological approach. It is also at this crossroads that we will place ourselves at the end of this second section in order to apperceive the articulation of the psychopathology and the phenomenology of volition. Let us start, then, with volition or choice.

The first structure offered to description is the voluntary intention itself. In a sense, everything is intention in consciousness: perception, memory, judgment, etc. In a broad sense there is an intention as soon as there is an intending, an aiming at something; but it is volition which is intention par excellence. If perception can be called an intention or, according to an earlier expression of Husserl, an act, it is to the extent that it expresses a power of thinking, and a power which depends upon us for its exercise. Every intention, in the strong sense of the term, is attention and every attention reveals an "I can" at the heart of the "I think." Thus, far from it being the case that the intentional analysis of volition is simply a transposition of that of perception—an area in which Husserl and his students excelled—it can be said that the analysis of volition places us at the very heart of the intentional function of consciousness. This central character of volition appears only if we break immediately with the old faculty psychology which, in the past, had prevented scholastic and Cartesian philosophy from fully completing their analyses. Nothing is more misleading in this regard than the opposition between understanding and will—as if only the operations of understanding had an object and as if the will were not intelligent in its fashion. The project of taking a trip is no less an intellectual operation than the observation of a state of affairs; such a project intends an aspect of the world just as much as the predicative proposition. Thus it is necessary to analyze the decision and the project while remaining completely oblivious to everything concerning the distinction of faculties. Faithful to the method indicated above, we will begin, then, with the "objective" side of "decision." In the project of

taking a trip, something is designated: something which I can indeed
designate also as a state of affairs; but this state of affairs is not the
term of an observation; it is an intending with a double quality: It is,
on the one hand, something which is "to be done" and not "already
there"—we will call it a "pragma"; on the other hand, it is something
which is "to be done by me," and not by another, as would be the
case with a wish, or an order addressed to another person. Thus we will
say that the project is a: "to be done by me." This second characteristic
designates the *pragma* as dependent upon me, as being within my
power. Thus, a dimension of the possible is discovered which is: neither a logical possibility—that is, the contrary of which does not imply
a contradiction; nor a physical eventuality—that is, something which is
compatible with the order of the world; nor a biological virtuality—
something which I can consider as a tendency of life. This "possible"
designates the capacity for the realization of the project inasmuch as
it is within my power; it is the correlate of my power over things themselves. It is a pure prejudice to maintain that this "possible" is more
"subjective" than the logically, physically or biologically possible. It
is no less objective than these: it is a signification directed toward the
world, *in the world;* the project is inserted into a future of the world,
which world includes voids, the indeterminate, the non-resolved; this
possible is projected upon the course of events, some of which do not
depend upon me and others of which do, to speak as the Stoics. Both
constitute the meaning of the world, and that to the same degree. The
world is such that a responsible agent bears the weight of a certain
number of events which happen because of him; the world is such
that it can be the object of prevision and of projects. It is by virtue of
an unjustifiable reduction that we decide to equate "world" with
the whole of observable facts; I inhabit a world in which there is something "to be done by me"; the "to be done by me" belongs to the
structure which is the "world."

A noetic quality corresponds to this noematic structure (the project
as being "to be done" and as being "in my power"): The voluntary intention is a "taking of a stand," a *Stellungnahme,* the affirmative intensity of which corresponds to the categorical modality of observational
judgments. It is this same modality which one finds in an order or an
imperative; it is the *fiat* aspect already described by William James; I
say: "Let it be this way." Moreover, this categorical modality presents
all degrees of affirmation, of doubt and conjecture, as could be revealed
by a close description of indecision, velleity, of unsteady or of firm
will. But this "taking a stand" itself has a double aspect; in taking a
position with respect to changes in the world which are "to be done by
me," I am taking a position with respect to myself; I commit myself
and I bind myself. In this regard, the analysis of a promise is richly

revealing—not at all that every decision is a promise, but a promise adds a particular consecration and a sort of solemn ritual to a more fundamental relation which one finds in all decisions which are not promises. This relation can be called an "imputing of" or an imputation. In determining something, I determine myself. Thus I myself figure in the project as the one to whom the action can be imputed. It is perhaps at this point that the privileged character of voluntary intention appears. Indeed, it is in the voluntary intention that the relation between the self and its acts is revealed in all its plenitude. Every act, in the strong sense of the term, possesses at the same time an objective intending and a relation of "imputation" which appears clearly in a decision; in making up my mind, I impute to myself the action, that is, I place it in a relation to myself such that, from then on, this action represents me in the world; if it is asked: "Who did this?" I hold myself ready to respond: "It is I who did this, *ego sum qui feci.*" I anticipated in a certain way the situation in which I will take the responsibility for the origin of the act before someone else; I answer for it; I take it upon myself; I assume it. Thus I posit myself as the agent in the intending of the action to be done. This analysis can be summarized in these terms: The voluntary intention is what reveals the subject pole of all my acts; and this original relation of me to myself is not at all that of an inspection, a looking which would transform me into an object and congeal me; the imputation of the self in its project is a nonspeculative imputation; it is an implication of myself which is rigorously contemporaneous with the act of decision; moreover, it may be said that it is a prereflective imputation. Far from looking at myself, it is in my acts that I affirm myself; the imputation is not a speculative construction; it is a practical affirmation, homogeneous with the project itself. It is even (and only) on the basis of this prereflective affirmation of myself in my projects that all my judgments of reflection can be understood. I conduct myself actively in relation to myself and I relate myself to my own being as to my own most proper possibility. This possibility of myself is the noetic correlate of the possibility which I open up in the world by means of my projects. In the same way that a project opens up possibilities in the world, it opens up new possibilities in myself and reveals me to myself as a possibility of acting. My power-to-be manifests itself in my power-to-do and this power-to-do is revealed to itself in the projects which it forms concerning things and in the world.

Let us consider the path which we have traversed before going on to the second moment of this phenomenological analysis, that is, to motivation. What new dimension does this intentional analysis bring to the philosophy of choice? On the one hand, it disengages the implicit phenomenology. One can indeed speak of a phenomenology of will in Aristotle, Augustine, Descartes and Kant (see Part I); but this phenomenology is mixed with other projects or considerations which limit its development: ethical and theological projects or epistemological and critical projects. The rule established by Husserl to return to things themselves and to abstain from every presupposition bears precisely and essentially on such considerations which hide the specificity of the structures of consciousness. In modern times, it is above all the concern to found science which impedes the development of pure description. An exclusive respect for observable facts follows in fact from this concern, a concern, that is, with objects considered as the correlates of a theoretical consciousness, and which are reducible to a physico-mathematical model. What we call experience is the product of such a reduction to the objective fact which is mathematized and inserted into a system which can be, in addition, formalized and axiomatized. The phenomenology of will even more than that of perception is entirely hidden in its proper character by a "prejudice" of this sort. With respect to objective experience, volition seems to be without object; only theoretical consciousness, one which is observational and quantifiable, has objects, it would seem; volition is, then, thrown back to the side of subjectivity, and the "possible" which it opens up is not a possible of "the world," but rather a possible which is "of thought only." In this regard, phenomenology represents a return to naïveté. It liberates sight and renders it attentive to all the richness of the real. For it, the perceived and the willed are original contours of the world; they are even dimensions of a reality more original than the scientific object, which appears later, at a second level of elaboration, while reality has already become a meaningful world at the stage of perception and action.

In thus giving to lived experience its complete amplitude, phenomenology prepares the way for the resolution of the Kantian antinomy. As we said, the Kantian antinomy represents a level of thought to which it is necessary to accede; in order to go beyond it, it is first necessary to have attained it. However, the Kantian antinomy is the result of the complete objectification of nature; human choice finds itself expelled, exiled from a nature which is entirely reduced to physical causality. Phenomenology leads back to a position which is prior to this total objectification, to a stage in which the world is not reduced to physical nature, but where it is still—following the expression of a pre-Socratic thinker—the gathering of gods, men and things. There is a world of *praxis,* of which the *theoria* is a second level; in the language of the early Heidegger, the world is the place of "care" (*Sorge*); there is a place for "care" which is more primitive than the world of scientific knowledge and which furnishes the latter with its first base, its preliminary ground. Will, as much as perception, reveals this enrooting of human existence in a world which is the field of its *praxis* before being a view for its theoretical reason.

This resolution of the Kantian antinomy does not signify that it was false or that a better reasoning process has enabled us to discover a new point of view capable of encompassing the thesis and the antithesis. The antinomy is confirmed at that level of theory attained by *thought about nature.* What phenomenology proposes is not a resolution of the antinomy at its level of rationality, but rather the rooting of it in a more original level of thought and existence, the very one in which perception and volition indeed reign. At this level, the world is at once both view and theatre of our action. This undividedness contains germinally the thesis and the antithesis of the antinomy which breaks apart only at a later level of rationality. Phenomenology only resolves the Kantian antinomy by carrying philosophical meditation back to a prereflective level which is prior to the antinomy; the antinomy manifests itself, then, as a cultural creation, contemporary with the advent of science; and its cultural creation is seen to be a conflict which is localized within a more fundamental relation of belonging, a belonging of man to the world. The antinomy does not receive an intellectual solution, but is located within the context of a more original ground.

It is this more original ground which we will continue to explore by means of the relation of motivation.

The concept of motivation has, as we have seen, a considerable philosophical past; but it is phenomenology which will render it full justice, both by restoring its complete signification and by resolving the antinomies to which it has given rise.

In the philosophical tradition—at least in that of classical rationalism—the field of motivation has too often been reduced to the canonical form of deliberation following the model of a parliamentary debate; anticipating the language of psychoanalysis, we can already say that deliberation thus understood is only a secondary elaboration, a rationalization. Behind it hides a more secret motivation with regard to which the "official" deliberation plays the role of screen or mask. The dimension of motivation can be given its complete amplitude by saying that a motive serves as a "support" or "base" for choice. This metaphor of "support" contains two different notions which are precisely coordinated in the concept of motive: the idea of a meaning and the idea of a force: a meaning inasmuch as the motive is a justification, a legitimization, a reason *to* or *for*; a force to the extent that the motive initiates a movement, inclines or entails. The connection of meaning and force is an essential one; there is no motive which is not to some degree a reason for, . . . thus a basis for value, and to some degree an energy, a power, in the sense in which Aristotle said that "the will moves by desire." In the third section [omitted in this selection], we will see to what extent this relation of force and meaning is essential for integrating psychoanalysis with the phenomenology of will. For psychoanalytic interpretation establishes itself precisely at this point of junction between force and meaning. At the moment, let us just say that this double function of legitimization and of motive constitutes the originality of the relation of motivation. When I say: I decide to take a trip because I *need* rest and because I *must* finish some work, the need and the duty both enter into the relation of motivation. In spite of their very different psychological function, they possess in common the characteristic of being related to voluntary intention as motives; it is this relation which is expressed in the: "because."

Here we find again the Leibnizian level of analysis. The motive is not the cause, of which the intention would be the effect. This relation is still too "physical" and does not account for the double function of motive which is to legitimize at the same time as to incline. It is necessary to avoid the suggestions of a too-clumsy imagery which would reduce the action of motives to that of weights tipping the balance of a scale. This is to forget that motives are themselves moving intentions and that the meaning of our motives is halted and completed only when that of our decisions is likewise; thus the relation: "motive-choice" is a circular relation: in cutting the knot of indecision, I also decide the meaning of my motives. And yet motivation is not a comedy which I play with myself; it has the function of binding the particular decisions of will to the whole of the personality. It is the second function which we have related to motives in the line of the Leibnizian monadology. But now we understand better this second function of motivation; it is because the motive gives meaning along with force that it can exercise its function of integration and of continuity at the level of the total personality. Without this relation of motivation, our choices would be discontinuous and as arbitrary as gratuitous acts or stupid wagers. Thanks to motivation, they are not reducible to discontinuous irruptions, but are integrated into the totality of experience and make our decisions themselves expressions of our total personality.

We will go beyond the Leibnizian level of description by making manifest a new relation, that of motivation to the body itself. By means of motivation, as a matter of fact, volition is placed in a living relation with bodily spontaneity—let us say, in general terms, with the sphere of the involuntary.

Why this new step? Because a theory of motivation which would not include the bodily field would not solve the new antinomy raised by the opposition between motive and cause. Physical cause is involved in the process of motivation through my body, inasmuch as it is *both* a part of the objective world and a part of my subjective experience, especially as a system of skills and abilities. It is in the experience of the *involuntary* that the objective and the subjective sides of experience are blended and that physical causality becomes psychical motivation. In order to understand this connection between the voluntary and the involuntary, we will have to complete our earlier description of volition. We have only underlined the active dimension of volition under the aspect of "taking a stand"; but the "taking of a stand" is itself correlative with an aspect of passivity, or better, of receptivity, which is expressed precisely in the relation of choice to its motives. Pfänder, whose analyses we have invoked several times, spoke of a *geistiges Gehör*, of a spiritual, that is, nonbodily listening, in order to designate that "reception" of reasons and forces which are incorporated in our volitions under the aspect of motives; some very suggestive metaphors will allow us to understand this: I say that I accept certain reasons, that I adhere to a point of view, that I go along with an opinion, that I adopt a position, etc. These metaphors of adhesion, or better, of adherence, reveal that there is a point of passivity or of receptivity in the heart of volition by which will renders itself sensitive to anything which can incline it without necessitating it, which can provide it with an impulsion and a legitimization. It is a proper characteristic of finite liberty to be able to decide only by becoming sensitive to motives.

But if motivation represents the moment of passivity of will, in return the relation of motive to volition gives to the human body a completely original significance. Our needs, our desires are not simply irresistible forces that can be measured and treated as physical magnitudes; they are also significations, evaluations, which are capable of entering into a field of motivation and of being confronted there with other values (esthetic, moral, religious, etc.). In the example which we gave earlier, a need and a duty find themselves combined in the same function of motivation. In other situations they can oppose each other; this is even more frequently the case. But even in this relation of opposition, they have in common the same function of motivation. What we just called the total field of motivation signifies precisely that needs can be incorporated in volition under the aspect of values of the vital level, confronted with other values of different levels; duty, in the Kantian sense, itself figures as a formal value in this total field of motivation, where it is confronted with the material values of multiple origin which constitute all the richness of our emotional life.

Thus, it is motivation that constitutes the living relation of volition to the body itself; this relation has a double meaning: on the one hand, it expresses the incarnation of human willing; on the other hand, it signifies that the body is a human body to the extent to which the living forces which constitute it are susceptible of entering into composition with other values in the total field of motivations. At the same time that the will becomes an embodied will, the body becomes a human body.

CHAPTER 5

Existential Phenomenology

Taken alone, the term "phenomenology" is not very illuminating. The word means science of appearances or of appearings. Thus, any inquiry or any work devoted to the way anything whatsoever appears is already phenomenology. The way in which things, animate beings, or human beings show themselves could be described. Thus, the phenomenology of a "region" of reality, the region thing, the region animal, the region man could be produced. Likewise, the phenomenology of a feeling (e.g., fear, if one descibes the way in which fear, the thing feared, and the world under the sign of fear show themselves) and in general the phenomenology of any subjective process of consciousness could be elaborated. In this diluted sense the word "phenomenology" covers every sort of popular presentation of appearances. The term is a long way from a disciplined limitation of its usage.

Phenomenology becomes strict when the status of the appearing of things (in the broadest sense of the term) becomes problematical. In short, it becomes strict when this question is raised: What does "appearing" signify for a thing, for an animate being, for a person, for a conscious experience, for a feeling, for an image, and the like? How do the "regions" of reality (thing, animal, man, etc.) relate to the subjective processes of consciousness (perceiving, imagining, positing an abstraction, judging, etc.)? In this strict sense the question of being, the ontological question, is excluded in advance from phenomenology, either provisionally or definitely. The question of knowing that which *is* in an absolute sense is placed "between parentheses," and the manner of appearing is treated as an autonomous problem. Phenomenology in the strict sense begins as soon as this distinction is reflected upon for its own sake, whatever the final result may be. On the other hand, whenever the act of birth, which brings appearing to emergence at the expense of being or against the background of being, is no longer perceived and systematized, then phenomenology ceases to be a philosophical discipline and falls back to the level of ordinary and popular description.

If what is implied in this first strict determination of the notion of phenomenology is developed, and if one calls "transcendental" any attempt at relating the conditions of the appearance of things to the structure of human subjectivity (in short, to the very life of the subject to whom and for whom things appear), then it will be said that all phenomenology is transcendental. Long before Husserl, Kant and Hegel understood the word "phenomenology" in this way: If this is how things stand, how can we speak of "existential" phenomenology? Is it another branch alongside transcendental phenomenology? But could there be another branch if all phenomenology is transcendental? We shall show that the phenomenology termed "existential" is not another division juxtaposed to "transcendental phenomenology"; rather, this phenomenology becomes a method and is placed in the service of a dominating problem-set, viz., the problems concerning existence.

Phenomenology of the existential sort brings together investigations and writings from several sources: (1) Under this rubric the last investigations of the founder of contemporary phenomenology, Edmund Husserl, can be placed. In these researches we can observe "transcendental" phenomenology turning toward an investigation of the various aspects of man's insertion in the world. (2) In addition, we must draw out the whole function of the rigorous description incorporated in the great philosophies which proceeded from Kierkegaard and Nietzsche in France and Germany (and also from the Hegel of the *Phenomenology of Mind*, not to mention that species of phenomenology of economic existence which can be discerned in the work of Karl Marx). These existential descriptions constitute an original source of contemporary phenomenology. In comparison with these philosophies born of the opposition to Hegel's *Logic,* in which classical philosophy is brought to its completion, Husserl's work seems to stand closer to certain currents of Neo-Kantianism than their author believed. (3) A third cycle of existential phenomenology is constituted by the works, particularly the French ones, which are situated at the confluence of the phenomenological method deriving from Husserl and the existential problem-set received from post-Hegelian philosophy. These works best merit the title "existential phenomenology."

I. THE "EXISTENTIAL" TURN OF "TRANSCENDENTAL" PHENOMENOLOGY

Husserlian phenomenology became more and more existential to the degree that the problem of perception took precedence over all other problems. This development deserves an explanation. In Husserl's first works, from the *Logical Investigations* to the *Cartesian Meditations,* consciousness is defined not by perception, that is to say, by its very presence to things, but rather by its distance and its absence. This distance and this absence are the power of signifying, of meaning. The intending of signifying can be empty (and even incapable of fulfillment, as is the case with absurd propositions): then perception is only a privileged mode of fulfillment by intuition. Thus, consciousness is doubly intentional, in the first instance by virtue of being a signification and in the second instance by virtue of being an intuitive fulfilling. In short, in the first works, consciousness is at once speech (*la parole*) and perception.

It is in the works and manuscripts of the last ten years that perception is described as the initial basis and genetic origin of all operations of consciousness. This is the consciousness which gives, which sees, which effects presences, and it supports and founds the consciousness which signifies, which judges, and which speaks. This shift in accent marks the passage to existential phenomenology. In fact, the sense of the existence of things and that of the existence of the subject are revealed simultaneously in perception thus reinterpreted.

From its encounter with the Platonic and then with the Galilean tradition, which suppose that the true reality is not what one perceives but what one conceives and measures, the "thing" acquires transcendence in relation to consciousness. This transcendence certainly is not the absolute transcendence of an "in-itself" which could do without any conscious witness but is the relative transcendence of an object (*un vis-à-vis*) into which consciousness comes to transcend itself (*se dépasser*). Consciousness defined by its intentionality is outside, beyond. It ties its own wandering to the "things" to which it can apply its consideration, its desire, its action. Correlatively, the world is "world-for-my-life," environment of the "living ego." And it has this sense only with reference to the "living present," where the pact between daily living and every revealed presence is continuously renewed. Retained and anticipated, time is once more, as Kant said of the imagination, "the art hidden in nature" thanks to which the living present never ceases to move beyond itself into the project of a total world.

Yet, in becoming more and more existential, the phenomenology of the late Husserl became more and more empirical, for the whole order of the understanding—predicative judgment, affirmation and negation, activity of synthesis and consecution—henceforth proceeds from "passive synthesis" initiated on the very level of perception. Thereafter it is clear that this progression toward an ever more originary original destroys every claim of constituting the world "in" consciousness or "beginning from" consciousness. The idealistic tendency of transcendental phenomenology is thus compensated for by the progressive discovery that one does not constitute the originary but only all that one can derive from it. The originary is just what could neither be constituted nor reduced.

The "world," consequently, is not what Kant said it was, viz., the Idea of reason, which commands us to unify scientific experience. For this cosmological Idea there is substituted the altogether existential notion of the horizon of subjective life. The "world" is prior to every "object." It is not only presupposed in the intellectualistic sense of a condition for possibilities, it is pre-given in the sense that every present activity surges into a world already there. Moreover, this world is the totality which, not being composed from parts and by means of addition, is inaccessible to doubt. It is the "passive pre-given universal of all judgmental activity," the "one basis of belief upon which every experience of particular objects is erected."

II. THE IMPLICIT PHENOMENOLOGY OF THE PHILOSOPHY OF EXISTENCE

1.   Not all of existential phenomenology is in Husserl—far from it. This is the place to recall that Hegel's first great work is called *The Phenomenology of Mind*. Now this great book nourished the most determined opponents of Hegelianism more than they believed, particularly the opponents of Hegel's *Logic*. It is one of the sources of the philosophy of existence.

In this book philosophy, passing from consciousness to self-consciousness, incorporated for the first time the most dramatic experiences of humanity which previously had yielded only to poetic, dramatic, or religious expression and not to essays having an economic, political, or historical turn. The pages on the desire of a desire which would be another self, on the struggle for recognition through the dialectic of master and slave, on stoicism and skepticism, on unhappy consciousness, and the like—today all of these pages are well-known. Hegel's concern to let human experience appear and speak for itself in its integrity is quite comparable to Husserl's precept: "Back to the things themselves." But at the same time Hegel introduced into the field of phenomenological analysis the "negative" experiences of disappearance, contradiction, struggle, and frustration which impart the tragic tone to his phenomenology. This tone is utterly foreign to Husserl's works which never drew on the "work of the negative"— as Hegel terms it—in the explication of self-consciousness.

This difference is fundamental. At the very moment that it promises an immense enrichment of the description, properly so-called, of human experience, this promotion of the "negative" paradoxically announces the end of phenomenology. In fact, these experiences of

the negative are intended to assure the "transitions" from one form
to another, and by that very fact to give a systematic cohesion which
the old logic of identity and noncontradiction was quite incapable of
introducing into the profusion of human experience. The "negative"
is the possibility of a system no longer of the analytical type, after the
fashion of the Leibnizian combinatorial logic, but of the dialectical
type in which the "negative" mediates the becoming of spirit through
its forms. Thus, phenomenology discovers the "negative." This negative
brought in the new logic, and this logic eliminated phenomenology.
This is why the philosophy of existence, though it may elaborate one
or another of the Hegelian analyses taken in isolation, is set up over
against the Hegelian system and against Logic, where tragedy is swallowed up.

2.   The term "existence," in the sense given it by contemporary philosophy, comes from Kierkegaard. The existent par excellence is the
individual who emerges in sadness and solitude, in doubt and exalta-
tion—and in passion—this is the individual whom the System does not
include. This strange and irrational birth to itself of the existential
thinker initially escapes every methodological concern; hence, it is beyond phenomenology—if its strict character as the science of phenomena be emphasized.

Nevertheless, in two respects Kierkegaard's thought contains the
outlines of a quite strict phenomenology. In the first place, his almost
sickly concern for self-justification initiates one of the most extraordinary apparatuses for the description of subjectivity ever constructed.
For example, the description of "stages on life's way" is set out in an
unusual key, one in which the intimacy of the most individual confession coincides with the generality of the barest abstraction. In the same
way a vertiginous dread, even fear of the vertigo, which grasps freedom
when confronted with the infinity of its possibilities and the finitude
of its engagements and under the goad of the forbidden—a dread in
which innocence turns aside to sin—elicits a description whose subtlety
mobilizes the resources of a casuistical psychology, of dramatic art, and
of theological anthropology. In short, the *Concept of Dread* is, properly
speaking, already a phenomenology of freedom.

Beyond this concern for justification which generates a pitiless lu-
cidity, Kierkegaard's work conceals within its irrationality a second
motive for rigor. In fact, as against Hegel, it was a matter of framing
the charter of the antisystem and thus little by little of rendering the
opposition to the System coherent. The *Philosophical Fragments* and
the *Postscript* develop this methodology of the antisystem by elaborating actual "categories" of the individual over against those of logic:
the instant in place of the eternity of logic, the individual in place of

the whole, paradox in place of mediation, and existence in place of the System. With the same stroke—and not without contradiction—the existential thinking tends toward a strict elaboration of the "concepts" of the antisystem and thus toward a phenomenology, which, unlike Hegel's, will never be swallowed up in logic. In these two ways, Kierkegaard is at the origin of existential phenomenology.

3. But Nietzsche is also one of its fathers. He also used strict description, though for other than Kierkegaard's reasons. To be sure, an aphoristic form and a symbolic, even mythological, construction belong to the essence of his thinking; an attempt to find a system in it would prove vain. But strict description is required by Nietzsche's plan just as it was by Kierkegaard's. It is set in motion not by concern for self-justification and for setting up a sort of indirect communication with the Other, but rather by the pitiless taste for unmasking the moral and spiritual falsehoods on which our culture is built. Nietzsche's work—at least the negative, nihilistic side of it—is an enormous enterprise of methodical disillusionment. The *Genealogy of Morals*—did Husserl not call one of his last works a "genealogy of logic"?—is a genuine phenomenology, at once reductive and genetic, applied to the totality of moral phenomena.

A powerful and wily instinct for dissimulation is discovered at the center of human existence, which philosophy vows to track down, to denounce, and to destroy. Thus, long before the Husserlian phenomenology issued from the technique of reduction, the philosopher of "suspicion" followed the path from the derived to the originary. It matters little to us that he mixed in with this technique of truth a dogmatism of instinct and an evolutionistic scientism which are antiquated today. It even matters little that Nietzsche should have lost himself in his destructive passion. The fact remains that he is the first to have practiced what Jean-Paul Sartre later called "existential psychoanalysis." The genesis of the spirit of humility from the will to power and of the demonic form from the project of saintliness are the most remarkable, and in certain respects the most frightening, examples of this critical phenomenology, a phenomenology noticeably more inclusive than the phenomenology of cognition to which the greatest part of Husserl's work had to be limited. This phenomenology includes both a critique of the self by the self, a coming to awareness of the sense of the times, and a recapitulation of Western history in its totality.

III. EXISTENTIAL PHENOMENOLOGY

It is now possible to distinguish the main themes of contemporary existential phenomenology deriving from the conjunction of Husserlian phenomenology and the philosophy of existence. But these descriptive themes cannot be torn out of their philosophical context without injury. Even when they are elaborated by the same method and at times in the same terms by different philosophers, they are each traversed by a different intention which profoundly alters the sense. Existential phenomenology never describes merely for the pleasure of describing. The examples of Hegel, Kierkegaard, and Nietzsche are sufficient indication that description is effective only in the service of a great plan: to denounce an alienation, to rediscover the place of man in the world, or, on the other hand, to recover his metaphysical dimension, and so on. For each of these senses given to man's existence, there are so many descriptive styles in existential phenomenology. Let us take as examples three themes which are like the three melodic lines of existential phenomenology:

1. First, the example of the "owned body." In Gabriel Marcel this theme has a function of break and recovery: on the one hand, break with the idolatry of the anonymous epistemological subject which is without situation, unmenaced, inaccessible to drama and to personal death, and, on the other hand, recovery of the concrete, restoration of an experience at once personal and integral which extends between the two poles of the carnal and the mysterious. This dual path, both critical and restorative, orients the patient, subtle, and sometimes evasive descriptions of the "owned body." It oscillates between being and having (I am it, and I have it), between the organ and the instrument, between the same and the different. Thought, misled by the object, works to restore the complete sense of "I exist." But at the very moment when this existential phenomenology seems to be identified with a philosophy of incarnation, it escapes this philosophy and repays it with an investigation of experiences which can be called ontological because they reveal the insertion of my being into being: fidelity, hope, etc. Existential phenomenology then signifies the "positing and concrete approach to the ontological mystery." In other words, the phenomenology of the "owned body" plays the equivocal role of a rerooting in the concrete and of a counterpole to the ontological mystery.

In Merleau-Ponty, on the other hand, the description of the "owned body" is entirely in the service of a philosophy of finitude or of an exorcism of standpointless thinking; ultimately it is in the service of a philosophy without an absolute. The *Phenomenology of Perception* should be followed from one end to the other without reference to the true object, seen from nowhere, which would justify the possibility of perception, even without ever denying the inherence of consciousness in a point of view. To be sure, this program assumes that the other operations of consciousness—principally science and also all that is amenable to speech and to the λόγος—bear the same fundamental structures, "the same syntheses of transition, the same sort of horizon" as perceptual experience; in short, it assumes that "every consciousness is perceptual, even the consciousness of ourselves." Thus, the first pact concluded between cognition and finitude orients the whole phenomenology of perception. The description of the "owned body" is its touchstone. This description, just as in both Husserl and Gabriel Marcel, goes hand-in-hand with a critique of sensation as reconstructed by psychophysiology, i.e., as the simple effect of a physical stimulus. Phenomenology calls description from the sensation, from that late developed object of scientific consciousness, to perception, just as it is given. This perception is given as at once significational, in contrast to the pretended sensation of sensualism, but not intelligible, in contrast to the judgment of experience according to the intellectualist tradition which runs from Lachelier and Lagneau to Alain and Brunschvicg.

The theory of the "owned body" is then the critical point where the breakdown of objective thinking is consummated and where the perspectivist doctrine of perception is established. Neither the psychic, according to reflective philosophy, nor the "physiological," according to scientific thinking, accounts for the owned body. For it is the movement of being-in-the-world (*être au monde*), indivisibly voluntary and involuntary, as projected and as given. Beginning at this point, every analysis of behavior is conducted in such a way as to avoid the alternatives of automatism and abstract intelligence. The "owned body" is the locus of all ambiguities between the nascent sense and facticity, between the enacted and the reflected. Merleau-Ponty's existential phenomenology thus represents the strictest disagreement with the Platonic conversion of the here-below to the beyond. Placed in the service of a reconversion from reflection to the prereflective, existential phenomenology becomes identified with the justification of being-in-the-world. One can only wonder, though, how the moment of reflection on the unreflected, how the devotion to universality and to truth, and finally how the philosophical act itself are possible if man is so completely identified with his insertion into his field of perception, action, and life.

2. The theme of freedom gives rise to contrasts even greater than those of the "owned body" and confirms the subordination of the descriptive method to the existential intention in this sector of phenomenology. The reason is clear: in the case of freedom the ontological status of man is in question. Heidegger had already placed phenomenology in the service of a fundamental ontology where the explication of the

being of man was to open the horizon to a theory of being qua being. Thereafter, it is not surprising that a phenomenology of freedom, such as is at the center of Jean-Paul Sartre's work, should carry an ontological title—*Being and Nothingness*—and a subtitle which combines phenomenology and ontology. Even so, we have scarcely left the field of existential phenomenology, for with freedom the existential and the ontological become synonymous. The being of man consists in existing, in the emphatic sense which Kierkegaard has conferred on this word.

The overthrow which Sartre introduced into the problem-set of freedom consists precisely in having inverted the ontological index of freedom. Did we just say that the being of man consists in existing? Let us rather say that existing consists in being its own nothingness. Here is where phenomenology comes into play, for it has the function of collecting the experiences where I discover my freedom in the negative style of absence, of rapture, of distance, of failure to cohere, and of constancy, of anguish, of rejection, in short, where freedom is revealed as the nihilation of the past, of the completed, in a word, of being. Evidently it is presupposed that being was previously reduced to the being of a thing, to thinghood. It is then clear that the abandonment of the great metaphysical tradition, whereby being is act par excellence, is what directs this phenomenology of nihilating acts. Moreover, this phenomenology manifests an abundance, a perspicacity, and a force rarely equaled. The "sense of the negative," of which Hegel took possession on behalf of philosophy (and to which, as we have seen, Husserl lost the key), reemerges in contemporary philosophy with Sartre. This dialectical sense is enriched along the way with the Kierkegaardian and Marxian themes of anxiety and conflict. In addition, Sartre uses an agile imagination of concrete situations which as philosopher he takes over from the playwright. Finally, Husserl's concept of intentionality takes on a new look after this bath in negativity. It becomes the original distance, the stepping away of the self from itself, the nothing which separates existence from its having-been. But the step which carries this phenomenology of nihilating acts to the level of an ontology of nothingness is made by the philosopher, not by the phenomenologist.

Yet the same patience, the same descriptive strictness can serve an entirely different purpose: for one can describe, with Gabriel Marcel, another level of freedom which consists less in tearing oneself away from oneself, in annulling every datum in-itself and beyond oneself, than in letting oneself be opened up by a liberating presence. A phenomenology of liberation, which describes the passage of unavailability to availability (*disponibilité*), from avarice to generosity, here becomes the harbinger of a quite different ontology, one where the main accent is on participation in being rather than on the nihilation of being. But this descriptive spirit is not what makes for the difference between the two phenomenologies. The difference lies rather in the sense of the word "being," which for one signifies act, the giving of existence, and for the other signifies the brute datum or dead thing.

In Merleau-Ponty the phenomenology of freedom can also take form within the phenomenology of the "owned body" which, as we have seen, joins the ego to the world instead of completing the break between the "for-itself" and the "in-itself." If in fact the body is the movement of my being-in-the-world, if it is a spontaneity which offers itself to a situation in order to form it, then the decisive experience of freedom is to be sought not in the dramatic moment of breaking away but rather in the moment of engagement which includes the whole involvement in situation. To project our past, our future, our human milieu around ourselves is precisely to situate ourselves. Henceforth, concrete freedom is not to be sought elsewhere than in this general power to place oneself in situation. And the all-or-nothing of Sartrean freedom appears to have no measure in common with actual experience, which does not know the sovereign "in-itself," and never encounters anything but a relative freedom which incessantly "busies itself in taking up some proposition about the world." The phenomenology of freedom follows up the metaphysics of finitude which the theory of the owned body began.

3. The theme of the Other supports our analysis of the relations between the phenomenological method and the ontological intention in existential phenomenology. Jean-Paul Sartre initiates his analysis of the existence of the Other with the experience of being seen, of being caught by a gaze which freezes me in my tracks, reduces me to the condition of an object, steals my world from me, and takes away my freedom along with my subject position. The existence of the Other thus constitutes my "original fall," that is to say, the movement by which I fall into the world and am condemned to parry and thrust, i.e., to the struggle which is pursued in incipient or indirect ways even in sexual activity. But the choice of this glance that encroaches, fixes, determines, this glance which menaces because it is menaced, this freezing gaze—this choice comes to phenomenology from far away. If the Other appears to me by primordial right as power of encroachment (*d'empiètement*) and of theft, is this not because freedom itself has been described without the experience of generosity or of giving? Is it not only in a foregone project of unavailability, as Emmanuel Mounier says somewhere, that the Other's gaze is a gaze that petrifies and not instead a gaze that overthrows?

However such things stand, when it is a question of the Other, just as when it is a question of freedom or of the owned body, the field of existential phenomenology is an oriented field. One does not describe just anything simply for the pleasure of making brilliant analyses. The privilege accorded to misunderstanding, to conflict, to encounter, to reciprocity, to the collaboration of a teammate or of a galley slave betrays a different ontological style, according to whether being renders the constitution of a *we* possible or not, wherein the difference and the distance between me and the Other would somehow be overcome.

Thus, existential phenomenology makes the transition between transcendental phenomenology, born of the reduction of every thing to its appearing to me, and ontology, which restores the question of the sense of being for all that is said to "exist."

CHAPTER 6

From Existentialism to the

Philosophy of Language

I have been asked to discuss the problems which I have been working
on during these last ten years. Nineteen sixty-one was the year that I
published *Fallible Man* and *The Symbolism of Evil,* and at that time
a specific problem occupied my mind: how is it possible to introduce
within the framework of a philosophy of will, on which I had written
ten years earlier,[1] some fundamental experiences such as guilt, bondage,
alienation, or, to speak in religious terms, sin? As such, this problem
could be expressed in terms of an existential philosophy. All existential
philosophies of the forties and fifties had met this problem. We may
speak of inauthentic life with Heidegger, or boundary situations (*Grenz-
situationen*) with Jaspers, or of Being and Having and of despair with
Gabriel Marcel. My problem belonged to this sphere of questions with
a somewhat more specific interest. My problem was to distinguish
between finitude and guilt. I had the impression, or even the conviction, that these two terms tended to be identified in classical existentialism at the cost of both experiences, guilt becoming a particular case
of finitude and for that reason beyond cure and forgiveness, and finitude, on the other hand, being affected by a kind of diffused sense of
sadness and despair through guilt. This is why I chose *Finitude and
Guilt* as a general title for the two volumes of which I spoke and the
problem was that of their difference and of their connection.

But at the same time a secondary problem emerged which tended
afterwards to pass to the forefront of my inquiries. This was the problem of language. Why? Because in order to introduce the dimension of
evil into the structure of the will, a fundamental change in the method
of description itself was required. In my first work I had relied heavily

on a reflective method which came from both Husserl and the existentialist pair, Jaspers and Marcel, to whom I had devoted two books.[2] I may now call this kind of first description an existential phenomenology, although at the time I did not dare call it phenomenology for I did not wish to cover my own attempt with the authority of Husserl, whom I was translating into French.[3] It was phenomenology, however, in the sense that it tried to extract from lived experience the essential meanings and structures of purpose, project, motive, wanting, trying, and so on.

I note in passing that phenomenology at that time had already attacked problems which now are in the forefront of the school of linguistic analysis with its philosophy of action. But if it was phenomenology, it was existential phenomenology in the sense that these essential structures implied the recognition of the central problem of embodiment, of *le corps propre.* Anyhow, whatever might be the relation between phenomenology and existentialism in this first attempt, this kind of philosophizing did not yet raise any particular problem of language, for a direct language was thought to be available. This direct language was ordinary language in which we find words like purpose, motive, and so on. This is why I now believe that there is an intersection of the philosophy of ordinary language and phenomenology at this first level.

Now the consideration of the problem of evil brought into the field of research new linguistic perplexities which did not occur earlier. These linguistic perplexities were linked to the use of symbolic language as an indirect approach to the problem of guilt. Why an indirect approach? Why symbolic language when we have to pass from a philosophy of finitude to a philosophy of guilt? This was the question that intrigued me. The fact is that we have a direct language to say purpose, motive, and "I can," but we speak of evil by means of metaphors such as estrangement, errance, burden, and bondage. Moreover, these primary symbols do not occur unless they are embedded within intricate narratives of myth which tell the story of how evil began: how at the beginning of time the gods quarreled; how the soul fell into an ugly body; or how a primitive man was tempted, trespassed a prohibition, and became an exiled rebel.

It seemed, therefore, that direct reflection on oneself could not go very far without undertaking a roundabout way, the detour of a hermeneutics of these symbols. I had to introduce a hermeneutical dimension within the structure of reflective thought itself. In other words, I could speak of purposive action without symbolic language, but I could not speak of bad will or of evil without a hermeneutics. This was the first way in which the problem of language appeared in a kind of philosophy which was not at first a philosophy of language, but a philosophy of the will. I had been compelled by my initial subject to inquire into the structure of symbolism and myth, and this inquiry by itself led me to the more general problem of hermeneutics. What is hermeneutics if there is something like an indirect language, a metaphorical language, if there are symbols and myths?

But I must now say that at that time I was not aware of the real dimension of the hermeneutical problem. Perhaps because I did not want to be drawn into the immensity of this problem, I tried to limit the definition of hermeneutics to the specific problem of the interpretation of symbolic language. I still held this position in my book on Freud which I shall come to in a moment. In the last chapter of *The Symbolism of Evil* and in the first part of *Freud and Philosophy*, I defined symbolism and hermeneutics in terms of each other. On the one hand, a symbolism requires an interpretation because it is based upon a specific semantic structure, the structure of double-meaning expressions. Reciprocally, there is a hermeneutical problem because there is an indirect language. Therefore I identified hermeneutics with the art of deciphering indirect meanings.

Today I should be less inclined to limit hermeneutics to the discovery of hidden meanings in symbolic language and would prefer to link hermeneutics to the more general problem of written language and texts (I shall come to this at the end). Nevertheless, such was the way I was introduced to the hermeneutical problem.

At the same time, or maybe somewhat later, I felt compelled to shift my interest from the original problem of the structure of the will to the problem of language as such, which had remained subsidiary even at the time when I was studying the strange structures of the symbolism of myths. I was compelled to do so for several reasons which I will now try to explain. First, my reflection on the structure of psychoanalytic theory; secondly, the important change in the philosophical scene, at least in France, where structuralism was beginning to replace existentialism and even phenomenology; thirdly, my continuing interest in the problem raised by religious language, and, more specifically, by the so-called theologies of the Word in the post-Bultmannian school; and finally, my increasing interest in the British and American school of ordinary language philosophy, in which I saw a way of both renewing phenomenology and of replying to the excesses of structuralism.

My interest in psychoanalysis was in a sense the result of my interest in the problem of will, bad will, and guilt. I could not go very far indeed in a reflection concerning guilt without encountering the psychoanalytic interpretation of guilt. But psychoanalysis was also directly linked to linguistic perplexities due to its own use of symbolic structures. Not only the problem of guilt, therefore, compelled me to consider the problem of psychoanalysis, but also the general structure of language according to psychoanalysis. Are not dreams and symptoms some kind of indirect language? What is more, psychoanalysis claims to give not only a specific interpretation of dreams and symptoms, but also of the whole fabric of cultural symbols and of religious myths, which I had previously approached with a merely descriptive method similar to that used in comparative history of religions and especially that used by Mircea Eliade. Therefore, I had to consider something which had escaped my reflections until then, the fact that there was not only one hermeneutics, but two hermeneutics, since psychoanalysis claimed to interpret symbols by reducing them. The idea of a reductive hermeneutics could no longer be overlooked. In fact, I had to understand that Freud was only one of the exponents of the reductive hermeneutics, and that Marx and Nietzsche, and before them Feuerbach, had to be understood as the fathers of this reductive method. The claim of psychoanalysis to explain symbols and myths as fruits of unconscious representations, as distorted expressions of the relation between libidinal impulses and the repressive structure of the superego, compelled me to enlarge my first concept of hermeneutics beyond a mere semantic analysis of double-meaning expressions.

Hermeneutics appeared henceforth as a battlefield traversed by two opposing trends, the first tending toward a reductive explanation, the second tending toward a recollection or a retrieval of the original meaning of the symbol. My problem was to link these two approaches and to understand their relation as dynamic and as moving from a first naïveté through a critique toward what I called, at the time, a second naïveté. Therefore, without giving up my earlier definition of hermeneutics as the general theory of symbolic language, I had to introduce into the theory the polarity between these two hermeneutical demands and to link philosophical reflection not only to a semantics of indirect language, but to the conflictual structure of the hermeneutical task. In this way a dramatic element was added to the previous recognition of the necessity of the detour through obscure and hidden meaning.

My book on Freud, published in 1965, reflects this double recognition, first of the necessity of the detour through indirect signs, and secondly of the conflictual structure of hermeneutics and thus of self-knowledge. Self-knowledge is a striving for truth by means of this inner contest between reductive and recollective interpretation.

Now a word about the second reason for shifting from existential phenomenology to a more linguistically concerned kind of philosophizing. I spoke of a general change in the philosophical scene in France, chiefly due to the emergence of structuralism as the main trend in philosophy. This new model of philosophizing came from linguistics; more precisely, it was an effort to extend to semantics and to all semiological disciplines the model which had succeeded in phonology. Inasmuch as there are signs in human life, the structural model was to be utilized. As you know, this structural model relies mainly on the affirmation that language, before being a process or an event, is a system, and that this system is not established at the level of the speaker's consciousness, but at a lower level, that of a kind of structural unconscious. Structuralism, as a philosophy, draws radical consequences from this epistemological model which directly affect the presuppositions of existentialism. First of all, the primacy of subjectivity, which was so strongly emphasized by existentialism, is overthrown by this displacement of analysis from the level of the subject's intentions to the level of linguistic and semiotic structures.

Hermeneutics is also called into question along with existential phenomenology and existentialism. The idea that language is a closed system of signs, within which each element merely refers to the other elements of the system, excludes the claim of hermeneutics to reach beyond the "sense"—as the immanent content of the text—to its "reference," i.e., to what it says *about* the world. For structuralism, language does not refer to anything outside of itself, it constitutes a world for itself. Not only the reference of the text to an external world, but also its connections to an author who *intended* it and to a reader who *interprets* it are excluded by structuralism. This twofold reference to a subject of the text, whether author or reader, is rejected as psychologism or "subjectivism."

Confronted by this situation, I tried to react in the following way. First, I tried to become more competent in linguistic problems. Secondly, I tried to incorporate within hermeneutics as much as I could of this structural approach by means of a better connection between the stage of objective explanation and the stage of subjective appropriation. My discussions about and with Lévi-Strauss reflect this effort.

The kind of hermeneutics which I now favor starts from the recognition of the objective meaning of the text as distinct from the subjective intention of the author. This objective meaning is not something hidden behind the text, rather it is a requirement addressed to the reader. The interpretation, accordingly, is a kind of obedience to this injunction starting from the text. The concept of "hermeneutical circle" is not ruled out by this shift within hermeneutics. Instead it is formulated in new terms. It does not proceed so much from an intersubjective relation linking the subjectivity of the author and the subjectivity of the reader as from a connection between two discourses: the discourse of the text and the discourse of the interpretation. This connection means that what has to be interpreted in a text is what it says and what it speaks about, i.e., the kind of world which it opens up or discloses; and the final act of "appropriation" is less the projection of one's own prejudices into the text than the "fusion of horizons"—to speak like Hans-Georg Gadamer—which occurs when the world of the reader and the world of the text merge into one another.

This shift within hermeneutics from a "romanticist" trend to a more "objectivist" trend is the result of this long journey through structuralism. At the same time, I had to depart from my previous definition of hermeneutics as the interpretation of symbolic language. Now I should tend to relate hermeneutics to the specific problems raised by the translation of the objective meaning of written language into the personal act of speaking which a moment ago I called appropriation. In that way, the broader question, What is it to interpret a text?,[4] tends to replace the initial question, What is it to interpret symbolic language? The connection between my first definition and the new emerging definition remains an unsolved problem for me, which will be the topic of my forthcoming work.

I want now to say a few words concerning the third field of inquiry in which I found an impulse and a help for my effort to coordinate phenomenology and the philosophy of language. The post-Bultmannian schools of theology, especially those of Ebeling and Fuchs, seemed to me to be following a parallel evolution. Bultmann had imposed two fundamental limitations upon the theory of religious language. On the one hand, myth was taken to be the opposite of Kerygma. In that way, demythologization became the central problem and this prevented grasping the question of religious language as a unique problem. On the other hand, understanding had to be opposed to objectification in a manner similar to the opposition between *Verstehen* and *Erklaren* inherited from Dilthey. Thus, Biblical theology remained trapped in the perplexities of a romanticized hermeneutics. The recognition of this led post-Bultmannian exegetes and theologians to subordinate the problem of demythologizing and the problem of existential interpretation to the broader problem of the "linguisticality" of human experience which makes possible both the emergence of texts and the response of interpretation to this emergence. The polarity between myth and Kerygma, on the one hand, and between interpretation and explanation, on the other hand, appeared to be only partial solutions to the more general question of how religious language functions.

Therefore studies devoted to the word "God" and in general to "God-talk" appear from the broader standpoint to be more fruitful than the studies of myth and of demythologizing. These inquiries intersect the linguistic and semantic question of how a word functions in different contexts. They also intersect the question of how a form of discourse—such as a narrative, an oracle, a psalm, or a parable—is linked to a specific theological content. This is why I am so interested in what

Donald Evans, John Macquarrie, and Langdon Gilkey are doing in the field of the semantics of religious discourse. And I am just as interested in what von Rad, Jeremias, Via, and Perrin are saying concerning the relation between the narrative form, or the form of the parable, and specific kinds of confession of faith.

What we need now is a new framework which would allow us to connect Biblical hermeneutics to general hermeneutics conceived as the question of what is understanding in relation to text-explanation. It is the function of general hermeneutics to answer problems such as: What is a text? i.e., what is the relation between spoken and written language? What is the relation between explanation and understanding within the encompassing act of reading? What is the relation between a structural analysis and an existential appropriation? Such are the general problems of hermeneutics to which a Biblical hermeneutics has to be submitted.

On the other hand, the problem of the specificity of Biblical hermeneutics is perfectly legitimate; but it could only be raised, in a consistent manner, against the background of a general hermeneutics. Questions like these would arise: What do we mean by the Kerygmatic kernel of "preaching"? What are the connections between faith and Word, between the character of "disclosure" belonging to all religious texts and even to nonreligious texts (tragedy, poetry, novels, etc.), and what is intended by the concept of revelation? What is the contribution of a general theory of discourse and of texts to the traditional notion of inspiration? All these classical problems may be renewed when related in some dialectical way to the topics and methods of a general hermeneutics.

I will finish this survey of the problems and methods which contributed to my present concern for a philosophical hermeneutics with a few words concerning the growing influence of the British and American school of ordinary language philosophy on my inquiries. I do not think that this philosophy has the last word, but I do think that it is at least a necessary first stage in philosophical inquiry. To my mind, the contribution of ordinary language philosophy is twofold. First, it has proved that ordinary language does not, cannot, and must not function according to the model of ideal languages constructed by logicians and mathematicians. The variability of semantic values, their sensitivity to contexts, the irreducibly polysemic character of lexical terms in ordinary language, these are not provisory defects or diseases which a reformulation of language could eliminate, rather they are the permanent and fruitful conditions of the functioning of ordinary language. This polysemic feature of our words in ordinary language now appears to me to be the basic condition for symbolic discourse and, in that way, the most primitive layer in a theory of metaphor, symbol, parable, etc.

Secondly, ordinary language now appears to me, following the work of Wittgenstein and Austin, to be a kind of conservatory for expressions which have preserved the highest descriptive power as regards human experience, particularly in the realms of action and feelings. This appropriateness of some of the most refined distinctions attached to ordinary words provides all phenomenological analysis with linguistic guidelines. Now the recapturing of the intentions of ordinary language experiences may become the major task of a linguistic phenomenology, a phenomenology which would escape both the futility of mere linguistic distinctions and the unverifiability of all claim to direct intuition of lived experience. Thanks to this grafting of linguistic analysis to phenomenology, the latter may be cured of its illness and find its second wind. (I surmise that the same thing may be said of ordinary language philosophy; that its conjunction with phenomenology could also enhance and renew it.)

Not only phenomenology, but also hermeneutics may draw some benefit from an accurate inquiry into the functioning of ordinary language. I have already alluded to the connection between the functioning of symbolic discourse and the polysemic structure of our ordinary words. We may extend the parallelism further: understanding, in the most ordinary sense of the word—let us say, in conversation—is already an intersubjective process. Inasmuch as ordinary language differs from an ideal language in that it has no fixed expressions independent of their contextual uses, to understand discourse is to interpret the actualisations of its polysemic values according to the permissions and suggestions proposed by the context. What happens in the far more intricate cases of text-interpretation, and what constitutes the key problem of hermeneutics, is already foreshadowed in the interpretive process as it occurs in ordinary language. Thus, the whole problem of text-interpretation could be renewed by the recognition of its roots in the functioning of ordinary language itself.

Such are the problems on which I am now working and reflecting.

PART III

Language
and Hermeneutics

III. LANGUAGE AND HERMENEUTICS

"Existence and Hermeneutics" deals with what Ricoeur calls "the graft of the hermeneutic problem *onto the* phenomenological method." *It is a general account of what he means by hermeneutics and how it can renew phenomenology. In "Structure, Word, Event," Ricoeur confronts structuralism, granting it a legitimate place, but also insisting on its strict limitations. This is Ricoeur's most important challenge to structuralism, written when the latter was at the height of its influence in France. With "Creativity in Language," Ricoeur offers an account of polysemy (the multiplicity of meanings of each of our words) and shows that, while scientific and ordinary language have strategies to reduce polysemy, it is essential to poetic language. This interest in poetic language is continued in "Metaphor and the Main Problem of Hermeneutics," which is Ricoeur's summary of his recent book* The Rule of Metaphor. *Finally, we have included in this section one of Ricoeur's most recent articles, "Explanation and Understanding," which was translated especially for this volume. In this essay Ricoeur shows how the antinomy of explanation and understanding is surpassed by a dialectic in the theory of the text, action theory, and the theory of history. This article gives a clear view of Ricoeur's characteristic dialectical method and the breadth of his philosophical interest.*

SOURCES

"Existence and Hermeneutics," in *The Conflict of Interpretations* (Evanston: Northwestern University Press, 1974), pp. 11–24. Used by permission.

"Structure, Word, Event," translated by Robert Sweeney, *Philosophy Today* 12 (1968):116–126. Used by permission.

"Creativity in Language," translated by David Pellauer, *Philosophy Today* 17 (1973): 97–111. Used by permission.

"Metaphor and the Main Problem of Hermeneutics," *New Literary History* 6 (1974–75):95–110. Used by permission.

"Explanation and Understanding," translated by Charles E. Reagan and David Stewart. A French version of this article appeared as "Expliquer et comprendre," *Revue Philosophique de Louvain* 75 (1977):126–147.

CHAPTER 7

Existence and Hermeneutics

THE LEVEL OF SEMANTICS

It is first of all and always in language that all ontic or ontological understanding arrives at its expression. It is thus not vain to look to semantics for an *axis* of reference for the whole of the hermeneutic *field.* Exegesis has already accustomed us to the idea that a text has several meanings, that these meanings overlap, that the spiritual meaning is "transferred" (Saint Augustine's *translata signa*) from the historical or literal meaning because of the latter's surplus of meaning. Schleiermacher and Dilthey have also taught us to consider texts, documents, and manuscripts as expressions of life which have become fixed through writing. The exegete follows the reverse movement of this objectification of the life-forces in psychical connections first and then in historical series. This objectification and this fixation constitute another form of meaning-transfer. In Nietzsche, values must be interpreted because they are expressions of the strength and the weakness of the will to power. Moreover, in Nietzsche, life itself is interpretation: in this way, philosophy itself becomes the interpretation of interpretations. Finally, Freud, under the heading of "dream work," examined a series of procedures which are notable in that they "transpose" (*Entstellung*) a hidden meaning, submitting it to a distortion which both shows and conceals the latent sense in the manifest meaning. He followed the ramifications of this distortion in the cultural expressions of art, morality, and religion and in this way constructed an exegesis of culture very similar to Nietzsche's. It is thus not senseless to try to zero in on what could be called the *semantic node* of every hermeneutics, whether general or individual, fundamental or particular. It appears that their common element—which is found everywhere from exegesis to psychoanalysis, is a certain architecture of meaning, which can be termed "double meaning" or "multiple meaning," whose role in every instance, although in a different manner—is to show while concealing. It is thus within the semantics of the shown-yet-concealed, within the semantics of multivocal expressions, that this analysis of language seems to me to be confined.

Having for my part explored a well-defined area of this semantics, the language of avowal, which constitutes the *symbolism of evil*, I propose to call these multivocal expressions "symbolic." Thus, I give a narrower sense to the word "symbol" than authors who, like Cassirer, call symbolic any apprehension, of reality by means of signs, from perception, myth, and art to science; but I give it a broader sense than those authors who, starting from Latin rhetoric or the neo-Platonic tradition, reduce the symbol to analogy. I define *symbol* as: *any structure of signification in which a direct, primary, literal meaning designates, in addition, another meaning which is indirect, secondary, and figurative and which can be apprehended only through the first.* This circumscription of expressions with a double meaning properly constitutes the hermeneutical field.

In its turn, the concept of interpretation also receives a distinct meaning. I propose to give it the same extension I gave to the symbol. *Interpretation,* we will say, *is the work of thought which consists in deciphering the hidden meaning in the apparent meaning, in unfolding the levels of meaning implied in the literal meaning.* In this way I retain the initial reference to exegesis, that is, to the interpretation of hidden meanings. Symbol and interpretation thus become correlative concepts; there is interpretation wherever there is multiple meaning, and it is in interpretation that the plurality of meanings is made manifest.

From this double delimitation of the semantic field—in regard to symbols and in regard to interpretation—there results a certain number of tasks, which I shall only briefly inventory.

In regard to symbolic expressions and the task of linguistic analysis, there is the matter of beginning an enumeration of symbolic forms which will be as full and as complete as possible. This inductive path is the only one accessible at the start of the investigation, since the question is precisely to determine the structure common to these diverse modalities of symbolic expression. Putting aside any concern for a hasty reduction to unity, this enumeration should include the cosmic symbols brought to light by a phenomenology of religion—like those of Van der Leeuw, Maurice Leenhardt, and Mircea Eliade; the dream symbolism revealed by psychoanalysis—with all its equivalents in folklore, legends, proverbs, and myths; the verbal creations of the poet, following the guideline of sensory, visual, acoustic, or other images or following the symbolism of space and time. In spite of their being grounded in different ways—in the physiognomical qualities of the cosmos, in sexual symbolism, in sensory imagery—all these symbolisms find their expression in the element of language. There is no symbolism before man speaks, even if the power of the symbol is grounded much deeper. It is in language that the cosmos, desire, and the imaginary reach expression; speech is always necessary if the world is to be recovered and made hierophany. Likewise, dreams remain closed to us until they have been carried to the level of language through narration.

This enumeration of the modalities of symbolic expression calls for a criteriology as its complement, a criteriology which would have the task of determining the semantic constitution of related forms, such as metaphor, allegory, and simile. What is the function of analogy in "transfer of meaning"? Are there ways other than analogy of relating one meaning to another meaning? How can the dream mechanisms discovered by Freud be integrated into this symbolic meaning? Can they be superimposed on known rhetorical forms like metaphor and metonymy? Do the mechanisms of distortion, set in motion by what Freud terms "dream work," cover the same semantic field as the symbolic operations attested to by the phenomenology of religion? Such are the structural questions a criteriology would have to resolve.

This criteriology is, in turn, inseparable from a study of the operations of interpretation. The field of symbolic expressions and the field of the operations of interpretation have in fact been defined here in terms of each other. The problems posed by the symbols are consequently reflected in the methodology of interpretation. It is indeed notable that interpretation gives rise to very different, even opposing, methods. I have alluded to the phenomenology of religion and to psychoanalysis. They are as radically opposed as possible. There is nothing surprising in this: interpretation begins with the multiple determination of symbols (with their overdetermination, as one says in psychoanalysis); but each interpretation, by definition, reduces this richness, this multivocity, and "translates" the symbol according to its own frame of reference. It is the task of this criteriology to show that the form of interpretation is relative to the theoretical structure of the hermeneutical system being considered. Thus, the phenomenology of religion deciphers the religious object in rites, in myth, and in faith, but it does so on the basis of a problematic of the sacred which defines its theoretical structure. Psychoanalysis, on the contrary, sees only one dimension of the symbol: the dimension in which symbols are seen as derivatives of repressed desires. Consequently, it considers only the network of meanings constituted in the unconscious, beginning with the initial repression and elaborated by subsequent secondary repressions. Psychoanalysis cannot be reproached for this narrowness; it is its *raison d'être*. Psychoanalytic theory, what Freud called his metapsychology, confines the rules of decipherment to what could be called a semantics of desire. Psychoanalysis can find only what it seeks; what it seeks is the "economic" meaning of representations and affects operating in dreams, neuroses, art, morality, and religion. Psychoanalysis will thus be unable to find anything other than the disguised expressions of representations and affects belonging to the most archaic of man's desires. This example well shows, on the single level of semantics, the fullness of a philosophical hermeneutics. It begins by an expanding investigation into symbolic forms and by a comprehensive analysis of symbolic structures. It proceeds by the confrontation of hermeneutical styles and by the critique of systems of interpretation, carrying the diversity of hermeneutical methods back to the structure of the corresponding theories. In this way it prepares itself to perform its highest task, which would be a true arbitration among the absolutist claims of each of the interpretations. By showing in what way each method expresses the form of a theory, philosophical hermeneutics justifies each method within the limits of its own theoretical circumscription. Such is the critical function of this hermeneutics taken at its purely semantic level.

Its multiple advantages are apparent. First of all, the semantic approach keeps hermeneutics in contact with methodologies as they are actually practiced and so does not run the risk of separating its concept of truth from the concept of method. Moreover, it assures the implantation of hermeneutics in phenomenology at the level at which the latter is most sure of itself, that is, at the level of the theory of meaning developed in *Logical Investigations.* Of course, Husserl would not have accepted the idea of meaning as irreducibly nonunivocal. He explicitly excludes this possibility in the "First Investigation," and this is indeed why the phenomenology of *Logical Investigations* cannot be hermeneutical. But, if we part from Husserl, we do so within the framework of his theory of signifying expressions; it is here that the divergence begins and not at the uncertain level of the phenomenology of the *Lebenswelt.* Finally, by carrying the debate to the level of language, I have the feeling of encountering other currently viable philosophies on a common terrain. Of course, the semantics of multivocal expressions opposes the theories of metalanguage which would hope to remake existing languages according to ideal models. The opposition is as sharp here as in regard to Husserl's ideal of univocity. On the other hand, this semantics enters into a fruitful dialogue with the doctrines arising from Wittgenstein's *Philosophical Investigations* and from the analysis of ordinary language in the Anglo-Saxon countries. It is likewise at this level that a general hermeneutics rejoins the preoccupations of modern biblical exegesis descending from Bultmann and his school. I see this general hermeneutics as a contribution to the grand philosophy of language which we lack today. We have at our disposal today a symbolic logic, a science of exegesis, an anthropology, and a psychoanalysis; and, for the first time perhaps, we are capable of encompassing as a single question the reintegration of human discourse. The prog-

ress of these dissimilar disciplines has at once made manifest and
worsened the dislocation of this discourse. The unity of human speech
is the problem today.

The preceding analysis, dealing with the semantic structure of expressions with double or multiple meanings, is the narrow gate through
which hermeneutical philosophy must pass if it does not want to cut
itself off from those disciplines which, in their method, turn to interpretation: exegesis, history, and psychoanalysis. But a semantics of
expressions with multiple meanings is not enough to qualify hermeneutics as philosophy. A linguistic analysis which would treat these significations as a whole closed in on itself would ineluctably set up language
as an absolute. This hypostasis of language, however, repudiates the
basic intention of a sign, which is to hold "for," thus transcending itself
and suppressing itself in what it intends. Language itself, as a signifying
milieu, must be referred to existence.

By making this admission, we join Heidegger once again: what animates the movement of surpassing the linguistic level is the desire for
an ontology; it is the demand this ontology makes on an analysis which
would remain a prisoner of language.

Yet how can semantics be integrated with ontology without becoming vulnerable to the objections we raised earlier against an Analytic
of Dasein? The intermediary step, in the direction of existence, is reflection, that is, the link between the understanding of signs and self-
understanding. It is in the self that we have the opportunity to discover an existent.

In proposing to relate symbolic language to self-understanding, I
think I fulfill the deepest wish of hermeneutics. The purpose of all
interpretation is to conquer a remoteness, a distance between the past
cultural epoch to which the text belongs and the interpreter himself.
By overcoming this distance, by making himself contemporary with the
text, the exegete can appropriate its meaning to himself: foreign, he
makes it familiar, that is, he makes it his own. It is thus the growth of
his own understanding of himself that he pursues through his understanding of the other. Every hermeneutics is thus, explicitly or implicitly, self-understanding by means of understanding others.

So I do not hesitate to say that hermeneutics must be grafted onto
phenomenology, not only at the level of the theory of meaning expressed in *Logical Investigations,* but also at the level of the problematic of the *cogito* as it unfolds from *Ideen I* to *Cartesian Meditations.* But neither do I hesitate to add that the graft changes the wild
stock! We have already seen how the introduction of ambiguous mean-

ings into the semantic field forces us to abandon the ideal of univocity extolled in *Logical Investigations.* It must now be understood that by joining these multivocal meanings to self-knowledge we profoundly transform the problematic of the *cogito.* Let us say straight off that it is this internal reform of reflective philosophy which will later justify our discovering there a new dimension of existence. But, before saying how the *cogito* is exploded, let us say how it is enriched and deepened by this recourse to hermeneutics.

Let us in fact reflect upon what the self of self-understanding signifies, whether we appropriate the sense of a psychoanalytic interpretation or that of a textual exegesis. In truth, we do not know beforehand, but only afterward, although our desire to understand ourselves has alone guided this appropriation. Why is this so? Why is the self that guides the interpretation able to recover itself only as a result of the interpretation?

There are two reasons for this: it must be stated, first, that the celebrated Cartesian *cogito,* which grasps itself directly in the experience of doubt, is a truth as vain as it is invincible. I do not deny that it is a truth; it is a truth which posits itself, and as such it can be neither verified nor deduced. It posits at once a being and an act, an existence and an operation of thought: I am, I think; to exist, for me, is to think; I exist *insofar as* I think. But this truth is a vain truth; it is like a first step which cannot be followed by any other, so long as the *ego* of the *ego cogito* has not been recaptured in the mirror of its objects, of its works, and, finally, of its acts. Reflection is blind intuition if it is not mediated by what Dilthey called the expressions in which life objectifies itself. Or, to use the language of Jean Nabert, reflection is nothing other than the appropriation of our act of existing by means of a critique applied to the works and the acts which are the signs of this act of existing. Thus, reflection is a critique, not in the Kantian sense of a justification of science and duty, but in the sense that the *cogito* can be recovered only by the detour of a decipherment of the documents of its life. Reflection is the appropriation of our effort to exist and of our desire "to be" by means of the works which testify to this effort and this desire.

The *cogito* is not only a truth as vain as it is invincible; we must add, as well, that it is like an empty place which has, from all time, been occupied by a false *cogito.* We have indeed learned, from all the exegetic disciplines and from psychoanalysis in particular, that so-called immediate consciousness is first of all "false consciousness." Marx, Nietzsche, and Freud have taught us to unmask its tricks. Henceforth it becomes necessary to join a critique of false consciousness to any rediscovery of the subject of the *cogito* in the documents of its life; a philosophy of reflection must be just the opposite of a philosophy of consciousness.

A second reason can be added to the preceding one: not only is the "I" able to recapture itself only in the expressions of life that objectify it, but the textual exegesis of consciousness collides with the initial "misinterpretation" of false consciousness. Moreover, since Schleiermacher, we know that hermeneutics is found wherever there was first misinterpretation.

Thus, reflection must be doubly indirect: first, because existence is evinced only in the documents of life, but also because consciousness is first of all false consciousness, and it is always necessary to rise by means of a corrective critique from misunderstanding to understanding.

At the end of this second stage, which we have termed the reflective stage, I should like to show how the results of the first stage, which we termed the semantic stage, are consolidated.

During the first stage, we took as a fact the existence of a language irreducible to univocal meanings. It is a fact that the avowal of guilty consciousness passes through a symbolism of the stain, of sin, or of guilt; it is a fact that repressed desire is expressed in a symbolism which confirms its stability through dreams, proverbs, legends, and myths; it is a fact that the sacred is expressed in a symbolism of cosmic elements: sky, earth, water, fire. The philosophical use of this language, however, remains open to the logician's objection that equivocal language can provide only fallacious arguments. The justification of hermeneutics can be radical only if one seeks, in the very nature of reflective thought, the principle of a logic of double-meaning. This logic is then no longer a formal logic but a transcendental logic. It is established at the level of conditions of possibility: not the conditions of the objectivity of a nature, but the conditions of the appropriation of our desire to be. It is in this sense that the logic of the double-meaning proper to hermeneutics can be called transcendental. If the debate is not carried to this level, one will quickly be driven into an untenable situation; in vain will one attempt to maintain the debate at a purely semantic level and to make room for equivocal meanings alongside univocal meanings, for the theoretical distinction between two kinds of equivocalness—equivocalness through a surplus of meaning, found in the exegetic sciences, and equivocalness through the confusion of meanings, which logic chases away—cannot be justified at the level of semantics alone. Two logics cannot exist at the same level. Only a problematic of reflection justifies the semantics of double-meaning.

THE EXISTENTIAL LEVEL

At the end of this itinerary, which has led us from a problematic of language to a problematic of reflection, I should like to show how we can, by retracing our steps, join a problematic of existence. The ontology of understanding which Heidegger sets up directly by a sudden reversal of the problem, substituting the consideration of a mode of being for that of a mode of knowing, can be, for us who proceed indirectly and by degrees, only a horizon, an aim rather than a given fact. A separate ontology is beyond our grasp: it is only within the movement of interpretation that we apperceive the being we interpret. The ontology of understanding is implied in the methodology of interpretation, following the ineluctable "hermeneutical circle" which Heidegger himself taught us to delineate. Moreover, it is only in a conflict of rival hermeneutics that we perceive something of the being to be interpreted: a unified ontology is as inaccessible to our method as a separate ontology. Rather, in every instance, each hermeneutics discovers the aspect of existence which founds it as method.

This double warning, nevertheless, must not deter us from clearing the ontological foundations of the semantic and reflective analysis which precedes it. An implied ontology, and even more so a truncated ontology, is still, is already, an ontology.

We will follow a track open to us, the one offered by a philosophical reflection on psychoanalysis. What can we expect from the latter in the way of a fundamental ontology? Two things: first, a true dismissal of the classical problematic of the subject as consciousness; then, a restoration of the problematic of existence as desire.

It is indeed through a critique of consciousness that psychoanalysis points to ontology. The interpretation it proposes to us of dreams, fantasies, myths, and symbols always contests to some extent the pretension of consciousness in setting itself up as the origin of meaning. The struggle against narcissism—the Freudian equivalent of the false *cogito*—leads to the discovery that language is deeply rooted in desire, in the instinctual impulses of life. The philosopher who surrenders himself to this strict schooling is led to practice a true ascesis of subjectivity, allowing himself to be dispossessed of the origin of meaning. This abandonment is of course yet another turn of reflection, but it must become the real loss of the most archaic of all objects: the self. It must then be said of the subject of reflection what the Gospel says of the soul: to be saved, it must be lost. All of psychoanalysis speaks to me of lost objects to be found again symbolically. Reflective philosophy must integrate this discovery with its own task; the self [*le moi*] must be lost in order to find the "I" [*le je*] . This is why psychoanalysis is, if not a philosophical discipline, at least a discipline for the philosopher: the unconscious forces the philosopher to deal with the arrangement of significations on a level which is set apart in relation to the immediate subject. This is what Freudian topography teaches: the most archaic significations are organized in a "place" of meaning that is separate from the place where immediate consciousness reigns. The realism of the unconscious, the topographic and economic treatment of representations, fantasies, symptoms, and symbols, appears finally as the condition of a hermeneutics free from the prejudices of the ego.

Freud invites us, then, to ask anew the question of the relationship between signification and desire, between meaning and energy, that is, finally, between language and life. This was already Leibniz's problem in *Monadology:* how is representation joined to appetite? It was equally Spinoza's problem in *Ethics,* Book III: how do the degrees of the adequacy of ideas express the degrees of the *conatus,* of the effort which constitutes us? In its own way, psychoanalysis leads us back to the same question: how is the order of significations included within the order of life? This regression from meaning to desire is the indication of a possible transcendence of reflection in the direction of existence. Now an expression we used above, but whose meaning was only anticipated, is justified: by understanding ourselves, we said, we appropriate to ourselves the meaning of our desire to be or of our effort to exist. Existence, we can now say, is desire and effort. We term it effort in order to stress its positive energy and its dynamism; we term it desire in order to designate its lack and its poverty: Eros is the son of Poros and Penia. Thus the *cogito* is no longer the pretentious act it was initially—I mean its pretension of positing itself; it appears as *already* posited in being.

But if the problematic of reflection can and must surpass itself in a problematic of existence, as a philosophical meditation on psychoanalysis suggests, it is always in and through interpretation that this surpassing occurs: it is in deciphering the tricks of desire that the desire at the root of meaning and reflection is discovered. I cannot hypostasize this desire outside the process of interpretation; it always remains a being-interpreted. I have hints of it behind the enigmas of consciousness, but I cannot grasp it in itself without the danger of creating a mythology of instinctual forces, as sometimes happens in coarse conceptions of psychoanalysis. It is behind itself that the *cogito* discovers, through the work of interpretation, something like an *archaeology of the subject.* Existence is glimpsed in this archaeology, but it remains entangled in the movement of deciphering to which it gives rise.

This decipherment—which psychoanalysis, understood as hermeneutics—compels us to perform, other hermeneutic methods force us to perform as well, although in different ways. The existence that psychoanalysis discovers is that of desire; it is existence as desire, and this existence is revealed principally in an archaeology of the subject. Another hermeneutics—that of the philosophy of the spirit, for example—suggests another manner of shifting the origin of sense, so that it is no longer behind the subject but in front of it. I would be willing to say that there is a hermeneutics of God's coming, of the approach of his Kingdom, a hermeneutics representing the prophecy of consciousness. In the final analysis, this is what animates Hegel's *Phenomenology of Mind.* I mention it here because its mode of interpretation is diametrically opposed to Freud's. Psychoanalysis offered us a regression toward the archaic; the phenomenology of the spirit offers us a movement in which each figure finds its meaning, not in what precedes, but in what follows. Consciousness is thus drawn outside itself, in front of itself, toward a meaning in motion, where each stage is suppressed and retained in the following stage. In this way, a teleology of the subject opposes an archaeology of the subject. But what is important for our intention is that this teleology, just like Freudian archaeology, is constituted only in the movement of interpretation, which understands one figure through another figure. The spirit is realized only in this crossing from one figure to another; the spirit is the very dialectic of these figures by means of which the subject is drawn out of his infancy, torn from his archaeology. This is why philosophy remains a hermeneutics, that is, a reading of the hidden meaning inside the text of the apparent meaning. It is the task of this hermeneutics to show that existence arrives at expression, at meaning, and at reflection only through the continual exegesis of all the significations that come to light in the world of culture. Existence becomes a self—human and adult—only by appropriating this meaning, which first resides "outside," in works, institutions, and cultural monuments in which the life of the spirit is objectified.

It is within the same ontological horizon that the phenomenology of religion—both Van der Leeuw's and Mircea Eliade's—would have to be interrogated. As phenomenology, it is simply a description of rite, of myth, of belief, that is, of the forms of behavior, language, and feeling by which man directs himself toward something "sacred." But if phenomenology can remain at this descriptive level, the reflective resumption of the work of interpretation goes much further: by understanding himself in and through the signs of the sacred, man performs the most radical abandonment of himself that it is possible to imagine. This dispossession exceeds that occasioned by psychoanalysis and Hegelian phenomenology, whether they are considered individually or whether their effects are combined. An archaeology and a teleology still unveil an *archē* and a *telos* which the subject, while understanding them, can command. It is not the same in the case of the sacred, which manifests itself in a phenomenology of religion. The latter symbolically designates the alpha of all archaeology, the omega of all teleology; this alpha and this omega the subject would be unable to command. The sacred calls upon man and in this call manifests itself as that which commands his existence because it posits this existence absolutely, as effort and as desire to be.

Thus, the most opposite hermeneutics point, each in its own way, to the ontological roots of comprehension. Each in its own way affirms the dependence of the self upon existence. Psychoanalysis shows this dependence in the archaeology of the subject, the phenomenology of the spirit in the teleology of figures, the phenomenology of religion in the signs of the sacred.

Such are the ontological implications of interpretation.

The ontology proposed here is in no way separable from interpretation; it is caught inside the circle formed by the conjunction of the work of interpretation and the interpreted being. It is thus not a triumphant ontology at all; it is not even a science, since it is unable to avoid the *risk* of interpretation; it cannot even entirely escape the internal warfare that the various hermeneutics indulge in among themselves.

Nevertheless, in spite of its precariousness, this militant and truncated ontology is qualified to affirm that rival hermeneutics are not mere "language games," as would be the case if their absolutist pretensions continued to oppose one another on the sole level of language. For a linguistic philosophy, all interpretations are equally valid within the limits of the theory which founds the given rules of reading. These equally valid interpretations remain language games until it is shown that each interpretation is grounded in a particular existential function. Thus, psychoanalysis has its foundation in an archaeology of the subject, the phenomenology of the spirit in a teleology, and the phenomenology of religion in an eschatology.

Can one proceed any further? Can these different existential functions be joined in a unitary figure, as Heidegger tried to do in the second part of *Being and Time?* This is the question the present study leaves unresolved. But, if it remains unresolved, it is not hopeless. In the dialectic of archaeology, teleology, and eschatology, an ontological structure is manifested, one capable of reassembling the discordant interpretations on the linguistic level. But this coherent figure of the being which we ourselves are, in which rival interpretations are implanted, is given nowhere but in this dialectic of interpretations. In this respect, hermeneutics is unsurpassable. Only a hermeneutics instructed by symbolic figures can show that these different modalities of existence belong to a single problematic, for it is finally through the richest symbols that the unity of these multiple interpretations is assured. These symbols alone carry all the vectors, both regressive and progressive, that the various hermeneutics dissociate. True symbols contain all hermeneutics, those which are directed toward the emergence of new meanings and those which are directed toward the resurgence of archaic fantasies. It is in this sense, beginning with our introduction, that we have insisted that existence as it relates to a hermeneutical philosophy always remains an interpreted existence. It is in the work of interpretation that this philosophy discovers the multiple modalities of the dependence of the self—its dependence on desire glimpsed in an archaeology of the subject, its dependence on the spirit glimpsed in its teleology, its dependence on the sacred glimpsed in its eschatology. It is by developing an archaeology, a teleology, and an eschatology that reflection suppresses itself as reflection.

In this way, ontology is indeed the promised land for a philosophy that begins with language and with reflection; but, like Moses, the speaking and reflecting subject can only glimpse this land before dying.

CHAPTER 8

Structure, Word, Event

THE PRESUPPOSITIONS OF
STRUCTURAL ANALYSIS

I will concern myself less with the results than with the presuppositions which constitute linguistic theory, in the epistemologically strong meaning of the word theory. Saussure, the founder of modern linguistics, noted these presuppositions but stated them in a language that often remained considerably behind the new conceptualization that he introduced; it is Louis Hjelmslev who theorized about these presuppositions in his *Prolegomena to a Theory of Language,* published in 1943. He is the first to have enunciated them in a treatment (*discours*) that is entirely homogeneous with its object. Let us enumerate these presuppositions:

1. Language is an object for an empirical science; empirical is taken here in the modern sense; it designates not solely the role and primacy of observation, but also the subordination of inductive operations to deduction and the calculus.

This possibility of constituting language as a specific object of a science was introduced by Saussure himself in his famous distinction between a language (*la langue*) and speech (*la parole*). By relegating to speech the psychophysiological execution, the individual performance and the free combinations of discourse, Saussure reserves for a language the rules constituting the code, the institution valid for the linguistic community, the collection of entities among which the choice of the free combinations of discourse takes place. Thus, a homogeneous object is isolated: everything which concerns a language falls, in effect, within the same domain, while speech is dispersed among the registers of psychophysiology, psychology, sociology, and does not seem to be able to constitute the unique object of a specific discipline.

2. Within a language itself we must still distinguish a science of states of system, or synchronic linguistics, and a science of changes, or dia-

chronic linguistics. Here again Saussure led the way by declaring emphatically that the two approaches cannot be mixed simultaneously and that in addition, it is necessary to subordinate the second to the first. Pushing Saussure's thesis to its most radical form, Hjelmslev says: "Behind every process one should be able to find a system." This second presupposition opens up a new range of intelligibility: change, considered as such, is unintelligible. We understand it only as the passage from one state of system to another, which is what the word "diachrony" signifies; it is, therefore, to the system, that is, the arrangement of elements in a simultaneous grouping that we give priority in understanding.

3. In a state of system there are no absolute terms, only relations of mutual dependence. Saussure expressed it, "language is not a substance but a form." And, if the intelligible form par excellence is opposition, again with Saussure, then "in a language there are only differences." This means that we need not consider the meanings attached to isolated signs as labels in a heteroclite nomenclature, but only relative, negative, oppositive values of signs with respect to each other.

4. The collection of signs must be maintained as a closed system in order to submit it to analysis. This is evident on the level of phonology which establishes the finite inventory of phonemes of a given language, but it is true also on the lexical level, which, as we can see in a unilingual dictionary, is immense but not infinite. But we can understand it better if we succeed in substituting for this practically innumerable list, the finite inventory of subsigns that underlie our lexicon and beginning from which one could reconstitute the immense richness of real lexicons. Finally, it is useful to recall that syntax is constituted by a finite system of forms and rules. If we add that on a still higher level linguistics always operates on a finite *corpus* of texts, we can formulate in a general fashion the axiom of closure that governs the work of analysis. Working thus at the interior of a closed system of signs, linguistics can consider that the system that it analyzes has no outside but only internal relations. It is in this way that Hjelmslev defines structure: *an autonomous entity of internal dependencies.*

5. The definition of the sign which satisfies these four presuppositions breaks entirely with the naïve idea that the sign is made to stand for a thing. If we have correctly separated a language from speech, the states of system from the history of changes, the form from the substance, and the closed system of signs from all references to a world, we must define the sign not only by its relation of opposition to all other signs of the same level but also in itself as a purely internal or immanent difference. It is in this sense that Saussure distinguishes the signifying and the signified, and Hjelmslev, expression and content. This

presupposition could be placed first, as Saussure does in his *Course;* but in the logical order of presuppositions, this definition of the sign serves only to sanction the set of anterior axioms. Under the rule of the closure of the universe of signs, the sign is either a difference between signs, or a difference, internal to each sign, between expression and content. This two-sided reality falls entirely within the linguistic closure.

Structuralism can thus be defined as the complete awareness of the exigencies contained in this series of presuppositions. Of course, Saussure does not use the word "structure," but the word "system." The word "structure" appeared only in 1928 at the *Premier Congrès international de linguistes* at the Hague, in the form "structure of a system." The word "structure" would appear then as a specification of the system and would designate the restrictive combinations, highlighted against the whole field of the possibilities of articulation and combination which create the individual configuration of a language. But in the form of the adjective "structural," the word has become synonymous with system. The structural point of view is thus globally opposed to the genetic point of view. It gathers together at the same time the idea of synchrony (the priority of the state of a language over its history), the idea of organism (a language as a unity of wholes enveloping parts), and finally the idea of combination or of the combinatory (a language as a finite order of discrete unities). Thus, from the expression "structure of a system," we have passed to the adjective "structural" to define the point of view which contains these diverse ideas, and finally to "structuralism," to designate the investigations which take the structuralist point of view as a working hypothesis, indeed as ideology and weaponry.

SPEECH AS DISCOURSE

The triumph of the structural point of view is at one blow a triumph of scientific quality. By constituting the linguistic object as an autonomous object, linguistics constitutes itself as science. But at what cost? Each of the axioms we have listed is both a gain and a loss.

The act of speaking is excluded not only as exterior execution, as individual performance, but as free combination, as producing new enunciations. Now, this is the essential aspect of language, properly speaking, its goal.

At the same time, history is excluded, not simply the change from one state of system to another, but the production of culture and of man in the production of his language. What Humboldt called production and what he opposed to the finished work is not solely diachrony, that is, the change and passage from one state of system to another, but rather the generation, in its profound dynamism, of the work of speech in each and every case.

The structural point of view also excludes, along with free combination and generation, the primary intention of language, which is to say something about something; speaker and hearer understand it immediately. For them language aims at something, or more exactly it has a double direction: an ideal direction (to say something) and a real reference (to say about something). In this movement, language leaps across two thresholds: the threshold of ideality of sense and, beyond this sense, the threshold of reference. Across this double threshold and by means of this movement of transcendence, language *"means"*; it has taken hold of reality and expresses the hold of reality on thought. Meillet already spoke of this: in language we must consider two things, its immanence and its transcendence. Today we would say: its immanent structure and the level of manifestation where its effects of meaning are offered to the bite of the real. It is necessary then to balance the axiom of the closure of the universe of signs by attention to the primary function of language, which is to say. In contrast to the closure of the universe of signs, this function constitutes its openness or its opening.

These considerations—still general and unanalyzed—lead us to question the whole first supposition of the science of language, namely, that language is an object for an empirical science. That language is an object goes without saying so long as we maintain the critical awareness that this object is entirely defined by the procedures, methods, presuppositions and finally the structure of the theory which governs its constitution. But if we lose sight of this subordination of object to method and to theory, we take for an absolute what is only a phenomenon. Now the experience which the speaker and listener have of language come along to limit the claim to absolutize this object. The experience we have of language reveals something of its mode of being which resists this reduction. For us who speak, language is not an object but a mediation. Language is that through which, by means of which, we express ourselves and express things. To speak is the act by which the speaker overcomes the closure of the universe of signs, in the intention of saying something about something to someone; to speak is the act by which language moves beyond itself as sign toward its reference and toward its opposite. Language seeks to disappear; it seeks to die as an object.

An antinomy begins to show itself here: on the one hand structural linguistics starts from a decision of an epistemological character, viz., to hold itself at the interior of the closure of the universe of signs. By virtue of this decision, the system has no outside; it is an autonomous entity of internal dependencies. But this is a methodological decision which does violence to linguistic experience. The task is then, on the other hand, to reclaim for the understanding of language what the structural model excluded and what perhaps is language itself as act of speech, as saying. It is necessary here to resist any intimidation, the veritable terrorism, which nonlinguists impose on the basis of a model naïvely extrapolated from the conditions of its functioning. The appearance of a "literature," which takes its own operations as its theme, introduces the illusion that the structural model exhausts the understanding of language. But a "literature" thus conceived is itself an exception in the field of language; it includes neither science nor poetry, which in different ways take up the vocation of language as saying. The conjunction of structural linguistics and of a "literature" of the same name should be considered as a quite contingent event and as having very limited importance. The claim of some, as they put it, to demystify speech and saying, ought itself to be demystified, as being noncritical and naïve.

Our task appears to me to be, rather, to go all the way with the antinomy, the clear conception of which is precisely the advanced fruit of structural understanding. The formulation of this antinomy is today the condition for the return to an integral understanding of language; *to think* language should be to think the unity of that very reality which Saussure has disjoined, the unity of a language and of speech.

But how? The danger here is to set up a phenomenology of speech in opposition to a science of language, at the risk of falling again into psychologism or mentalism, from which structural linguistics has rescued us. To think correctly the antinomy of a language and speech, it would be necessary to be able to produce the act of speech at the very center of a language, in the fashion of a setting forth meaning, of a dialectical production, which makes the system occur as an act and the structure as an event.

So, this promotion, this production, this advance can be thought, if we undertake a precise understanding of the hierarchical levels of language. We have said nothing about this hierarchy so long as we have simply superimposed two levels of articulation: phonological articulation and lexical articulation (indeed three levels, if we add syntactical articulation). We have not yet surpassed the point of view according to which a language is a taxonomy, a *body* of already emitted texts, a repertory of signs, an inventory of units, and a combinatory system of elements. The hierarchy of the levels of language includes something more than a series of articulated systems: phonological, lexical, and syntactic. We actually change levels when we pass from the units of a language to the new unit constituted by the sentence or the enunciation. This is no longer the unit of a language, but of speech or of discourse. By changing the unit, one also changes function, or rather, one passes from structure to function. We then have the opportunity of encountering language as saying.

The new unit which we shall now consider is in no way semiological —if by this we understand everything concerning the relations of internal dependence between signs or components of signs. This large unit is properly semantic, if we take this word in its strong sense, which is not solely to signify in general but to say something, to refer the sign to the thing.

The enunciation or sentence includes all the traits that underlie the antinomy of structure and event. By its own characters, the sentence attests that this antinomy does not oppose language to something other than itself, but traverses it at its center, at the heart of its own accomplishment.

1. For discourse has an *act* as its mode of presence—the instance of discourse (Benveniste) which, as such, is of the nature of an event. To speak is an actual event, a transitory, vanishing act. The system, in contrast, is atemporal because it is simply virtual.

2. Discourse consists in a series of choices by which certain meanings are selected and others excluded. This choice is the counterpart of a corresponding trait of the system—constraint.

3. These choices produce *new* combinations: to emit new sentences, to understand such sentences—such is the essence of the act of speaking and of comprehending speech. This production of new sentences in virtually infinite number has as its counterpart the finite and closed collection of signs.

4. It is in discourse that language has a reference. To speak is to say something about something. It is here that we again encounter Frege and Husserl. In his famous article *"Uber Sinn und Bedeutung"* (expressions which Peter Geach and Max Black have translated as "Sense and Reference"), Frege showed precisely that the aim of language is double: the aim of an ideal sense (that is, not belonging to the physical or psychic world) and an aim of reference: if the sense can be called inexistent, insofar as it is a pure object of thought, it is the reference—*Bedeutung*—which roots our words and sentences in reality. "We expect a reference of the proposition itself: it is the exigency of truth (*das Streben nach Wahrheit*) which drives (*treibt*) us to advance (*Vordringen*) toward the reference." This advance of (ideal) sense toward the (real) reference is the very soul of language. Husserl does not say anything different in his *Logical Investigations:* the ideal sense is a void and an absence which demand to be fulfilled. By such fulfilling, language comes into its own, that is to say, dies to itself. Whether we distinguish, with Frege, *Sinn* and *Bedeutung* or, with Husserl, *Bedeutung* and

Erfüllung, what we thus articulate is a signifying intention that breaks the closure of the signs, which opens the sign onto the other, in brief, which constitutes language as a saying, a saying something about something. The moment when the turning from the ideality of sense to the reality of things is produced, is the moment of the transcendence of the sign. This moment is contemporaneous with the sentence. It is on the level of the sentence that language says something; short of it, it says nothing at all. In effect, the double articulation of Frege is the source of predication, insofar as "to say something" designates the ideality of sense and "to say about something" designates the movement of sense to the reference.

It is not necessary, therefore, to oppose two definitions of the sign, the one as internal difference of the signifying to the signified, the other as external reference of sign to thing. There is no need to choose between these two definitions. One relates to the structure of the sign in the system, the other to its function in the sentence.

5. This is the last trait of the instance of discourse. The event, choice, innovation, reference also imply a specific manner of designating the subject of discourse. Someone speaks to someone—that is the essence of the act of communication. By this trait, the act of speech is opposed to the anonymity of the system. Rather, we should say that the system has no subject, not even "someone"; the question, who speaks, has no meaning on the level of a language. A language is a neutral instrument, an organon that is simply available; a language has no one, is no one. With the sentence comes the question, "who speaks?" The answer is not necessarily, "I." But the question, who speaks, even if it must remain simply a question, a question without an answer, takes on a meaning only on this level. There is speech wherever a subject can take up in an act, in a single instance of discourse, the system of signs which a language puts at his disposal. This system remains virtual as long as it is not actualized, realized, operated by someone who, at the same time, addresses himself to another. The subjectivity of the act of speech is from the beginning the intersubjectivity of an allocution....

Thus, it is at the same level and in the same instance of discourse that language has a reference and a subject, a world and an audience. It is not surprising, then, that reference to the world and self-reference are excluded together by structural linguistics, as not constitutive of the system as such. But this exclusion is only the presupposition that must be set up in order to constitute a science of articulations. It is no longer of value when it is a matter of attaining the level of actuation where a speaker realizes his signifying intention relative to a situation and to an audience. Allocution and reference merge with act, event, choice, innovation.

STRUCTURE AND EVENT

Having arrived at this point, we might be tempted to let ourselves be split apart by the antinomy. Doubtless, structuralism leads to that. But this journey by way of antinomy is not in vain: it constitutes the first level—the properly dialectical level—of a constituting thought. That is why, in a first phase, nothing else can be done than to reinforce this antinomy of the systematic and the historical, and to oppose, term for term, the "event-ual" to the virtual, choice to constraint, innovation to institution, reference to closure, allocution to anonymity.

But in a second phase, it is necessary to explore new ways, to try to find new models of intelligibility, where the synthesis of the two points of view would be thinkable once again. It is a matter then of finding instruments of thought capable of mastering the phenomenon of language, which is neither structure nor event, but the incessant conversion of one into the other in discourse.

1.   It is in the order of *syntax* that poststructuralist linguistics is now making spectacular progress. The Chomsky school in the United States is currently working on the notion of "generative grammar." Turning its back on the taxonomies of the original structuralism, this new linguistics concerns itself from the beginning with the sentence and the problem posed by the production of new sentences. At the beginning of *Current Issues in Linguistic Theory* (Mouton, 1964), Chomsky writes:

> The central fact to which any significant linguistic theory must address itself is this: a mature speaker can produce a new sentence of his language on the appropriate occasion, and other speakers can understand it immediately, though it is equally new to them. Most of our linguistic experience, both as speakers and hearers, is with new sentences; once we have mastered a language, the class of sentences with which we can operate fluently and without difficulty or hesitation is so vast that for all practical purposes (and, obviously, for all theoretical purposes), we can regard it as infinite. Normal mastery of a language involves not only the ability to understand immediately an indefinite number of entirely new sentences, but also the ability to identify deviant sentences and, on occasion, to impose an interpretation on them ... it is clear that a theory of language that neglects this 'creative' aspect of language is of only marginal interest (pp. 7–8).

A new concept of structure is thus required to take into account what Chomsky calls the grammar of a language. He defines it in these terms: "Grammar is a device which specifies the infinite set of well-formed sentences and assigns to each of these one or more structural descriptions" (ibid., p. 9). Thus, the traditional structural description, which is concerned with dead inventories, is the result of the assignment of a dynamic rule of generation which undergirds the competence of the reader (*lecteur*). Chomsky continually opposes a generative grammar to the inventories of elements characteristic of the taxonomies favored by the structuralists. And we are led back to the Cartesians (Chomsky's latest book is titled *Cartesian Linguistics*), and to Humboldt, for whom language is not a product but production, generation.

In my understanding, this new conception of structure as a regulated dynamism will overcome the original structuralism. It will overcome it by integrating it, by situating it exactly at its own level of validity. I will return to this problem in a later study. But I wish to speak now of someone who has a real kinship with this new development in linguistics. I have in mind the great but too little recognized French linguist, Gustave Guillaume. Guillaume's theory of morphological systems—that is, the parts of speech—is a kind of generative grammar. His studies on the article and the tenses of the verb show how the task of discourse is to put words in a sentence position. What we call parts of speech—the categories of noun, verb, etc.—have as their function to complete, to terminate, to close the word in such a way as to insert it into the sentence, into discourse. By placing the word in a sentence position, the system of categories allows our words and our discourse to be applied to reality. More particularly, the noun and the verb are parts of speech thanks to which our signs are in a certain sense "returned to the universe" under the aspect of space and of time. By completing the word as noun and verb, these categories render our signs capable of grasping the real and keep them from closing up in the finite, closed order of a semiology.

But morphology fulfills this function only because the science of discourse and of systems such as those of the article, the verb, etc. . . . is a science of operations and not a science of elements. And let no one raise the accusation of mentalism. This accusation, which inhibits too many investigators, is valid against a psychologism of the image and of the concept, against the claim of psychic contents accessible to introspection alone. It is foolish when directed against operations.

More than anything else, recourse to Guillaume at this point in our investigation helps break down a prejudice and bridge a lacuna. The prejudice is this: We readily think of syntax as the most interior form of language, as the completion of the self-sufficiency of language. Nothing is more false. Syntax does not assure the division of language, which has already been accomplished by the constitution of the sign in the closed and taxonomic system. Because it relates to discourse and not to a language, syntax is on the path of the return of the sign toward reality. That is why the parts of speech, such as the noun and the verb, mark the endeavor of language to apprehend reality under its spatial and temporal aspects: what Gustave Guillaume calls "returning the sign to the universe." This shows that a philosophy of language must not simply account for the distance and the absence of the sign from reality (Lévi-Strauss). One can hold to this point of view as long as he considers the closed system of discrete units which compose a language; it no longer suffices when one approaches discourse in act. It would appear then that the sign is not only that which is lacking to things, it is not simply absent from things and other than them; it is what wishes to be applied, in order to express, grasp, apprehend, and finally show, to make see.

That is why a philosophy of language need not be limited to the conditions of possibility of a semiology: to account for the absence of the sign from things, the *reduction* of relations of nature and their mutation into signifying relations suffices. It is necessary, in addition, to satisfy conditions of possibility of discourse insofar as it is an endeavor renewed ceaselessly to express integrally the thinkable and the sayable in our experience. Reduction—or any act comparable to it by reason of its negativity—no longer suffices. Reduction is only the inverse, the negative facet, of a wanting-to-say which aspires to become a wanting-to-show.

Whatever is the fate of the work of Chomsky in France and of the assistance that Gustave Guillaume can offer toward its assimilation, the philosophical interest of this new phase of linguistic theory is evident: a new relation, of a non-antinomic character, is in process of being instituted between structure and event, between rule and invention, between constraint and choice, thanks to dynamic concepts of the type, *structuring operation* and no longer *structured inventory.*

I hope that anthropology and the other human sciences will know how to draw the consequences of this, as they are doing now with the original structuralism at the moment when its decline is beginning in linguistics.

2.   I would like to sketch a parallel overcoming of the antinomy of structure and event in the *semantic* order. It is here that I again meet my problem of the word.

The word is much more and much less than the sentence. It is much less because there is not yet any word before the sentence. What is there before the sentence? Signs, that is, differences in the system, values in the lexicon. But there is not yet any meaning, any semantic entity. Insofar as it is a difference in the system, the sign says nothing. That is why it is necessary to say that, in semiology, there is no word but only relative, differential, oppositive values. In this respect, Hjelmslev is right: if we remove from semiology the substance of sounds and that of meaning, such as they are, each of them, accessible to the feeling of speakers, it is necessary to say that phonetics and semantics do not belong to semiology. Each of them relates to *usage* or *use*, not to the *schema*. Now the schema alone is essential to a language. Usage or use is at the intersection of a language and speech. We must conclude that the word names at the same time that the phrase says. It names in sentence position. In the dictionary, there is only the endless round of terms which are defined circularly, which revolve in the closure of the lexicon. But then, someone speaks, someone says something. The word leaves the dictionary; it becomes word at the moment when man becomes speech, when speech becomes discourse, and the discourse a sentence. It is not by chance that in German, *Wort*—the word—is also *Wort*, speech (even if *Wort* and *Wort* do not have the same plural). Words are signs in speech position. Words are the point of articulation of semiology and semantics, in every speech event.

Thus, the word is, as it were, a trader between the system and the act, between the structure and the event: on the one hand it is then only a semantic virtuality; on the other hand, it relates to the act and to the event in the fact that its semantic actuality is contemporaneous with the vanishing actuality of the enunciation.

But it is here also that the situation is reversed. The word, I have said, is less than the sentence in that its actuality of meaning is subject to that of the sentence. But it is more than the sentence from another point of view. The sentence, we have seen, is an event: as such, its actuality is transitory, passing, vanishing. But the word survives the sentence. As a displaceable entity, it survives the transitory instance of discourse and holds itself available for new uses. Thus, heavy with a new use-value—as minute as this may be—it returns to the system, it gives it a history. . . .

CHAPTER 9

Creativity in Language:

Word, Polysemy, Metaphor

This essay is about the creative aspects of language. However, we must avoid platitudes about this formidable topic. A helpful suggestion and guide may be found, I think, in the famous aphorism of Wilhelm von Humboldt which describes language as an infinite use of finite means. Looking for a striking illustration of this contrast, I found it in some recent interpretations of metaphor which depart from the traditional interpretation of rhetoric and show it to be not an ornament of language nor a stylistic decoration, but a semantic innovation, an emergence of meaning. In order to introduce this theme, I thought that it might be fruitful to present it as an alternative strategy of discourse distinct from and opposed to other strategies, particularly those of ordinary language and scientific language.

These diverse strategies seem to me to be different answers which may be given to the specific perplexity and challenge proposed by the crucial phenomenon of natural languages, which we call polysemy. By polysemy I shall mean that remarkable feature of words in natural languages which is their ability to mean more than one thing. I was thus led to inquire into the creative potentialities already contained in this nuclear phenomenon and to connect it to the focus of all creativity in language, the sentence.

Hence the strategy of this essay about the strategy of language. First, we shall speak of the sentence as the actual bearer of all creativity in language. Then we shall consider polysemy as the potential creativity contained in the word. Third, we shall consider the range of alternate strategies opened by polysemy, and finally, and this will be the aim of this paper, we shall describe metaphor as the main procedure of the third kind of strategy of discourse considered in this paper, that of poetic discourse. My goal will be to show that this strategy preserves best the potential creativity of the words of our language.

THE SENTENCE AS INFINITE USE OF FINITE MEANS

My first task is to relate the fundamental structures of language to the Humboldtian opposition between finite means and infinite use. As I already suggested in my introductory remarks, it is not first the word, but the sentence which has to be considered as the focus of creativity. It is not that I identify infinite use with the sentence and finite means with the words. The relation is more complex, since as we shall see the word as related to the sentence is itself the depository of the creativity of language. Therefore the first opposition is not between the sentence and the words, but between the sentence and some other entities which are more fundamental than words, signs.

I am using here the terminology of the great French Sanskritist Emile Benveniste, from his *Essays on General Linguistics.* According to him, language relies not on one, but on two kinds of entities: the semiotic entities, that is to say the signs, and the semantic entities, the bearers of meaning. I want to explain this distinction and to relate it to the Humboldtian distinction between finite means and infinite use.

Semiotic entities or signs are merely distinctive and oppositive units within specific systems: phonemes within phonological codes, morphemes or sememes within lexical codes, syntactic forms of rules within syntactic systems. In saying that they are merely distinctive and oppositive units, we mean that they are defined by their difference with regard to other units of the same system. It follows from this main trait that these entities are not related to extralinguistic realities such as things, events, properties, relations, actions, passions, or states of affairs. They are purely intralinguistic phenomena. This feature is true even of the most primitive difference which we may find within the linguistic signs themselves and which distinguishes them from other semiotic systems. I mean the difference which Saussure introduced between the signifier and the signified, which Hjelmslev reformulated as the difference between the expression and its content. This difference borrowed from the Stoic tradition is a difference within the sign itself and not an external relation between sign and thing. Signifier and signified—or in psychological terms, acoustic images and concepts—represent the two sides of the same sign like the two sides of one and the same coin. Like the coin the sign is the unity of both.

Now how does this description of semiotic entities satisfy Humboldt's aphorism? In what sense can semiotic entities be said to be finite? It follows from the immanent nature of all the relations between signs and within signs that semiotic systems are closed systems and for that reason they constitute finite sets of entities. Furthermore, among all semiotic systems, linguistic systems have the peculiarity of being twice closed or twice finite. On the one hand, the analysis of the signifier, or of the expression, yields a finite number of distinctive elements: the phonemes, a few dozen in each language. On the other hand, the signified, or the content, may be submitted to a similar analysis which at least in principle should lead to those symbols which would constitute the elementary constituents of all lexical systems. In conjunction with specific combinatory rules, these elementary constituents should provide a basis for a complete analysis of all lexical codes. If this hypothesis holds, we should have to assume that lexical systems, too, are finite systems. As concerns the syntactic systems, it is obvious that the paradigms of tenses constitute finite lists of forms and imply a finite enumeration of rules. Now in what sense may we speak of an infinite use of these finite sets? The first entity which has to be considered is not the word, but the sentence. Our task will be to describe the features of the sentence which contribute to the creative process of language that we call discourse. The first trait to be noticed is the temporal character of these new entities. Language as sentence and as discourse appears and disappears. It happens. Whereas systems of signs are merely virtual, language as discourse is actual.

As a second trait, we can consider the remarkable capacity of an instance of discourse to refer back to its own speaker thanks to specific procedures such as the personal pronouns, the tenses of the verbs, the demonstratives, and so on. Whereas systems of signs are properly anonymous, discourse requires a speaker who may express himself in it.

In the same manner, the instance of discourse refers to a hearer to whom it is addressed as the second person. This I-thou structure of discourse belongs to the semantic order and has no place in semiotic systems.

Finally, the sentence as a whole is the bearer of the meaning. Here we mean to designate something other than and something more than the signified of the individual signs. It is a distinctive feature which may be identified as the predicative function. (The sentence, of course, may be reduced to its predicate. Then we have a one-word sentence as in the imperative, but it is a sentence nevertheless inasmuch as it is a predicate.) The predicative constitution of the sentence provides it with a meaning. This meaning should be called the intended rather than the signified of the sentence, if we want to preserve the distinction between the semiotic and the semantic order. This intended is what we seek to translate when we transpose a discourse from one language into another. The signified is untranslatable in principle. It cannot be transposed from one system to another since it characterizes one system in opposition to the other. The intended, on the contrary, is fundamentally translatable since it is the same intended unit of thought transposed from one semiotic system into another. Let us therefore say that the intended is the semantic element in discourse. As we shall see later, the intended of discourse is the focus of all creative process in language. But before considering the aspect of creativity and infinity which belongs to the semantic element as such, let us consider a last semantic feature of the sentence.

The intended can be considered from two different points of view. It is something immanent within the sentence, merely resulting from the connection between the terms in the predicative operation of a sentence, and at the same time a claim to express reality. To this claim is linked the possibility of truth and error in discourse. Let us call the immanent character of the meaning "sense," and its truth-claim "reference." Then we may say that where there is meaning there is also a question of reference, that is, a claim which can be fulfilled or which can remain null or void. As you may see, I am using the expressions coined by Gottlob Frege in a very free way. This thinker called *Sinn* (sense) the ideal content, the objective side of the meaning, the intended-as-such. And he called *Bedeutung* (reference or denotation) the directedness of discourse toward reality which it may reach or miss. With this consideration of reference, the opposition between semiotic and semantic is complete. Whereas semiotic units are systems of inner dependencies, and for that reason constitute closed and finite sets, the sentence, as the first semantic unit, is related to extralinguistic reality. It is open to the world.

Now, in what sense are semantic entities infinite? Discourse is infinite because sentences are events, because they have a speaker and a hearer, because they have meaning, and because they have reference. Each of these traits has an infinite character. With the event comes the openness of temporality; with the speaker and hearer, the depth of individual fields of experience; with meaning, the limitlessness of the thinkable; and with reference, the inexhaustibility of the world itself. On all these counts language-as-discourse appears as an open process of mediation between mind and world. To return to Humboldt, discourse is the creative process of giving form to both the human mind and the world, of forming (*Bildung*) man and reality at the same time. This process is infinite in the sense that the boundary between the expressed and the unexpressed endlessly keeps receding. Discourse is this power of indefinitely extending the battlefront of the expressed at the expense of the unexpressed.

We may now relate the function of the word to that of discourse and introduce polysemy.

The main implication of the preceding analysis is that words have meaning only inasmuch as sentences have meaning. Once again I am taking meaning in its semantic sense as an intended content and as a claim to refer to something outŝide language. In this sense, words do not have meaning outside the sentence. Their intended content is a part of the whole, intended content of the sentence, and they designate something inasmuch as sentences themselves refer to states of affairs. In brief, words function as meaningful entities only within the framework of the sentence. That they have partial meaning only in connection with the whole meaning of the sentence could be very easily demonstrated by showing that words have no meaning before they are used either as logical subjects of a proposition or as predicates, that is, before they serve either to identify individuals or to assert universal characteristics of these individuals. In this sense, words belong to the linguistics of the sentence, not to the linguistics of the sign. They are semantic entities, not semiotic entities.

Of course words are based on lexical entities which are undoubtedly semiotic things. But a lexical entity is not yet a word. It is only the possibility of a word. This is why a lexical entity is defined merely by its opposition to other lexical entities within the same system. It has nothing to do with reality. This is not the case with the word in the sentence. It bears a part of the sentence meaning and shares the referential function of the whole discourse. It is about things, it points to things, it represents things. When *Sprache spricht*, then words themselves cooperate in the shaping of reality.

We are now prepared to consider our second theme, the polysemy of words. As I said in my introduction, I relate this specific topic to the general topic of my paper in the following way. If metaphor is one of the strategies of discourse which exploits the creativity of language, then we may ask about the kind of challenge which this strategy claims to come to grips with. It is this question which leads me to focus on polysemy as the crucial phenomenon of natural languages and to ask about the place of the word itself in the fabric of language. Having done the required analysis of the word, we can now consider polysemy.

Polysemy is readily defined as the property of words in natural language of having more than one meaning. As Stephen Ullmann puts it in his *Principles of Semantics,* polysemy means one name with several senses. This feature is a universal feature of words in natural languages. Before considering the challenge which results from this constitutive trait, let us describe its functional character. Before all other possible

advantages, a polysemic language satisfies the most elementary requirement of a natural language, I mean economy. A lexicon which would
be based on the opposite principle of total univocity of all its elements,
that is to say, on the principle of only one sense for one name, would
be infinite if it were destined to convey from one person to another
the richness of concrete and qualitative experience. It would even be
doubly infinite because of the limitless variety of each individual sphere
of experience and because of the innumerable plurality of individual
perspectives on the world.

This first functional trait has for its counterpart a second feature
which we shall call the sensibility to context. Thanks to the contextual
use, language based on polysemy may draw practically innumerable
meanings from the finite set of lexical entities codified by the dictionary. We shall see in a moment how ordinary language proceeds to make
this procedure appropriate to its ends. Let us say, in general terms, that
polysemic language is characterized by its sensibility to the context.

By context we mean not only the linguistic environment of the
actual words, but the speaker's and the hearer's behavior, the situation
common to both, and finally the horizon of reality surrounding the
speech situation. Furthermore, the context is already implied in the
very definition of the words. Each of the partial values enumerated by
the dictionary represents a potential use in a typical context which has
been identified and classified by lexicology. The sum of these potential uses in potential contexts is what we call, in an improper sense,
the meaning of the word. This is an improper sense because the lexical
entities are not yet words in the strong sense. But this way of speaking
is not wholly improper since the partial meanings of a word summarize
previous uses which have been classified according to corresponding
contexts. In this sense, a polysemic language is contextually determined not only in its use, but in its very constitution.

Such are the two functional traits of a polysemic language: economy
at the level of the code, and contextual dependence at the level of the
message. This dialectics of economy and novelty foreshadows the dialectics of finite means and infinite use which will be unfolded when we
consider the various strategies by which we make use of these polysemic
traits. This dialectic takes place in the concrete process by which we
decode a given message and which we may call interpretation in the
most general sense of the word. The simplest message conveyed by the
means of natural language has to be interpreted because all the words
are polysemic and take their actual meaning from the connection with
a given context and a given audience against the background of a given
situation. Interpretation in this broad sense is a process by which we
use all the available contextual determinants to grasp the actual meaning of a given message in a given situation.

It was already in this broad sense, or maybe an even broader sense, that Aristotle used the word *hermeneia* (that is to say, interpretation) in the second treatise of the *Organon,* which its editors have called by the same name. His sense may have been still broader than ours because it seems that language has to be interpreted not only because words are the symbols of states of mind, and written signs of oral signs, but because discourse is fundamentally the interpretation of reality. We shall return to this still broader sense of interpretation at the end of this study. Let us therefore call interpretation the decoding of messages based on polysemic words. It is interpretation which calls for the various strategies which we shall now consider.

Why this diversity of strategies? Because of a challenge, a threat which is implied in all processes of interpretation. This challenge is the threat of ambiguity or of equivocity which appears to be the permanent counterpart of polysemy or, so to speak, the price to pay for a polysemic language. But let us be accurate. Ambiguity or equivocity is not the same thing as polysemy. Polysemy is a feature of words, several senses for one name. Ambiguity is a feature of discourse, that is to say, of the stretch of speech longer than or equal to the sentence. Ambiguity or equivocity means that for one string of words we have more than one way of interpreting it. Whereas polysemy is a normal phenomenon, ambiguity may be a pathological phenomenon. I say "may be" because, as we shall see, we must preserve the possibility of highly significant ambiguities, the possibility of a functional ambiguity. That will be the case with poetic language. But ambiguity remains a case of dysfunction each time that the situation of discourse requires only one interpretation for reasons which will be proper to each type of strategy. Each time that the present stretch of discourse gives no sufficient clue to eliminate equivocity in interpretation, then misunderstanding becomes unavoidable and, as Schleiermacher said, there is a hermeneutical task where there is misunderstanding and when understanding proceeds from the rectification of misunderstanding.

In the preceding remarks, I used equivocity, ambiguity, and misunderstanding as synonymous terms. In order to distinguish these terms, we could perhaps call ambiguity the character of the discourse itself as opened to several interpretations; and call equivocity the process of interpretation hesitating between these interpretations. Misunderstanding would be the effect of both ambiguity and equivocity on the inter-subjective process of communication.

Such is the balance of advantages and disadvantages of a polysemic language. On the one hand, it satisfies the principle of economy, which is the basic principle for all kinds of languages, at the same time that it allows the contextual game to draw an infinite variety of meaningful effects from this economic structure. But on the other hand, it delivers language to the precarious and haphazard work of interpretation and, therefore, to the risks of ambiguity, equivocity, and misunderstanding.

POLYSEMY AND THE STRATEGIES OF LANGUAGE

Let us now introduce the various strategies capable of meeting the challenge of misunderstanding. I shall consider three of them: ordinary language, scientific language, and poetic language—without pretending that these are the only possible solutions.

By ordinary language I mean that use of natural languages (English, French, German, and so on) whose aim is communication and whose means are a tactic of polysemy reduction. By communication I mean the attempt to convey information from speaker to hearer concerning the concrete situations of everyday life which are differently experienced by the individual members of the speech community. A certain amount of univocity is reached by specific means requiring a minimal technicity in the use of words which I call the reduction of polysemy. This tactic relies mainly on the clever use of the context's effect on the individual terms of discourse. This reductive action of contexts is easy to understand. The use of language is not only governed by syntactic rules of grammaticality, but also by semantic rules of sense composibility. In order to make sense together, words must have a mutual appropriateness, a semantic pertinence. This rule of semantic pertinence requires that when we speak, only a part of the semantic field of a word is used. The remainder is excluded or rather repressed by the process of mutual selection exerted by the sentence as a whole and by the context of discourse on its parts. If the sentence is not enough to screen the convenient contextual values, the topic will help to eliminate the unwanted meaning under the control of the whole speech situation. Finally it is the function of the exchange of questions and answers within the dialog or conversation to allow the hearer to check the semantic choice of the speaker and to allow the speaker to verify that the message has been correctly decoded by the hearer. The speaker's utterances must provide the hearer's interpretation with some specific clues or guidelines for this screening of polysemy.

Such is the way in which ordinary language succeeds to a certain extent in reducing the initial polysemy of the words and in making relatively univocal statements with polysemic words. But if this strategy is enough in everyday life, it does not radically exclude polysemy. It cannot claim more than to reduce it. The threat of misunderstanding, as we too well know, is not fundamentally dispelled. Very often a long speech, if not a whole book, is not enough to insure understanding and agreement. Misunderstanding finally prevails.

This ultimate failure of ordinary language to meet the challenge of misunderstanding explains why a quite different strategy had to be introduced, a strategy which would no longer aim at reducing polysemy, but at eradicating it. This strategy is that of scientific language.

In the following analysis I shall not speak of scientific language in general, but only from the point of view of the therapy of misunderstanding and therefore in connection with the treatment of ambiguity.

From this limited point of view scientific language may be defined by the defensive measures it takes against ambiguity. I will mention only the most striking of them.

As a first step, scientific language only pushes further a procedure rooted in ordinary language, that of definition. As is well known, language is constructed in such a way that it is always possible to designate an element of our lexical code by means of other elements belonging to the same code. It is possible in principle to say that a bachelor is an unmarried man. Thanks to this reflective action of language, we expand our vocabulary and control the meaning of our words. Scientific language pushes this definatory procedure further by refining it with the help of classificatory and taxonomic measures.

The second step is to introduce technical terms into our vocabulary which satisfy a specific rule, that of denoting only quantitative entities to the exclusion of the qualitative aspect of our experience. Some previous words borrowed from ordinary language such as "stream," "mass," "speed," may be retained, but they are reformulated and redefined according to the requirements of a *mathesis universalis.*

At a further stage of abstraction, words similar to those of our dictionaries are replaced by mathematical symbols, that is to say, by signs which can be read but not vocally uttered. The link with natural language is broken. Scientific language henceforth is beyond the boundary line which divides artificial language from natural language.

Finally, at a stage corresponding to an advanced degree of formalization, the meaning of all the formulas and all the laws of a formal system are governed by a set of axioms which assign each elementary meaning its place in the theory and prescribe the rules for reading the whole symbolism. Of course there is still room for interpretation in the sense that a formal system has still to be applied to a diversity of empirical domains of experience, but this interpretation is itself governed by new rules of translation which exclude all ambiguity. These rules of translation and the prescription which they imply take the place of contextual interpretation in ordinary discourse. Therefore, the constitution of formal systems and the rules for interpreting them in relation to empirical fields constitute the ultimate procedure directed by scientific language against ambiguity.

At this point we might be tempted to reformulate the whole fabric of our language according to the procedures which we just defined.

Does it not seem reasonable to construct a *langue bien faite* ruled by the principle of a one-to-one relation between signs and entities, of one meaning for each word, and to extend this artificial language to ethical and political problems, and why not even to conversation? This dream of a radical and complete reformulation of the whole of our language haunted philosophers like Leibniz, conceiving his *characteristica universalis,* Russell writing the *Principia Mathematica,* and Wittgenstein in his *Tractatus* stating the rules of a language which would be the exact picture of the structure of facts.

But there are fundamental reasons for thinking that this project must fail. Ordinary language and artificial language not only belong to two irreducible strategies, but have different aims. The theme of ordinary language is communication, and its field of application is reality as it is differently experienced by the individual members of the speech community. Strictly speaking, however, communication is not the aim of a scientific language. When we read a scientific paper, we are not in the position of an individual member of the speech community just invoked. All readers are, in a sense, one and the same mind, and the purpose of discourse is not to build a bridge between two spheres of experience, but to insure the identity of meaning from the beginning to the end of an argument. This is why there are no contextual variations of meaning in a *langue bien faite.* The meaning is contextually neutral, or, if you prefer, insensible to the context because the main purpose of this language is that the meaning remain the same all through the arguments. This continual sameness of the meaning is secured by the one-to-one relation between name and sense and by the indifference to the context. Thus, I should say that the aim of a scientific language is not communication, but argumentation. It follows that there is something irreducible in ordinary language. The variability of meanings, their displacibility, and their sensibility to the context are the condition for creativity and confer possibilities of indefinite invention on both poetic and scientific activity. Here, indeterminateness and creativity appear to be completely solidary. This is why *langues biens faites* are at best insular languages. The conclusion could be, as Roman Jakobson says, that both mathematical and ordinary languages are required, and that each of them has to be considered as the metalanguage required for the structural analysis of the other.

METAPHOR AND POLYSEMY

In the last part of this chapter, I want to consider metaphor within the limits of my present concern, that is, with respect to creativity in language and in continuity with my previous remarks about polysemy. In other words, I shall treat metaphor as a creative use of polysemy and in that way as a specific strategy of language. Instead of reducing or suppressing polysemy, metaphor uses polysemy as a means to preserve polysemy and to make it work in a most effective way. For what purpose? We shall reserve the answer for the end of this essay.

The decisive step in the direction we are now taking has been indicated by writers like I. A. Richards, Max Black, Colin Turbayne, Monroe Beardsley, Douglas Berggren, and others who departed from the tradition of rhetoric for which metaphor conveyed no information and appeared merely as a stylistic ornament whose function it was to please. They could break with this tradition because they approached the problem of metaphor from a quite new perspective. For traditional rhetoric, metaphor was one of the figures of speech called tropes because they proceeded from a deviating use of the meaning of words. Tropes, therefore, affected just the names and the giving of names. Instead of giving their proper names to certain things, or facts, or experiences, the writer chooses to use the name of something else by extending the meaning of this foreign name. The task of rhetoric, thus, is to classify the different figures according to the kind of deviation which generated them. Metaphor was traditionally classified as a trope by resemblance or by analogy. This treatment of metaphor by rhetoric has been characterized by Richards and his followers as a substitution theory. The decisive factor is that the borrowed word taken with its deviating use is substituted for a potential proper name which is absent in the context, but which could be used in the same place. The writer chooses not to use the convenient word in its proper sense and to replace it with another word which seems to be more pleasant.

To understand the metaphor, then, is to restitute the term which has been substituted. It is easy to understand that these two operations—substitution and restitution—are equivalent. Therefore, it is possible to give an exhaustive paraphrase of a given metaphor. From these presuppositions, it follows that metaphor offers no new information. It teaches nothing. For the same reason, metaphor is a mere decorative device. It has no informative value, it merely adorns language in order to please. It gives color to speech, it provides a garment to cover the nudity of common usage.

Such is the train of presuppositions implied in a rhetorical treatment of metaphor. Between the starting point that metaphor is an accident in the process of naming, and the conclusion that metaphor is merely decorative and intended to please, the road is continuous and the turning point is constituted by the action of substitution. The weakness of this model is obvious. It is impossible on its basis to give an account of the difference between a bad metaphor, like "the leg of a chair," and a novel metaphor, like the poetic verse, "La terre est bleue comme une orange," or "time is a beggar." The aspect of semantic novelty which,

I believe, is the fundamental problem of metaphor, remains unexplained in a substitution theory which covers both cases. Furthermore, the theory is unable to explain the process itself by which the meaning of a word is extended beyond its common use. What Beardsley called the "metaphorical twist" remains an enigma. This is why rhetoric contented itself with classifying the figures of speech, being unable to generate them.

The reason why rhetoric could not give an account of the process which generates metaphor is that it limited its description to the words and, more precisely, to the name. As we shall see, the metaphorical process occurs at another level, at the level of the sentence and of discourse as a whole. This is why rhetoric could only identify the effects of the process on the word, the lexical impact, so to speak, and classify the metaphor among other figures such as metonymy, synecdoche, irony, and so on. . . .

Could we not say, therefore, that the dynamics of metaphor consists in confusing the established logical boundaries for the sake of detecting new similarities which previous categorization prevented our noticing? In other words, the power of metaphor would be to break through previous categorization and to establish new logical boundaries on the ruins of the preceding ones. If we take this last remark seriously, we may wish to draw the ultimate consequence and say that the dynamics of thought which breaks through previous categorization is the same as the one which generated all classifications. In other words, the figure of speech which we classify as metaphor would be at the origin of all semantic fields, since to contemplate the similar or the same—and we know now that the similar is also the same—is to grasp the genus, but not yet as genus, to grasp the same in the difference, and not yet as above or beside the difference. To grasp the kinship in any semantic field is the work of the metaphoric process at large. We are now allowed to speak of metaphoric process in so general a way because the so-called metaphor, the metaphor as trope or as a figure as it is defined by rhetoric, presents the same process, but under the paradoxical structure of sameness in spite of difference. This is why we may say from the likeness at work in metaphor, what we say about the genus as it is grasped in logical thought. We may say that we learn from it, that it teaches us something. Aristotle once more observes that it is from metaphor that we can best get hold of something fresh, for "when Homer calls old age stubble, he teaches and informs us through the genus, for both have lost their bloom. . . ."

We will now relate this analysis of metaphor to our previous analysis of polysemy. It is essential to the structure of metaphor that the old and the new are present together in the metaphorical twist. The kind of tension which we described at the level of the sentence and even within the copula itself, now dwells in the words themselves. When we receive a metaphorical statement as meaningful, we perceive both the literal meaning, which is bound by the semantic incongruity, and the new meaning, which makes sense in the present context. Metaphor is a clear case where polysemy is preserved instead of being screened. Two lines of interpretation are opened at the same time and several readings are allowed together and put into tension. This effect has been compared to stereoscopic vision. Several layers of meaning are noticed and recognized in the thickness of the text.

This first relation between metaphor and polysemy is not the only one. We have treated it as a synchronistic phenomenon, but it is also a diachronic one. If we consider the long history of a metaphor, we may say that it passes from the state of novelty to that of faded or dead metaphor. At the first stage, metaphor does not belong to the lexicon. It exists only in discourse, in the present and actual instance of discourse. But as soon as it is received by a speech community, it tends to be used in the same way as the literal meanings already classified by our dictionaries. At the last stage, when the tension between literal and metaphorical sense is no longer perceived, we may say that the metaphorical sense has become a part of the literal sense. Then it is merely added to the previous polysemy of the word. In this way we may say that metaphor is the procedure by which we extend polysemy.

In this way we come to the following hypothesis. If metaphor extends polysemy, is not polysemy the result of previous metaphor? But now metaphor is no longer a rhetorical device, no longer a trope; it designates the general process by which we grasp kinship, break the distance between remote ideas, build similarities on dissimilarities.

We are now prepared to answer the decisive question: What is the function of metaphor? By this question we are sent back to the strategy underlying the use of metaphor. If ordinary language aims at communication by cleverly reducing ambiguity, and if scientific language aims at univocity in argumentation by suppressing equivocity, what is the finality of metaphorical language? Our concept of likeness as the tension between sameness and difference implies that a discourse which makes use of metaphor has the extraordinary power of redescribing reality. This is, I believe, the referential function of a metaphorical statement. . . .

If this analysis is sound, we should have to say that metaphor not only shatters the previous structures of our language, but also the previous structures of what we call reality. When we ask whether metaphorical language reaches reality, we presuppose that we already know what reality is. But if we assume that metaphor redescribes reality, we must then assume that this reality as redescribed is itself novel reality. My conclusion is that the strategy of discourse implied in metaphorical language is neither to improve communication nor to insure univocity in argumentation, but to shatter and to increase our sense of reality by shattering and increasing our language. The strategy of metaphor is heuristic fiction for the sake of redescribing reality. With metaphor we experience the metamorphosis of both language and reality.

CHAPTER 10   Metaphor and the Main Problem

of Hermeneutics

I assume in this paper that the main problem of hermeneutics is that of interpretation. Not interpretation in any undetermined sense of the word, but interpretation with two qualifications: one concerning its scope or field of application, the other its epistemological specificity. As concerns the first point, I should say that there are problems of interpretation because there are *texts, written* texts, the autonomy of which (as regards either the intention of the author, or the situation of the work, or the destination to privileged readers) creates specific problems; these problems are usually solved in spoken language by the kind of exchange or intercourse which we call dialogue or conversation. With written texts, the discourse must speak by itself. Let us say, therefore, that there are problems of interpretation because the relation writing-reading is not a particular case of the relation speaking-hearing in the dialogical situation. Such is the most general feature of interpretation as concerns its scope or application field.

Secondly, the concept of interpretation occurs, at the epistemological level, as an alternative concept opposed to that of explanation (or explication); taken together, they both form a significant contrasting pair, which has given rise to many philosophical disputes in Germany since the time of Schleiermacher and Dilthey: according to that tradition, interpretation has specific subjective implications, such as the involvement of the reader in the process of understanding and the reciprocity between *text*-interpretation and *self*-interpretation. This reciprocity is usually known as the "hermeneutical circle" and has been opposed—mainly by logical positivists, but also for opposite reasons by Romantic thinkers—to the kind of objectivity and to the lack of self-involvement which is supposed to characterize a scientific explanation of things. I shall say later to what extent we may be led to amend, and even to rebuild on a new basis, the opposition between interpretation and explanation.

Anyhow, this schematic description of the concept of interpretation is enough to delineate the two main problems of hermeneutics: that of the status of written texts versus spoken language, and that of the status of interpretation versus explanation.

Now enters the metaphor!

The aim of this essay is to connect together the problems raised in hermeneutics by *text-interpretation* and the problems raised in rhetoric, semantics, stylistics—or whatever may be the discipline concerned—by metaphor.

I. TEXT AND METAPHOR AS DISCOURSE

Our first task will be to find a common ground for the theory of text and for that of metaphor. This common ground already has a name—discourse; it has still to receive a status.

One first thing is striking: the two kinds of entities which we are now considering are of different length and may be compared from the standpoint of length of the basic unity of discourse, the sentence. Of course a text may be reduced to only one sentence, as in proverbs or aphorisms; but texts have a maximal length which may go from paragraphs, to chapters, to books, to "selected works," to "complete works" (*Gesammelte Werke!*), and even to full libraries. I shall call a *work* the closed sequence of discourse which may be considered as a text. Whereas texts may be identified on the basis of their maximal length, metaphors may be identified on the basis of their minimal length, that of the words. Even if the remainder of the analysis tends to show that there are no metaphors, in the sense of metaphorical *words*, without certain contexts, even therefore if we shall have to speak of metaphorical *statements* requiring at least the length of a sentence, or of a phrase, nevertheless the "metaphorical twist" (to speak like Monroe Beardsley) is something which happens to words; the shift of meaning which requires the whole contribution of the context affects the word; it is the word that has a "metaphorical use," or of a nonliteral meaning, or a novel, "emergent meaning" in specific contexts. In that sense the definition of metaphor by Aristotle—as a transposition of an alien *name* (or word) (ὄνομα)—is not cancelled by a theory which lays the stress on the contextual action which creates the shift of meaning in the word. The word remains the "focus," even if this focus requires the "frame" of the sentence, to use the vocabulary of Max Black.

This first remark—merely formal—concerning the difference of length between text and metaphor, that is, between *work* and *word*, will help us to elaborate our initial problem in a more accurate way: To what extent may we treat metaphor as a work in miniature? The answer to this first question will help us afterwards to raise the second question: To what extent may the hermeneutical problem of text-interpretation be considered as a large-scale expansion of the problems condensed in the explication of a local metaphor in a given text?

Is a metaphor a work in miniature? May a work—say, a poem—be considered as an expanded metaphor? The answer to the first question relies on the general properties belonging to *discourse*, since both text and metaphor, work and word, fall under one and the same category, that of discourse.

I shall not elaborate the concept of discourse at length, but limit my analysis to those features which are necessary for the comparison between text and metaphor. For the sake of this analysis, I shall consider only the following characteristics. All of them present the form of a paradox, that is, of an apparent contradiction.

First, all discourse occurs as an *event;* it is the opposite of language as "langue," code, or system; as an event, it has an instantaneous existence, it appears and disappears. But, at the same time—here lies the paradox—it can be identified and reidentified as the same; this sameness is what we call, in the broad sense, its *meaning.* All discourse, let us say, is effectuated as an event, but all discourse is understood as meaning. We shall see in what sense metaphor concentrates on the character of event and of meaning.

Second, metaphor as a pair of contrasting traits: the meaning is carried by a specific structure, that of the proposition, which involves an inner opposition between a pole of singular identification (this man, the table, Mr. Jones, London), and a pole of general predication (mankind as a class, lightness as a property, equality with such and such as a relation, running as an action). Metaphor, as we shall see, relies on this "attribution" of characters to the "principal subject" of a sentence.

Third, discourse, as an act, may be considered from the point of view of the "content" of the propositional act (it predicates such and such characters of such and such things), or from the point of view of what Austin called the "force" of the complete act of discourse (the "speech act" in his terms): what is *said* of the subject is one thing; what I "do" *in* saying that is another thing: I may make a mere description, or give an order, or formulate a wish, or give a warning, etc. Hence the polarity between the locutionary act (the act *of* saying), and the illocutionary act (that which I do *in* saying); this polarity may seem to be less useful than the preceding ones, at least at the level of the structure of the metaphorical statement; it will play a significant role when we shall have to replace the metaphor in the concrete setting, say, of a poem, of an essay, of a fictional work.

Fourth, metaphor as a pair of opposite features: discourse, mainly as sentence, implies the polarity of *sense* and *reference,* that is, the possibility to distinguish between *what* is said, by the sentence as a whole and by the words as parts of the sentence, and *about what* something is said. To speak is to say something about something. This polarity will play the central role in the second and the third parts of this paper, since I shall try to connect the problems of explanation to the dimension of "sense," that is, to the immanent design of the discourse— and the problems of interpretation to the dimension of "reference" understood as the power of discourse to apply to an extralinguistic reality *about* which it says what it says.

But, before developing this dichotomy of sense and reference as the ground for the opposition between explanation and interpretation, let us introduce a last polarity which will play a decisive role in the hermeneutical theory. Discourse has not only one kind of reference, but two kinds of reference: it refers to an extralinguistic reality, say, the world, or a world, but it refers equally to its own speaker by the means of specific devices which function only in a sentence, therefore in discourse, such as personal pronouns, verbal tenses, demonstratives, etc. In that way, language has both a *reality*-reference and a *self*-reference. And it is the same entity—the sentence—which has this twofold reference, intentional and reflective, thing-bound and self-bound. As we shall see, this connection between the two directions of reference will be the key of our theory of interpretation and the basis of our reappraisal of the hermeneutical circle.

I enumerate the basic polarities of discourse in the following condensed way: event and meaning, singular identification and general predication, propositional act and illocutionary acts, sense and reference, reference to reality, and self-reference.

Now, in what sense may we say that text and metaphor rely on this same kind of entity which we called discourse?

It is easy to show that all texts are discourse, since they proceed from the smallest unit of discourse, the sentence. A text is at least a set of sentences. We shall see that it has to be something more in order to be a work. But it is at least a set of sentences, therefore a discourse.

The connection between metaphor and discourse requires a specific justification, precisely because the definition of metaphor as a transposition occurring to *names,* or to words, seems to put it in a category of entities smaller than the sentence. But the semantics of the word demonstrates very clearly that words have *actual* meanings only in a sentence and that lexical entities—words in the dictionary—have only potential meanings and for the sake of their potential uses in sentences. As concerns the metaphor itself, semantics demonstrates with the same strength that the metaphorical meaning of a word is nothing which may be found in a dictionary. (In that sense we may continue to oppose the metaphorical sense to the literal sense, if we call literal sense *whatever* sense may occur among the partial meanings enumerated in the dictionary, and not a so-called original, or fundamental, or primitive, or proper meaning.) If the metaphorical sense is more than the actualization of one of the potential meanings of a polysemic word (and all our words in common discourse are polysemic), it is necessary that this metaphorical use is only *contextual;* by that I mean a sense which emerges as the result of a certain contextual action. We are led in that way to oppose *contextual* changes of meaning to *lexical* changes, which concern the diachronistic aspect of language as code, system, or *langue.* Metaphor is such a *contextual* change of meaning.

By saying that, I agree partially[1] with the modern theory of metaphor, from I. A. Richards to Max Black and Monroe Beardsley; more specifically, I agree with these authors on the fundamental issue: a word receives a metaphorical meaning in specific contexts within which they are opposed to other words taken literally; this shift in meaning results mainly from a clash between literal meanings, which excludes a literal use of the word in question, and gives clues for the finding of a new meaning which is able to fit in the context of the sentence and to make sense in this context.

This contextual action creates a word-meaning which is an event, since it exists only in this context; but it can be identified as the same when it is repeated; in that way the innovation of an "emergent meaning" (Beardsley) may be recognized as a linguistic creation; if it is adopted by an influential part of the speech community, it may even become a standard meaning and be added to the polysemy of the literal entities, contributing in that way to the *history* of language as *langue*, code, or *system.* But, at that ultimate stage, metaphor is a dead metaphor. Only genuine metaphors are at the same time "event" *and* "meaning."

The contextual action requires, in the same way, our second polarity, that between singular identification and general predication: a metaphor is said of a "principal subject"; as a "modifier" of this subject, it works as a kind of "attribution." The three theories to which I refer here rely on this predicative structure, either when they oppose the "vehicle" to the "tenor," or the "frame" to the "focus," or the "modifier" to the "principal subject."

That metaphor requires the polarity between sense and reference will demand a complete section of this essay; the same must be said of the polarity between reference to reality and self-reference. You will understand later why I am unable to say more about sense and reference, and about reality-reference and self-reference at the level of metaphoric statements. Here the mediation of the theory of text will be required.

We have so far delineated the framework of our comparison. We are now prepared for the second part of our task, in which we shall answer our second question: To what extent may *text*-explanation and interpretation, on the one hand, and the explication of metaphor, on the other hand, be said to be similar processes, only applied at two different levels of discourse, the level of the *work* and the level of the *word?*

II. EXPLANATION AND METAPHOR

I want to explore the following working hypothesis. From one standpoint the process of understanding a metaphor is the key for that of understanding larger texts, say, literary works; this point of view is that of explanation and develops only this aspect of the meaning which we called the *sense*—the immanent design of discourse. But, from one other standpoint, it is the understanding of a work as a whole which gives the key to metaphor; this other point of view is that of interpretation, properly said, which develops the second aspect of the meaning, which we called the reference, that is, the intentional direction toward a world and the reflective direction toward a self. Therefore, if we apply explanation to sense as the immanent design of the work, we may reserve interpretation to the kind of inquiry devoted to the power of a work to project a world of its own and to initiate the hermeneutical circle between the apprehension of those projected worlds and the expansion of self-understanding in front of these novel worlds.

Our working hypothesis invites us, therefore, to proceed from metaphor to text at the level of the "sense" and of the "explanation" of the sense—then from text to metaphor at the level of the reference of the work to a world and to a self, that is, at the level of interpretation, properly said.

What aspects of metaphor-explication may serve as paradigms for text-explication or explanation?

These aspects are features of the *work* of explanation which do not appear when we start from trivial cases, such as—man is a wolf, or a fox, or a lion. (You could look at most of the good authors on metaphor and notice interesting variations within the bestiary which furnishes them with examples!) With those examples we elude the major difficulty, that of *identifying a meaning which is a word-meaning.* The only way of doing it is to *construct* it so that the whole sentence makes sense.

On what do we rely in the case of trivial metaphors? Max Black and Beardsley argue that the meaning of a word does not only depend on the semantical and syntactical rules which govern its use as *literal* use, but by other rules—which are nevertheless rules—to which the members of a speech-community are committed, and which determine what Black calls the "system of associated commonplaces," and Monroe Beardsley the "potential range of connotations." In the statement "man is a wolf," the principal subject is qualified by one of the traits of the animal which belong to the "wolf-system of related common-places" (p. 41);[2] this implication-system works as a filter or as a screen; it does not only select, but brings forward aspects of the principal subject.

What may we think of this explication in the light of our description of metaphor as a word-meaning occurring in a new context?

I agree entirely with the "interaction view" implied by this explication; the metaphor is more than a mere substitution for another literal word which an exhausting paraphrase could restitute at the same place. The algebraic sum of these two operations, of substitution by the speaker and of restitution by the hearer or the reader, equals zero. No new meaning emerges and we learn nothing. As Max Black says: "Interaction-metaphors are not expendable . . . this use of a subsidiary subject to foster insight into a principal subject is a distinctive intellectual operation"; this is why you cannot translate an interaction metaphor in plain language without "a loss in cognitive content" (ibid., p. 46).

But are we doing better justice to the power of metaphor "to inform and enlighten" by merely adding to the semantic polysemy of the word in the dictionary and to the semantic rules which govern the literal use of the lexical terms, the "system of associated commonplaces" and the cultural rules—I coin the term—which govern their use? Is not this system something dead, or at least something already established?

Of course, this system of commonplaces has to be assumed in order that the contextual action follow the guidelines of some directions for the construction of the new meaning. And Max Black's theory reserves the possibility that metaphors are "supported by specially constructed systems of implication as well as by accepted commonplaces" (ibid., p. 43). The problem is precisely that of these "specially constructed systems of implication." We have, therefore, to inquire into the process of interaction itself in order to explain the cases of novel metaphors in novel contexts.

Beardsley's theory of metaphor leads us a step further in that direction when he emphasized the role of logical absurdity—or of clash between literal meanings within the same context. "And in poetry," he says, "the chief tactic for obtaining this result is that of *logical absurdity*" (p. 138).[3] How? Logical absurdity creates a situation in which we have the choice between either preserving the literal sense of both the subject and the modifier and concluding to the meaninglessness of the whole sentence—or attributing a new meaning to the modifier, such as the whole sentence makes sense. Then we have not only a self-contradictory attribution, but a significant self-contradictory attribution. When I say "man is a fox" (the fox has chased the wolf), I must shift from a literal to a metaphorical attribution *if* I want to save the sentence. But, from where do we have this new meaning?

As long as we raise this kind of question—*from where*—we are sent back to the same kind of solution; the potential range of connotations does not say more than the system of associated commonplaces; indeed, we enlarge the notion of meaning by including the "secondary meanings" as connotations within the scope of the full meaning; but we keep linking the creative process of metaphor-forming to a noncreative aspect of language.

Is it sufficient to add to this "potential range of connotations," as Beardsley does in the "revised theory of controversion" (*the metaphorical twist*), the range of *properties* which do not yet belong to the range of connotations of my language? At first sight this addition improves the theory; as Beardsley says very strongly, "the metaphor transforms a property actual or attributed into a sense." The shift in the theory is important, since we have now to say that "the metaphors would not only actualize a potential connotation, but establish it as a stable one"; and further: "some of the relevant properties are given a new status as elements of verbal meaning."

But to speak of properties *of things* (or *of objects*) which were not yet meant is to concede that the novel meaning is not *drawn from* anywhere, in language at least (property is a thing-implication, not a word-implication). And to say that a novel metaphor is *not drawn at all* is to recognize it for what it is, that is, a momentaneous creation of language, a semantic innovation which has no status in language, as already established, neither as designation nor as connotation.

At that point it could be asked how one can speak of a semantic innovation, of a semantical *event* as of a *meaning*, which can be identified and reidentified (such was the first criterion of discourse in our first part).

Only one answer remains possible: to take the standpoint of the hearer or of the reader and to treat the novelty of an emergent meaning as the counterpart, from the side of the author, of the *construction* from the part of the reader. Then the process of explanation is the only access to the process of creation.

If we don't take this way, we do not get rid of the theory of *substitution;* instead of substituting for the metaphorical expression some literal meaning restituted by the paraphrase, we substitute the system

of connotations and commonplaces. This task must remain a prepara-
tory task which relates literary criticism to psychology and sociology.
The decisive moment of explication is that of the construction of the
network of interaction which makes of this context an actual and
unique context. In doing that, we point to the semantic event as to
the point of intersection between several semantic lines; this construction is the means by which all the words taken together make sense.
Then—and only then—the "metaphorical twist" is both an event *and*
a meaning, a meaningful event and an emerging meaning in language.

Such is the fundamental feature of the explication of metaphor
which makes of it a paradigm for the explanation of a literary work.
We construct the meaning of a text in a way which is similar to the
way in which we make sense of all of the terms of metaphorical statement.

Why have we to "construct" the meaning of a text? First, because it
is a *written* thing: in the asymmetric relation of the text and the reader,
only one of the partners speaks for two. Bringing a text to speech is
always something else than hearing somebody and listening to his
words.

A second reason concerns more specifically the fact that a text is not
only a *written* thing, but a work, that is, a closed chain of meaning.
Now, a work has to be constructed because a text—especially if it is
a literary work—is more than a linear succession of sentences. It is a
cumulative, holistic process.

From these two reasons, what we may give for the necessity of con-
struing the meaning of a *text,* or more precisely of a *work,* of a literary
work, we may draw more suggestions concerning the "how" of this
construction. It is at that stage that the pole of text-understanding is
homologous to the understanding of a metaphorical statement.

On the one hand, this construction necessarily takes the form of a
guess. As Hirsch says in his book *Validity in Interpretation,* there are
no rules. As concerns the place of *guessing* in the construction, it follows from what we said about the absence of the author's intention
as a guideline and the character of a work as a system of whole and
parts. We may summarize in this way the corresponding features which
are the grounds for the analogy between the explication of a metaphoric statement and a literary work as a whole.

In both cases the construction relies on the "clues" contained in the
text itself: a clue is a kind of index for a specific construction, both
a set of permissions and a set of prohibitions; it excludes some unfitting
constructions and allows some others which make more sense of the
same words.

Secondly, in both cases a construction may be said more probable
than another, but not true. The most probable is that which: (1) ac-

counts for the greatest number of facts provided by the text, including potential connotations, and (2) offers a better qualitative convergence between the traits which it takes into account. A poor explication may be said to be narrow or far-fetched.

I agree here with Beardsley that a good explication satisfies two principles: that of congruence and that of plenitude. I have spoken so far of convergence. The principle of plenitude will provide us with a transition to our third part. This principle reads: "All the connotations that can fit are to be attached; the poem means all it can mean." This principle leads us farther than mere concern for the "sense." It already says something of the reference, since it takes as a measure of plenitude the requirements raised by an expression which wants to be said and to be equated by the semantic density of the text. The principle of plenitude is the corollary at the level of the *sense* of a principle of integral expression, which draws our inquiry in a quite different direction.

A quotation from Humboldt will help us approach this new field of inquiry: "A language," he said, "language as discourse (*die Rede*) stands on the boundary line between the expressed and the unexpressed. Its aim and its goal is to always repel this boundary a bit farther."

Interpretation conforms to this aim.

III. FROM HERMENEUTICS TO METAPHOR

1. At the level of interpretation, text-understanding gives the key for metaphor-understanding.

Why? Because some features of discourse begin to play an explicit role only when discourse takes the form of a literary *work*. These features are those which we put under the two headings of reference and self-reference. I oppose reference to sense by identifying "sense" with "what," and "reference" with "about what" of discourse. Of course, these two traits may be recognized in the smallest unity of language as discourse, in sentences. The sentence is about a situation which it expresses and refers back to its own speaker by the means of specific devices. But reference and self-reference do not give rise to perplexing problems until discourse has become a text and has taken the form of a work.

Which problems? Let us start once more from the difference between written and spoken language. In spoken language, what a dialogue ultimately refers to is the situation common to the interlocutors, that is, aspects of reality which can be shown or pointed at; we say then that reference is "ostensive." In written language, reference is no longer ostensive: poems, essays, and fictional works speak of things, events, states of affairs, characters which are evoked, but which are not there.

Nevertheless, literary texts are something. About what? About a world, which is the world of this work. Far from saying that the text is there without a world, I will now say without paradox that only man has a world, and not just a situation, a *Welt* and not just an *Umwelt*. In the same manner that the text frees its meaning from the tutelage of the mental intention, it frees its reference from the limits of ostensive reference. For us, the world is the ensemble of references opened up by texts. Thus we speak about the "world" of Greece, not to designate any more what were the situations for those who lived then, but to designate the nonsituational references which outlive the effacement of the first and which henceforth are offered as possible modes of being, of symbolic dimensions of our being-in-the-world.

This nature of reference in the case of literary works has an important consequence for the concept of interpretation. It implies that "the meaning of a text is not behind the text, but in front of it. It is not something hidden, but something disclosed." What has to be understood is what points toward a possible world thanks to the nonostensive references of the text. Texts speak of possible worlds and of possible ways of orientating oneself in those worlds. In that way disclosure becomes the equivalent for written texts of ostensive reference for spoken language. And interpretation becomes the grasping of the world-propositions opened up by the nonostensive references of the text.

This concept of interpretation expresses a decisive shift of emphasis within the Romanticist tradition of hermeneutics; here the emphasis was put on the ability of the hearer or of the reader to transfer himself in the spiritual life of another speaker or writer. The emphasis now is less on the *other*, as a spiritual entity, than on the world that the work displays. *Verstehen*—understanding—is to follow the dynamics of the work, its movement from what it says to that about which it speaks. "Beyond my situation as reader, beyond the author's situation, I offer myself to the possible ways of being-in-the-world which the text opens up and discovers for me." This is what Gadamer calls "fusion of horizons" (*Horizontverschmelzung*) in historical knowledge.

The shift of emphasis, from understanding the other to understanding the world of his work, implies a corresponding shift in the conception of the "hermeneutical circle." By "hermeneutical circle," Romanticist thinkers meant that the understanding of a text cannot be an objective procedure in the sense of scientific objectivity, but necessarily involves a precomprehension which expresses the way in which the reader has already understood himself and his world. Therefore, a kind of circularity occurs between understanding a text and understanding oneself. Such is, in condensed terms, the principle of the "hermeneutical circle." It is easy to understand that thinkers taught in the tradition of logical empiricism could only reject as sheer scandal the mere idea of a hermeneutical circle and consider it as an outrageous violation of all the canons of verifiability.

For my part, I do not want to deny that the hermeneutical circle remains an unavoidable structure of interpretation. No genuine interpretation which does not end in some kind of appropriation—of *Aneignung,* if by that term we mean the process of making one's own *(eigen)* what was other, foreign *(fremd)*. But my claim is that the hermeneutical circle is not correctly understood when it is presented (1) as a circle between two subjectivities, that of the reader and that of the author, and (2) as the projection of the subjectivity of the reader in the reading itself. Let us correct the first assumption in order to correct the second one: That which we make our own, we appropriate for ourselves, is not a foreign experience or a distant intention, it is the horizon of a world toward which this refers: the appropriation of the reference no longer finds any model in the fusion of consciousness, in empathy or in sympathy. The coming to language of the sense and the reference of a text is the coming to language of a world and not the recognition of another person.

The second correction of the Romanticist concept of interpretation follows from the first one: If appropriation is the counterpart of disclosure, then the role of subjectivity is not correctly described as projection. I should rather say that the reader understands himself before the text, before the world of the work. To understand oneself before, in front of, a world is the contrary of projecting oneself and one's beliefs and prejudices; it is to let the work and its world enlarge the horizon of my own self-understanding.

Hermeneutics, therefore, does not submit interpretation to the finite capacities of understanding of a given reader; it does not put the meaning of the text under the power of the subject who interprets. Far from saying that a subject already masters his own way of being in the world and projects it as the a priori of his reading, I would say that interpretation is the process by which the disclosure of new modes *of being*—or, if you prefer Wittgenstein to Heidegger, of new "forms of life"—gives to the subject a new capacity of knowing himself. If there is somewhere a project and a projection, it is the reference of the work which is the project of a world; the reader is consequently enlarged in his capacity of self-projection by receiving a new mode of being from the text itself.

In that way the hermeneutical circle is not denied, but it is displaced from a subjectivistic to an ontological level; the circle is between my way (or my mode) of being—beyond the knowledge which I may have of it—and the mode (or the way) of being disclosed by the text as the work's world.

2. Such is the model of interpretation which I want now to transfer from texts as long sequences of discourse to metaphor as "a poem in miniature" (Beardsley). Indeed, the metaphor is too short a discourse to display this dialectic between disclosing a world and understanding one's self in front of this world. Nevertheless, this dialectic points toward some features of metaphor which the modern theories I quoted above do not seem to consider, but which were not absent from Greek theory of metaphor.

Let us return to the theory of metaphor in the *Poetics* of Aristotle. Metaphor is only one of the "parts" (μερή, *merê*) of that which Aristotle calls "diction" (λέξις, *lexis*); as such, it belongs to a family of language procedures—use of foreign words, coining of new words, shortening or lengthening of words—all of which depart from common (κυριον, *kyrion*) use of words. Now, what makes the unity of *lexis*? Only its *function* in poetry. *Lexis*, in its turn is one of the "parts" (μερή, *merê*) of tragedy, taken as the paradigm of the poetic work. Tragedy, in the context of the *Poetics*, represents the level of the literary work as a whole. Tragedy, as a poem, has sense and reference. In the language of Aristotle, the "sense" of tragedy is secured by what he calls the "fable," or the "plot" (μῦθος, *mythos*). We may understand the *mythos* of tragedy as its sense, since Aristotle keeps putting the emphasis on its structural characters; the *mythos* must have unity and coherence and make of the actions represented something "entire and complete." As such, the *mythos* is the principal "part" of tragedy, its "essence"; all the other "parts" of tragedy—the "characters," the "thoughts," the "diction," the "spectacle"—are connected to the *mythos* as the means, or the conditions, or the performance of the tragedy as *mythos*.

We must draw the inference that it is only in connection with the *mythos* of tragedy that its *lexis* makes sense, and, with *lexis*, *metaphora*. There is no local meaning of metaphor besides the regional meaning provided by the *mythos* of tragedy.

But, *if* metaphor is related to the "sense" of tragedy by the means of its *mythos*, it is related to the "reference" of tragedy thanks to its general aim which Aristotle calls *mimesis* (μίμησις).

Why do poets write tragedies, elaborate fables and plots, and use such "strange" words as metaphors? Because tragedy itself is related to a more fundamental project—that of *imitating* human action in a *poetic* fashion. With these master words—*mimesis* and *poiesis*—we reach the level of what I called the referential world of the work. Indeed, the Aristotelian concept of *mimesis* actually includes all the paradoxes of reference. On the one hand, it expresses a world of human action which is already there; tragedy is bound to express human reality, the tragedy of life. But, on the other hand, *mimesis* does not mean duplication of reality; *mimesis* is *poiesis*, that is, fabrication, construction, creation. Aristotle gives at least two hints of this creative dimension of *mimesis:* the fable itself as a coherent construction of its own, and above all the definition of tragedy as the imitation of human actions as better, nobler, higher than they actually are. Could we not say, then, that *mimesis* is the Greek name for what we called the unostensive reference of the literary work, or in other words, the Greek name for world-disclosure?

If we are right, we may now say something about the *power* of metaphor. I say here the "power," and no longer the "structure," no longer even the "process of metaphor." The power of metaphor proceeds from its connection, within a poetic and work, *first* with the other procedures of "diction" (*lexis*), *secondly* with the "fable," which is the essence of the work, its immanent "sense," *thirdly* with the intentionality of the work as a whole, that is, its intention to represent human actions as *higher* than they actually are: and this is *mimesis*. In that sense the power of metaphor proceeds from that of the poem as a whole.

Let us apply these remarks borrowed from Aristotle's *Poetics* to our own description of metaphor. Could we not say that the feature of metaphor that we put above all other features—its nascent or emerging character—is related to the function of poetry as a creative imitation of reality? Why should we invent novel meanings, meanings which exist only in the instance of discourse, if it were not for the sake of the *poiesis* in the *mimesis*? If it is true that the poem creates a world, it requires a language which preserves and expresses its creative power in specific contexts.

Link together the *poiesis* of the *poem* and metaphor as an emergent meaning, then you will make sense of both at the same time: poetry and metaphor.

Such is the way in which the theory of interpretation paves the way for an ultimate approach to the power of metaphor. This priority given to text-interpretation in this last stage of the analysis of metaphor does not imply that the relation between both is not reciprocal. The explication of metaphor as a local event in the text contributes to the interpretation itself of the work as a whole. We could even say that, if the interpretation of local metaphors is enlightened by the interpretation of the text as a whole and by the disentanglement of the kind of world it projects, then the interpretation of the poem as a whole is controlled, reciprocally, by the explication of metaphor as a local phenomenon. I should venture, as an example of this reciprocal relation between regional and local aspects of the text, the possible connection, in Aristotle's *Poetics,* between the function of *imitation,* as making human actions *higher* than they actually are, and the structure of metaphor, as *transposing* the meaning of ordinary language into *strange* uses. Is there not a mutual affinity between the project of making human actions look *better* than they actually are and the special procedure of metaphor as an emerging meaning?

Let us express that relation in more general terms: Why should we draw new meanings from our language if we had nothing *new* to say, no new worlds to project? Linguistic creations would be meaningless if they did not serve the general project of letting new worlds emerge from poetry.

Allow me to conclude in a way which would be consistent with a theory of interpretation which lays the stress on "opening up a world." Our conclusion should also "open up" some new vistas. On what? Maybe on the old problem of imagination, which I cautiously put aside. We are prepared to inquire into the power of imagination, no longer as the faculty of deriving "images" from sensory experiences, but as the capacity to let new worlds build our self-understanding. This power would not be conveyed by emerging images but by emerging meanings in our language. Imagination, then, should be treated as a dimension of language. In that way, a new link would appear between imagination and metaphor.

CHAPTER 11   Explanation and Understanding:

On Some Remarkable Connections Among the Theory of

the Text, Theory of Action, and Theory of History

The ancient debate between explaining and understanding concerns both epistemology and ontology. More precisely, it is a debate which begins as a simple analysis of our way of thinking and talking about things, but which, as the argument proceeds, turns to the things themselves on which our concepts bear. At first, the question is to know if the sciences, whether natural or human, constitute a homogeneous, single continuum, or whether there must be an epistemological break between the natural sciences and the social sciences. At this first level, the terms "explanation" and "understanding" are the flags of the two camps. In this duel, the term "explanation" stands for the thesis of nondifferentiation, that is, of the epistemological continuity between the natural and social sciences, while the term "understanding" signifies the claim that the social sciences are peculiar and irreducible. But what is it, in the final analysis, that establishes this dualism if not the presupposition that in the things themselves even the order of signs and institutions is not reducible to that of facts subsumed under natural laws. Thus, it would be the job of philosophy to base the pluralism of methods and the epistemological discontinuity between the natural and the social sciences on the ultimate difference between the mode of being of nature and that of spirit.

The goal of this essay is to call into question the dichotomy which assigns to the two terms "explanation" and "understanding" two distinct epistemological fields which refer, respectively, to two irreducible modes of being.

I would like to draw my argument from the resemblance, or better, the homology that can be established among three general problems, those of the text, of action, and of history. In fact, in each of these theoretical areas similar difficulties have led, by independent paths, to a questioning of methodological dualism of explanation and understanding and the substitution of a refined dialectic for this blunt opposition. By dialectic, I understand the view that explanation and understanding would not constitute mutually exclusive poles, but rather relative moments in a complex process called interpretation. This alternative solution also has epistemological and ontological dimensions. Epistemological dimension: If there is a relation of mutual implication between the methods, we should find between the natural and the social sciences a continuity as well as a discontinuity, a family resemblance as well as a particularity in their methods. Ontological dimension: If explanation and understanding are inextricably bound together on the epistemological level, it is no longer possible to make an ontological dualism correspond to a methodological dualism. By the same stroke, the destiny of philosophy is no longer bound to that of a difference of methods. That would be to believe that philosophy is united with a discipline or with a group of disciplines which would escape the universal reign of mathematical or experimental sciences. If philosophy is to survive, it is not by inciting methodological schisms. Its destiny is bound to its capacity to subordinate the very idea of method to a more fundamental concept of the relation of truth to things and to beings. I will say a few words in my conclusion about this movement of radicalization by which philosophy is defined.

But, before coming to this ultimate question, let us go back to work on the debate at the epistemological level. Before seeing the problem divided among the three domains where it plays a role today, let us consider what should lead, in the theory of *Verstehen* itself, to a complete revision of the purely dichotomous idea of the relation between explanation and understanding.

In the mind of Dilthey, the most typical German representative of the theory of *Verstehen* at the turn of the century, it was not at all a matter of opposing some kind of Romantic obscurantism to the scientific spirit handed down from Galileo, Descartes, and Newton. Rather, it was a matter of giving understanding a scientific respectability equal to that of explanation. Thus, Dilthey was not able to restrict himself to founding understanding on our ability to transfer ourselves into another's psychic life on the basis of signs the other gives us. These signs may be direct, such as gestures or speech, or indirect, such as writing or monuments or generally the inscriptions that human reality leaves behind. We would only have the right to speak of social sciences if we could build a true knowledge on this "understanding" which, while keeping the mark of its origin in the understanding of signs, would nevertheless have the characteristics of a true knowledge: organization, stability, and coherence. Thus, we must admit right off that only signs fixed by writing or by some other equivalent inscription lend themselves to the sort of objectification required by science. Next, if we are to inscribe psychic life, it must be made up of stable connections, a sort of institutional structure. From there, Dilthey was led to reintroduce the characteristics of the Hegelian "objective spirit" into a philosophy which, nevertheless, remained romantic, to the extent that it is life which expresses itself in signs and which thus interprets itself.

These internal difficulties with the theory of *Verstehen* make a good introduction to the attempt to reformulate the relation between explanation and understanding that I would now like to sketch out. I will do this by putting myself successively in the three major *places* where this problem is discussed today: the theory of the text, action theory, and the theory of history. We will derive the idea of a general dialectic between explanation and understanding from the correlation among these three theories.

I. THEORY OF THE TEXT

I will begin with the theory of texts because it remains in the line of the problem of *signs* on which Dilthey had constructed his plea for *Verstehen*. But I would not like, however, to limit myself to a purely semiotic consideration. That is why I will use the theories of action and of history in order to expand to the dimensions of a *philosophical anthropology* the debate which was at first limited to the semiological level. In this respect, nothing is more interesting than the interplay among *text, action,* and *history.* I will say something about this presently. In fact, it is through this triple theoretical articulation of the anthropological field that the subtle dialectic of understanding and explanation unfolds.

The theory of the text offers a good starting point for a radical revision of the methodological problem because semiology does not permit us to claim that the explanatory procedures are foreign to the domain of the sign and are imported from the neighboring field of the natural sciences. New models of explanation have appeared which belong properly to the domain of signs, both linguistic and nonlinguistic. These models, as is well known, are more frequently structural than genetic, that is to say, they rest on stable correlations among discrete unities rather than on regular sequences of events, phases, or stages of a process. Henceforth, a theory of interpretation has a semiological rather than a naturalistic look.

I will not give a history of the development of the semiological model. To do so would require that we begin with the Saussurian distinction between language and speech, then consider the establishment of a purely synchronic science of systems of differences, oppositions, and combinations, and then go on to the theoretical work not only of the Geneva school, but also of the Prague and the Danish schools. I will mention only very briefly the progressive extension of the semiological model: First, the conquest of the phonological foundation, then its application to its principal area, the lexicon of the natural languages; then comes its extension to units of speech larger than the sentence, such as the *story* (where structuralism has had its greatest success) and, finally, the extrapolation of the model to the level of systems as complex as the *myth* with the *Mythologiques* of Lévi-Strauss—to say nothing of the as yet tentative attempts to extend the model to the order of nonlinguistic signs, to the world of techniques, to economic, social, political, and religious institutions.

I will consider only that part of this remarkable development which concerns the debate between explanation and understanding, and I will concentrate on the single example of the story. First, because as I just said, it has been the object, since Propp and the Russian formalists and with Roland Barthes, Bremond, and their school, of the most brilliant and convincing work. Secondly, because the parallelism among theory of the text, theory of action, and theory of history is immediately suggested by the *narrative* genre of discourse.

A purely dichotomic position of the problem would amount to saying that there is no relation between a structural analysis of the text and an understanding which would remain faithful to the Romantic, hermeneutical tradition. For analysts favoring an explanation without understanding, the text would be a machine with purely internal functioning to which no (so-called psychologizing) questions must be put, whether about the author's intention or the audience's reception, or even from the heart of the text itself about a *meaning,* or of a message distinct from the form itself, that is, from the intersection of the *codes* put in action by the text. For Romantic hermeneutics, on the other hand, the structural analysis would proceed from an objectification foreign to the message of the text, itself inseparable from the intention of its author: to understand would be to establish between the mind of the reader and that of the author a communication, even a communion, similar to that which occurs in a face-to-face dialogue.

Thus, on the one hand, for the sake of an objectivity of the text, every subjective and intersubjective relation would be eliminated; on the other hand, for the sake of a subjectivity of the appropriated message, every objectifying analysis would be declared foreign to understanding.

In place of this mutual exclusion I offer the more dialectical concept of an interpretation between understanding and explanation. Let us follow the line from one to the other in both directions, beginning by going from understanding toward explanation.

Understanding calls for explanation as soon as there is no longer a dialogue, where the give and take of questions and answers permits an interpretation to be verified as it unfolds. In the simple situation of a dialogue, understanding and explanation almost coincide. When I do not spontaneously understand, I ask you for an explanation; and the explanation that you offer allows me to understand you better. Here explanation is only understanding developed by questions and answers. It is completely different with written works which have broken their initial link with the intention of the author, with the original audience, and with the situation common to the parties. The semantic autonomy of discourse constitutes, as Dilthey had already seen, one of the most fundamental conditions for its objectification. Without doubt we must add, against any hypostasis of writing, that the first condition of any inscription is, in discourse itself, even oral, the smallest gap that inserts itself between saying and what is said. This, of course, we have already seen in the first chapter of Hegel's *Phenomenology of Mind.* I say, "It is night," but when day breaks, what I said remains said. That is why it can be written. But *literature,* in the etymological sense of the word, infinitely exploits this gap and creates a totally different situation from that of dialogical understanding. Reading is not simply a kind of listening. It is regulated by *codes* comparable to the grammatical code which guides the understanding of sentences. In the case of a story, these codes are precisely those which a structural analysis develops under the name of narrative codes.

Thus, we cannot say that passing through explanation is destructive of inter-subjective understanding. It is a mediation required by discourse itself. I say explicitly discourse and not simple *speech,* which is the fleeting manifestation of language. For it is discourse which calls for the ever more complicated process of exteriorization to itself; it begins with the separation of the act of speaking and what is said, is continued by alphabetic inscription, and culminates in the complex codifications of works of discourse, among which is that of the story. This exteriorization into material marks, and this inscription in the codes of discourse, make not only possible *but necessary the mediation of understanding by explanation,* of which the structural analysis of the story constitutes the most remarkable achievement.

But going in the other direction is no less required. Explanation is finally completed by understanding. Here structural analysis has reduced the story to the functioning of codes which crisscross there. But by this series of operations the given story has somehow been made virtual, I mean stripped of its actuality as an event of discourse and reduced to the state of a variable in a system which has no other existence than that of a unified ensemble of permissions and prohibitions. Now we must take the opposite path, from the virtual to the actual, from system to event, from language to speech. This is the road that Gadamer calls *Anwendung,* recalling the *applicatio* dear to Renaissance hermeneutics. The activity of analysis thus appears as a simple segment of an interpretative arc which goes from naïve understanding through explanation to knowledgeable understanding. In the case of the story, taken here as paradigm, *applicatio* corresponds to the overall operation that can be called, to use Barthes's expression, "narrative communication." This is the operation by which the narrator tells a story and his listener hears it.

I understand full well that structuralism, remaining within the confines of the story, will not look elsewhere than in the signs of narration for the mark of the narrational level. Refusing any psychologizing about the narrator and listener and any sociology of the audience, it restricts itself to "describing the code through which the narrator and the reader are signified throughout the story itself."[1] Thus, structuralism does not transgress the rule of immanence which is the methodological postulate of all structural analysis. But what motive does the analyst have in looking for the signs of the narrator and the listener *in* the text of the story itself, if not the understanding which envelops all of the analytic steps and places the narrative back into a movement of transmission, into a living tradition, as a story told by someone to someone? The story thus belongs to a chain of speeches by which a cultural community is constituted and by which this community interprets itself by means of narratives. This belonging to a tradition says, in its turn, something about the fundamental belonging (that I will mention in my conclusion) and which is the theme of philosophy. To the extent that this belonging is fundamentally constituted in and by tradition, we can say that it is this radical problematic which is on the same all-encompassing level as narrative communication. Narration—in the operational sense of the word—is thus the action which opens the story to the world, where it wastes away and dissolves, and this openness is the counterpart of what the semiologist knows only as the self-containedness of the story. It is the same narration which constitutes the crest between these two slopes.

Is this to say that in thus passing from explanation to understanding, from the explanation of the story-object to the understanding of the narrative operation, we are slipping again into the rut of psychologism? Nothing has done more damage to the theory of understanding than identification (central for Dilthey) between understanding and understanding others, as if it were always a matter of first understanding someone else's psychological life behind a text. What must be understood in a story is not first the one who speaks behind the text, but that which is spoken about, the *subject matter of the text,* that is, the sort of world that the work lays out in front of the text. In this respect, Aristotle gave, in his theory of tragedy, a key which seems valuable to me for all stories: The poet, in writing a fable, a plot, a *mythos,* gives us a *mimesis,* a creative imitation of men in action. In the same way, a logic of narrative possibilities, which a formal analysis of narrative codes claims to be about, is completed only in the mimetic function by which the story remakes the world of human action. Thus, there is no question of denying the subjective character of understanding in which explanation is completed. It is always someone who hears, makes his own, appropriates the meaning. But there is no abrupt short circuit between the completely objective analysis of the structures of the story and the subjective appropriation of meaning: between the two lies the world of the text, the meaning of the work, that is, in the case of a story-text, the world of possible paths of a real action. If a subject is called upon to understand himself in the presence of the text, it is to the extent that the text is not closed on itself, but open to the world which it redescribes and refashions.

I will say no more about the dialectic of explanation and understanding within the framework of the theory of the text. As I mentioned at the beginning, I do not want to be confined to a semiological discussion. On the contrary, I would like to show that the theory of the text is, for a philosophical anthropology, only one of the "places" where the present debate can be enriched. The *theory of action* is another. I will say a few words later about the somewhat structural reasons which allow the theory of the text and that of action to be interchanged. But at first, I prefer to take advantage of the distance between the two. It is not the same authors, in fact, who are interested in these two domains. Nor is it the same problems that have been raised, since the theory of action, in its contemporary form, is an Anglo-American specialty. It is even more instructive that the debate about action has led to the same difficulties and to the same search for a dialectical solution as the debate about the text. We can take as evidence the very title of Georg Henrik Von Wright's book *Explanation and Understanding,*[2] which I will talk about later.

II. THEORY OF ACTION

During the first phase, in fact, from about 1955 to 1960, under the influence of Wittgenstein and Austin, the discussion—primarily in English

—produced the same dichotomy between explanation and understanding as that which existed fifty years before in the German language, even if the vocabulary was different. The theory of "language games," by insisting on the irreducibility of these language games, reproduced in fact a comparable epistemological situation, as shown, for example, by Anscombe's *Intention,*[3] published in 1957. The outline of the argument is the following: Events produced by nature and actions done by men do not participate in the same language game. For to talk about events, we enter into the language game containing notions such as cause, law, fact, explanation, and so on. Rather than mix language games, we must keep them separate. Thus, we speak of human actions in another language game, in another conceptual network, because if we have begun to speak of actions we will go on in terms of projects, intentions, motives, reasons for acting, agents, etc. To recognize and distinguish language games is thus the job of clarification, the essentially therapeutic task of philosophy.

I will mention right off that the struggle has been carried on to a great extent over the word "cause." Perhaps this was a mistake, for it was too quickly accepted that the word "cause" has only one meaning, that which Hume gave it. For him, the relation between cause and effect implies that the antecedents and the consequents are logically independent, that is, they are capable of being separately identified (e.g., if a match ignites an explosive material, I can describe the match perfectly without describing the explosion). There is thus no logical bond of implication between the cause and the effect. But this is not the case between intention and action, or between motive and project. I cannot identify a project without talking about the action I am going to do. Here the connection is logical and not causal (in Hume's sense). In the same way, I cannot talk about my motives without connecting these motives with the action for which they are the motives. There is thus an implication between motive and project which does not fit into the schema of the logical heterogeneity of cause and effect. As a consequence, if I use the word "because" in this language game, it is a different sense of "because." In one case I am asking for a cause, in the other a reason. Anscombe has sharply distinguished between these two language games by using the two expressions *why* and *because of.* With one I am speaking in the order of motivation, with the other that of causality.

On another specific point, an equally ardent debate has arisen: What is the relation between the agent and his action? Can we say that the agent is the cause of his actions? No, if cause means constant antecedent; yes, if we can say that the relation between the agent and his actions follows a non-Humean model of causality, for instance one closer to the Aristotelian model.

This is the state of the problem that I take as a starting point for our discussion. I propose not to give the reasons why this simple dichotomy is untenable, a dichotomy which at once tends to solve, but also to evaporate, the problem. All of the language games having, in effect, an equal right, philosophy no longer has the task of articulating, of ranking, of organizing knowledge, but rather of maintaining the difference between heterogenous language games. This apparently conciliatory position is, in fact, untenable. I will consider two arguments:

The first concerns the debate between motive and cause. Can we relegate them to two heterogenous language games? Already at the level of ordinary language it is not true that the two language games are completely separate. Rather, we need to establish a spectrum where we would have at one extreme a causality without motivation, and at the other a motivation without causality. Causality without motivation would correspond to ordinary experiences of constraint (when we give an account of a functional problem, we explain it not by intention but by the disturbing cause). Causal explanation also wins out in the case that Aristotle would call "violence," taken in its most general sense (*bia*). In the same context, there are forms of motives which are very close to these external causes. It is in this sense that we ask quite naturally, what incited him to do that? What led him to do that? All the unconscious motives of the Freudian type are modeled for the most part on an interpretation in economic terms, which is very close to causality-constraint. At the other end of the spectrum, we would find the rarer forms of purely rational motivation, where the motives would be reasons, such as in intellectual games (chess, for example) or in strategic models. The human phenomenon is situated between the two: between a causality that requires explanation and not understanding, and a motivation requiring a purely rational understanding.

The properly human domain is this in-between in which we are constantly moving in order to compare more rational and less rational motives, to make a relative appreciation, put them on a scale of preference (cf. the concept of preference in Aristotle), and finally to use them as a premise in practical reasoning. In this respect, Anscombe and others have done a great deal of work on the form of practical reasoning and the practical syllogism. And, in fact, it is always possible to introduce the verbal expression of a desire into practical reasoning. By its character of desirability—that is, that by virtue of which we desire something—it can be treated as a reason for acting and can be implicitly put on the level of rationality and discursivity. This double face of desire—desire as *force* which pushes and moves, desire as *reason* for acting —is at the origin of the opposition between what can be explained (the cause) and what can be understood (the motive-reason). But this opposition is purely abstract. Reality presents, rather, the combination of the two extreme cases in the properly human field of motivation, where the motive is at the same time motion of will and justification. The linguistic stage of the discussion is quite inadequate here. A linguistic analysis quickly gives rise to much more radical questions. What sort of being is it who makes possible this double allegiance of motive both to force and to meaning, to nature and to culture, to *bios* and to *logos?* We must reflect on the very position of the body in nature: it is simultaneously a body among bodies (a thing among things) and the mode of existence of a being capable of thinking, of taking charge of himself, and of justifying his conduct. The epistemological argument is purely superficial and in fact hides the extremely profound gamble on an anthropology which must be made explicit. Man is precisely the being who belongs at the same time to the regime of causality and to that of motivation, thus of explanation and of understanding.

A second argument against the semantic and epistemological dualism appears when we examine the conditions under which an action is inserted in the world. Too often we examine the interior of intentions and motives while forgetting that to act means above all to make a change in the world. Consequently, how can a project change the world? What must be, on the one hand, the nature of the world in order that man can introduce changes? What must be, on the other hand, the nature of action that it can be seen in terms of changes in the world?

The Finnish philosopher Von Wright (to whom I owe a great deal for this part of my essay) proposes, in the book I mentioned earlier, a reformulation of the conditions of explanation on the one side, and the conditions of understanding on the other, so that these conditions can be combined in the notion of an "intentional intervention" in the world.

Von Wright's argument rests essentially on the theory of systems. According to him, we can think only of a partial, closed system which excludes, as a consequence, extrapolation to the whole universe conceived as a system of all systems. Using this notion of a "closed system," he will later try to conceive of man in the world as a closed system allowing us to define an initial state, stages, and a terminal state. But the earlier and longest part of his book establishes the formal logical conditions to his model of a closed system. On the basis of this, he contests the idea of a universal determinism: causal relations between an initial state and a final state proceed, in principle, in an asymmetrical way, since the sufficient conditions of the progressive order cannot be exchanged for the necessary conditions of the regressive order. According to Von Wright, a refined model should have a sequence of phases, each open to a greater or lesser number of alternatives in the progressive order.

Human action can now be placed in the context of this notion of a closed system, with an initial state, internal alternatives, and terminal states. Indeed, the possibility of action is introduced by the consideration of the conditions of isolation of a closed system. We learn to isolate a closed system essentially by putting the system into action; this is what Von Wright calls "to put the system into motion." But how do we start a movement? By producing the initial state, by exercising a power or capacity, by *intervening* in the course of things. For Von Wright, the simplest model of intervention is the experimentation of the scientist in his laboratory. The scientist acts in such a way with his hands that the initial state of the system which he puts into motion corresponds with the exercise of one of his abilities. The notion of an initial state is thus essential. But what we are able to do we know with a knowledge that Anscombe, ten years earlier, called a "knowledge without observation." I know that I can move my hand, I can open a window, etc. I know from experience that the window does not open itself, but that I can open it, and if I open it I produce a number of effects. I let in fresh air; I make the papers blow; etc. If we move backward from the most distant effects of an action, we always end up with actions that we know how to do because we are able to do them. To act is essentially to make something happen, or to do one thing in order to make something else happen, or simply to do something, but not by means of something else. This last type of action can be called "basic action" (Danto). The notion of an ability is absolutely irreducible and consequently represents the counterpart of any theory of closed systems. By exercising an ability I make some event happen as the initial state of a system. The relation between doing something immediately (basic action) and making something happen mediately (by doing something else that I can do) follows the lines of the causal analysis of closed systems. Thus, we see here a highly interesting intersection, which requires a similar intersection at the level of method between what can be called the theory of systems and the theory of action. This intersection implies a mutual relation, since "knowing how to do" (that which I am able to do) is necessary for identifying the initial state of a system, isolating it, and defining its conditions of closedness. Inversely, action under its programmed form (to do something in order to make something else happen) requires a specific concatenation of systems, considered as a fragment of the history of the world.

Let us draw some conclusions from this analysis. First, and obviously, we definitively turn our backs on the dichotomy between explanation and understanding. If explanation is in the province of the theory of systems and understanding in that of motivation (of intentional and motivated human action), we realize that these two elements —the course of things and human action—overlap in the notion of *intervention* in the course of things. Next, this notion of intervention leads us to an idea of cause quite different from Hume's and synonymous with the initiative of an agent. But it is not opposed to motive; rather it includes it, since intervention in the course of things implies that we follow the articulation of natural systems.

Furthermore, the notion of intervention puts an end to the intolerable state of opposition between a mentalistic order of understanding and a physicalistic order of explanation. On the one hand, there is no system without initial state, no initial state without intervention, and no intervention without the exercise of a capacity. To act is always to do something to make something else happen in the world. On the other hand, there is no action without a relation between knowing-how-to-do (being able to do) and what it makes happen. Causal explanation applied to a fragment of the history of the world cannot function without recognizing and identifying an ability which belongs to the repertory of our own capacities of action.

Finally, with respect to determinism, the analysis shows to what extent the idea of universal determinism is pure illusion: it rests on the extrapolation to the totality of things from the knowledge that we have of some causal connections relative to fragments of the history of the world. For, in order for the extrapolation to succeed, it would be necessary to eliminate, by becoming a passive observer, one of the conditions which makes the system possible, precisely the condition of closedness. This condition is tied to the exercise of a capacity, the ability to put the system into motion. Human action and physical causality are too intertwined in this completely primitive experience of the intervention of an agent in the course of things to permit the abstraction of the first term and the absolute extension of the second.

Without borrowing anything from the theory of the text, there is an extraordinary convergence between it and the theory of action. The same difficulties and the same requirements for a dialectical solution arose in two fields where there were few mutual influences.

I would like to suggest that this convergence is not accidental. Serious reasons justify the similarities between the theory of the text and the theory of action. But I can give only an outline of these reasons here because they in themselves constitute an important problem for a philosophical anthropology. I will say, briefly, that in one way the notion of the text is a good *paradigm* for human action, in another the action is a good *referent* for a whole category of texts. With respect to the first point, human action is in many ways a quasi-text. It is exteriorized in a manner comparable to the fixation characteristic of writing. In becoming detached from its agent, the action acquires an autonomy similar to the semantic autonomy of a text; it leaves a trace, a mark. It is inscribed in the course of things and becomes an archive and document. Even more like a text, of which the meaning has been freed from the initial conditions of its production, human action has a stature that is not limited to its importance for the situation in which it initially occurs, but allows it to be reinscribed in new social contexts. Finally, action, like a text, is an open work, addressed to an indefinite series of possible "readers." The judges are not contemporaries, but subsequent history.

Thus, it is not surprising that the theory of action gives rise to the same dialectic of understanding and explanation as the theory of the text.

The right to proceed to such a transfer will appear even stronger if, in turn, we consider that certain texts—if not all texts—have as a referent action itself. In any case this is true of the story. We mentioned earlier Aristotle's remark in the *Poetics:* the *mythos* of tragedy, that is, at once the fable and the plot, is *mimesis,* the creative imitation of human action. Poetry, he also says, shows men as in action. The analogy between text and action does not seem risky once we can show that at least one area of discourse has action as its subject; it refers to it, redescribes it, and repeats it.

III. THEORY OF HISTORY

The interesting correlations between the theory of the text and the theory of action are reinforced in the third area where the dialectic of explanation and understanding can be studied, that is, in the theory of history.

That history—I mean the history of historians—engenders the same problems and the same debates as the theory of the text and the theory of action should not surprise us. For, on the one hand, history—historiography—is a type of *story,* a "true" story in contrast to myths or fictional stories such as epics, drama, tragedies, novels, and short stories. On the other hand, history is about the *actions* of men in the past.

This double affinity with the theory of action and with the theory of the story justifies our having saved for the last our account of the historical method, in which the characteristics of the other two theories are brought together.

In the theory of history, too, we can identify two opposing camps which confront one another in a nondialectical way. Then we can see a more nuanced and dialectic opposition being worked out as a result of the failure of the one-sided positions.

On the side of understanding, we find the antipositivist objections of French-speaking historians such as Raymond Aron and Henri Marrou, influenced by the comprehensive German sociology—Rickert, Simmel, Dilthey and Weber—but also of English-speaking historians influenced by Collingwood. The former essentially underline two characteristics of the historical method. First, history is about human actions, directed by intentions, projects, motives, which must be under-stood by an *Einfühlung,* by an intropathy similar to that by which, in daily life, we understand the intentions and motives of others. Accord-ing to this argument, history is only an extension of understanding others. Secondly, this understanding, contrary to the objective knowl-edge of the facts of nature, is not possible without the personal involve-ment of the historian, of his subjectivity. In a different but convergent terminology, Collingwood said almost the same thing in his well-known work *The Idea of History.* On the one hand, history proposes to under-stand events which have an interior and an exterior: an exterior because they happen in the world, an interior because they express ideas, in the broadest sense of the word. Action is thus the unity of this interior and exterior. On the other hand, history consists in reactivating, that is to say, in rethinking past thought in the present thought of the his-torian.

This is a schema of the *Verstehen* position in history. It does not differ fundamentally from the *Verstehen* position in the theory of the text and theory of action, precisely because of the kinship mentioned earlier.

It is not surprising, consequently, that the same obstacles, the same ambiguities, the same difficulties of a pure theory of *Verstehen* are also found in the theory of history. The difficulty here is to introduce the *critical* moment in a theory based on the immediate transfer into an alien psychic life, in short, to introduce mediation into the immediate relation of intropathy. But the explanatory procedures—of which a scientific history consists—are connected to this critical moment. History begins when we no longer have immediate understanding, and when we undertake to reconstruct the sequence of antecedents along lines other than that of the motives and reasons alleged by the actors in the history. The difficulty for epistemology is precisely to show how explanation is added to, or superimposed on, or even substituted for, the immediate understanding of the course of past history.

We are thus tempted to begin from the pole of explanation and to construct explanation in history on the model of explanation in the natural sciences, even if one never again meets the original and specific work of the historian, and imposes on him an artificial schema that satisfies only the epistemologist. This is what happened in the English-speaking analytic school following Carl Hempel's article, "The Function of General Laws in History," published in 1942 (which later authors never tired of commenting on, refining, or refuting). Hempel's thesis is that historical explanation is not specific and original. It follows the same schema as the explanation of a physical event, such as the burst-ing of a water tank by freezing, or a geological event like an avalanche or a volcanic eruption. In all these cases, we deduce an event from two kinds of premises. The first contains the description of the initial conditions (anterior events, circumstances, contexts, etc.) while the second contains a statement of a general law, in other words, the assertion of a regularity. It is the general law which provides a basis for the explanation. If history appears to oscillate between a true science and a popular explanation, it is because its laws, most often unformulated rather than rationally adduced, are themselves only regularities of varying degrees of scientific rigor. They may be the sayings of popular wisdom, or even prejudices or mythical assertions, such as the historic mission of the chief, of the race, and the like. Or we may find poorly verified psychological laws or, rarely, the relatively trustworthy laws of demography, economics, and sociology. But there is always a conjunction of two kinds of statements: singular, initial conditions and (alleged or verified) universal hypotheses. The scientific weakness of history is entirely due to the epistemological weakness of the alleged or tacitly accepted general laws.

This discussion should have made obvious the difficulties, which are the inverse of those of the *Verstehen* theory. The latter made it difficult to account for the critical separation of historical explanation from the ordinary understanding of human action. Hempel's model makes it difficult to account for the effective work of the historian. For it seems obvious that the historian is never in a position to satisfy his own epistemological idea. Hempel himself admitted in the same article that history must most often be content with an "explanation-sketch," which an always more elaborate explanation tries to complete, to refine, and to raise to a higher degree of scientific rigor. In spite of this concession, Hempel maintains that history sees imposed on itself an epistemological model that does not come from its own practice.

In fact, as soon as we consider this practice, it is the characteristics different from the Hempelian model which, paradoxically, become significant. The laws are never more than "explanation-sketches." The explanation has no predictive value. It only gives conditions judged important because of certain types of questions, therefore of interests. The language of history never succeeds and perhaps does not even seek to free itself from ordinary language. Generalizations are not ordinarily eliminated by counter-examples, but are preserved by specifying more precisely the places, times, and circumstances for which the explanation is held valid. All these anomalies with respect to the pure model suggest that we must start afresh and dialectically articulate understanding and explanation, instead of seeing them as polar opposites.

I propose to say, with certain authors, that historical understanding, onto which explanation is grafted, puts in action a specific competence, the competence to follow a history, in the sense of a history that one retells. There is a reciprocal relation between recounting and following a history which defines a completely primitive language game. We take up again the notion of the story, but add to it the new traits that are seen and developed by the theory of history. To follow a history, in fact, is to understand a succession of actions, of thoughts, of feelings presenting at the same time a certain direction, but also some surprises (coincidences, recognitions, revelations, etc.). Consequently, the conclusion of the history is never deducible and predictable. That is why it is necessary to follow the development. But neither can the history be disconnected: even though not deducible, its ending must be plausible. Thus, in every retold history there is a bond of logical continuity which is completely specific, because the outcome must at the same time be contingent and plausible.

Such is the basic understanding without which there would be neither narratives nor history, neither *story* nor *history.* The reader does not direct his interest to the so-called underlying laws but to the turns taken by this unique history. To follow a history is a completely specific activity by which we continuously anticipate a final course and an outcome, and we successively correct our expectations until they coincide with the actual outcome. Then we say that we have understood.

This starting point for understanding differs from the one proposed by the intropathic theory, which entirely neglects the specificity of the narrative element in the recounting as well as in the following of the history. That is why a theory in which understanding depends on a narrative element allows us more easily to go from understanding to explanation. While explanation appeared to do violence to understanding, taken as the immediate apprehension of the intentions of others, it naturally prolongs understanding, taken as putting into action the competence to follow a story. For a story is rarely self-explanatory. Contingency along with acceptability call for questioning, for interrogation. Thus, interest in what follows—"And then?" asks the child—is replaced by an interest in reasons, motives, causes—"Why?" asks the adult. The story thus has a lacunary structure so that *why* spontaneously comes from *what.* Conversely, explanation has no autonomy. As a virtue and as an effect, it allows us to follow better and further a history when spontaneous understanding of the first degree fails.

To come back to Hempel's model, I will say that it is not at all contestable that explanation is done by recourse to general laws. Hempel's thesis on this point is invincible, and his explanatory syllogism is well constructed. What Hempel's thesis does not consider is the function of explanation. Its structure is well described, but its function is misunderstood: explanation is what allows us to again follow a history when spontaneous understanding is blocked. This accounts for the fact that explanation can be moved to various levels of generality, regularity, and thus of scientific rigor, provided that the historian does not intend to subsume a case under a law, but to interpolate a law in a story in order to make understanding possible again.

This is the alternating play of understanding and explanation in history. This play does not differ fundamentally from that in the theory of the text or the theory of action, as we have already seen. This result, I repeat again, is not surprising to the extent that history combines the theory of the text and that of action, in a theory of the true story of the actions of men in the past.

My conclusion is twofold.

On the epistemological level, I say that there are not two methods, the explanatory method and the method of understanding. Strictly speaking, only explanation is methodic. Understanding is rather the nonmethodic moment which, in the sciences of interpretation, comes together with the methodic moment of explanation. Understanding precedes, accompanies, closes, and thus *envelops* explanation. In return, explanation *develops* understanding analytically. This dialectical bond between explanation and understanding has as a consequence a very complex and paradoxical relation between the social sciences and the natural sciences. In fact, to the extent that the explanatory procedures of the social sciences are homologous to those of the natural sciences, the continuity of the sciences is assured. But to the extent that understanding contributes a specific ingredient—be it an understanding of signs in the theory of the text, or an understanding of intentions and motives in the theory of action, or in the competence to follow a story in the theory of history—to this extent, the discontinuity between the two areas of knowledge is insurmountable. But discontinuity and continuity come together *between* the sciences just as understanding and explanation do *in* the sciences.

Second conclusion: The epistemological reflection leads, by the very flow of the argument—as I suggested in the beginning—to a more fundamental reflection on the ontological conditions of the dialectic between explanation and understanding. If philosophy is concerned with "understanding," it is because it testifies, in the heart of epistemology, to a belonging of our being to the being which precedes every objectification, every opposition between subject and object. If the word *understanding* has such a density it is because, at the same time, it designates the nonmethodic pole, dialectically opposed to the pole of explanation in every interpretive science, *and* it designates the indicator, no longer methodological but verifying, of the ontological relation of belonging of our being to beings and to Being. The rich ambiguity of the word *understanding* is that it designates a moment in the theory of method, the one we call the nonmethodic pole, *and* the apprehension, at a level other than scientific, of our belonging to the whole of what is. But we will again fall into a ruinous dichotomy if philosophy, after having given up making or maintaining a methodological schism, reconstitutes a reign of pure understanding at this new level of radicality. It seems to me that philosophy has not only the job of accounting, in a discourse other than scientific, for the primordial relation of *belonging* between the being that we are and some region of being that a science elaborates as an object by the appropriate methodological procedures. It must also be able to account for the movement of *distanciation* by which this relation of belonging requires objectification, the objective and objectifying treatment of the sciences, and thus the movement by which explanation and understanding are called forth on the properly epistemological level. I shall stop at the threshold of this difficult investigation.

PART IV

Freud and Psychoanalysis

IV. FREUD AND PSYCHOANALYSIS

The first article, "A Philosophical Interpretation of Freud," is Ricoeur's summary of his massive work Freud and Philosophy. *The second selection, "The Question of Proof in Freud's Psychoanalytic Writings," is one of Ricoeur's most recent contributions to the philosophy of psychoanalysis. In this essay he questions why psychoanalysis "has never quite succeeded in stating how its assertions are justified, how its interpretations are authenticated, how its theory is verified." To answer the question of validity requires that we first find out what will count as a fact in psychoanalysis, and secondly, what is the* relation *between theory and analytic experience. Ricoeur claims that the failure to answer these preliminary questions has vitiated previous discussions of validity in psychoanalysis.*

SOURCES

"A Philosophical Interpretation of Freud," translated by Willis Domingo, in *The Conflict of Interpretations* (Evanston: Northwestern University Press, 1974), pp. 160–76. Used by permission.

"The Question of Proof in Freud's Psychoanalytic Writings." *Journal of the American Psychoanalytic Association* 24 (No. 4, 1977). Used by permission.

CHAPTER 12

A Philosophical Interpretation

of Freud

It is important to distinguish two attitudes a philosopher may adopt toward Freud's written work: These are a "reading" or a "philosophical interpretation." The reading of Freud is the work of a historian of philosophy. It does not pose problems which differ from those we would encounter in a reading of Plato, Descartes, or Kant, and it makes a claim to the same sort of objectivity. A philosophical interpretation is the work of a philosopher. It presupposes the sort of reading which makes a claim to objectivity, but goes on to take a position toward the work. It adds a relocation in a different discourse to the architectonic reconstitution of the work. The new discourse is that of the philosopher who thinks from Freud—that is, after, with, and against him. I propose "one" philosophical interpretation of Freud.

1. The reading I presuppose considers Freudian discourse to be a mixed discourse. It intermingles questions of meaning (the meaning of dreams, symptoms, culture, etc.) and questions of force (cathexis, economic accounting, conflict, repression, etc.). I allow here that this mixed discourse is not equivocal but is appropriate to the reality which it wishes to take into account, namely, the binding of force and meaning in a semantics of desire. This reading does justice to the most realistic and naturalistic aspects of Freudian theory, while it never neglects to treat "instincts," the "unconscious," and the "id" as significations to be deciphered in their effects of meaning.

2. The question which gives birth to the present interpretation is the following: Can a reflective philosophy make sense of analytical

experience and theory? I will assume here that the *Ego cogito* and the *Ego sum* are the foundations of all legitimate propositions about man. If that is true, one can understand Freud by formulating the concept of the archaeology of the subject. This concept defines the philosophical position of analytical discourse. It is not Freud's concept. I formulate it in order to understand myself in my understanding of Freud. It is in and for reflection that psychoanalysis is an archaeology.

But of what subject?

The reading of Freud is also the crisis of the philosophy of the subject. It imposes the dispossession of the subject such as it appears primarily to itself in the form of consciousness. It makes consciousness not a given but a problem and a task. The genuine *cogito* must be gained through the false *cogitos* which mask it.

It is thus that the reading of Freud becomes an adventure of reflection.

3. The question which follows is: Can a subject have an archaeology without having a teleology? This question does not exist without the preceding one. It is not posed by Freud but by reflective thought, which says that only a subject with a *telos* can have an *archē*. The appropriation of a meaning constituted in the past presupposes the movement of a subject drawn ahead of itself by a succession of "figures" (such as in Hegel's *Phenomenology of Mind*) each of which finds its meaning in those to follow.

This dialectic of archaeology and teleology allows us to reinterpret some Freudian concepts, such as sublimation and identification, which do not, in my opinion, have a satisfactory status in Freud's own systematics.

Finally, this dialectic is the philosophical ground on which the complementarity of rival hermeneutics of art, morality, and religion can be established. Outside it, these interpretations either confront one another without any possible arbitration or else are thrown together in idle eclecticisms which are the caricature of thought.

DEVELOPMENT

I will not act as counsel for a book in this lecture, but will rather devote myself to a free reflection on its difficulties.

Two questions immediately come to mind: (1) Can we, as I have just done, distinguish between *the* reading and *a* philosophical interpretation of Freud? (2) Do we have the right to construct a philosophical interpretation which consists, as I said in my exposition, in relocating the work in a different discourse, especially if this discourse is reflective philosophy?

I will answer the first question both generally and specifically. I can answer generally that philosophy (or, as is awkwardly said, general philosophy) and the history of philosophy are two distinct philosophical activities. A tacit and distinct consensus among historians of philosophy concerning the objectivity that can be attained in their discipline has, I believe, been established. It is possible to understand an author in himself without necessarily deforming or repeating him. I used a term devised by Guéroult in speaking of the "architectonic reconstitution" of a work. But I believe that all other historians—even if they speak in a more Bergsonian sense of philosophical intuition—admit that it is impossible to duplicate a work. The most one can do is grasp it anew from a constellation of themes which have been produced by intuition and especially from a network of articulations which in a sense constitute its substructure and underlying framework. This is why one does not repeat but reconstruct. From a different viewpoint, however, the historian does not falsify the work he studies if he manages to produce, if not a copy of the work (which would be useless), its homologue in the strict sense of a vicarious *object* which presents the same arrangement as the work. This is how I understand objectivity, because—in a negative sense, of nonsubjectivity—the philosopher brackets his own convictions, positions, and above all his manner of beginning, attacking, and strategically handling his thought, and because—in a positive sense—he submits his reading to what the work itself—which remains the *quid* which guides his reading—wants and means.

And so I say that Freud can be read just as our colleagues and teachers read Plato, Descartes, and Kant. This is what I claim; it is my first wager and has not yet necessarily been won. The reference of doctrine to an experience which requires apprenticeship and competence, which is a craft and even a technique—does this reference not completely separate Freud from the thinkers and philosophers cited above? I still think that such an objection is not invincible and that the reading of Freud poses no different problem from the reading of Plato, Descartes, and Kant and can claim the same type of objectivity. Why? First, because Freud wrote works which were not addressed simply to his students, colleagues, and patients but to all of us. By giving lectures and publishing books, he agreed to occupy in the minds of his readers and listeners the same field of discourse as do philosophers. He is the one who took the risk, not me. But my argument is still too contingent and too bound to the hazards of communication. I claim that what appears in the analytical relationship is not radically different from what someone who has not been analyzed can understand. I say "understand" and not "live," for no comprehension gained from books will ever be a substitute for the factual experience of psychoanalysis. However, the meaning of what is thus lived is essentially communicable.

Because it is communicable, the analytical experience can be transposed through doctrine to the level of theory with the aid of descriptive concepts which result from a second level of conceptuality. Just as in the theater I can understand situations, feelings, and conduct which I have not experienced myself, so I can understand in a mode of reflective empathy the meaning of an analytical experience I have not undergone. This is why, in spite of serious misunderstandings which I do not underestimate, a philosopher, as a philosopher, is capable of understanding psychoanalytic theory and even in part the psychoanalytic experience. Should I add an even more decisive argument? It is Freud who came onto our territory. How? Because the object of his investigation is not, as is too hastily assumed, human desire, the wish, libido, instincts, Eros (all of these words having a precise sexual context), but rather desire in a more or less conflicting relationship with a world of culture, a father and mother, authorities, imperatives, prohibitions, works of art, social ends, and idols. This is why Freud does not, when he writes about art, morality, and religion, transpose to cultural reality a science and practice which found their definite place in human biology or psychophysiology. From the beginning, his science and practice are held at the point of interaction between desire and culture. Take *The Interpretation of Dreams* or *Three Essays on the Theory of Sexuality,* just to consider two of the major works, where the instinctual level is taken in its relationship with "censorship," "repression," "prohibitions," and "ideals." The nuclear figure of the father in the Oedipal episode is merely this system's center of gravity. This is why in the first and then in the second topography we are faced from the beginning with a plurality of "places" and "roles" in which the unconscious is diametrically opposed to consciousness and preconsciousness and where the id is at once in a dialectical relationship with the ego and the superego. This dialectic is that of the very situation explored by psychoanalysis, namely, the interlacing of desire and culture. This is why I said that Freud came onto our ground; for, even when he speaks to us of instincts, he speaks of them in and from the level of expression, that is, in and from certain effects of meaning which give themselves to be deciphered and can be treated as texts: dream texts or symptomatic texts—yes, texts which occur in the network of communications, of exchanges of signs. It is precisely in this milieu of signs that the analytical experience (as the work of speech, an encounter between speaking and listening, a complicity between speech and silence) takes place. The fact that the analytical experience belongs, as much as Freudian doctrine, to the order of signs is what fundamentally justifies not only the communicability of analytical experience but also its fundamentally homogeneous character with the totality of human experience which philosophy undertakes to reflect upon and understand.

These, then, are the presuppositions which guided my decision to read Freud as I read other philosophers.

I will say very little about this reading here because I have chosen to speak about the philosophical interpretation which I propose. I will simply comment upon what I called architectonic reconstitution and will intentionally give my development a more systematic presentation than I did in my book.[1]

Freud's work seems to me to be divided into three great masses, each of which has its own architecture and can be considered as a conceptual level. These three levels find their fullest expression in different states of system, which can be charted diachronically. The first network is constituted with the interpretation of dreams and neurotic symptoms and ends up, in the writings of *The Papers on Metapsychology,* in a state of system which is known by the name of the first topography (the series ego, id, superego constituting rather, in Lagache's terms, a "personology"). The next great mass of facts and notions, which constitutes the second theoretical network, contains the interpretation of culture: works of art, ideals, and idols. This second network comes out of the former one, in that the first already contained the dialectic of desire and culture. But, by applying the dream model of wish-fulfillment to all the meaning effects which we may encounter in the life of culture, we are led to profoundly alter the equilibrium attained in *The Papers on Metapsychology.* The result of this alteration is a second state of system which is expressed in the sequence ego, id, superego. It does not replace the first system but is superimposed on it. The final great mass of facts and notions, which constitutes the third theoretical network, arises from the alteration imposed by the introduction of the death-instinct into the preceding edifice. This alteration reaches the very foundations of existence, for it involves a redistribution of forces in terms of the polarity, Eros-Thanatos. As the relation between instinct and culture remains the principal leading thread, however, this basic alteration also affects every aspect of culture. Indeed, the entry of the death-instinct implies the most important reinterpretation of culture, that which is expressed in *Civilization and Its Discontents.* It is in guilt, in the discontent of the civilized individual, and in the clamor of war that the mute instinct begins to cry out.

This, in broad terms, is the architecture of Freudianism.

As we can see, there is a development, but it is comprehensible only if we move from one state of system to another. We can thus pick out a sensible continuum which goes from a mechanistic representation of the psychic mechanism to a romantic dramaturgy of life and death. But this development is not incoherent. It proceeds by successive alterations of structures. This parade of alterations is produced within a homogeneous milieu, namely, the desire's effects on meaning. It is the homogeneous milieu of all the restructuring of Freudian doctrine which I called the *semantics of desire.*

Let us return to the principal object of this essay, however, which is *a* philosophical interpretation of Freud. We might begin to consider it by the second objection that could be brought against such an undertaking. Can one not legitimately challenge all attempts to relocate a work like Freud's in a *different* discourse? It will be argued that Freud's work is a totality sufficient unto itself and that we are falsifying it if we place it in another field of thought from that which it generates. This argument has considerable force. It would work for any other thinker, but it has a particular force in Freud's case. It is always possible to consider the philosophical enterprise which would claim to integrate it as the supreme denial and the craftiest of resistances. That is probably true. Still, my opinion is that, even though victorious, the objection does not affect the problem of a philosophical interpretation of Freud.

Two arguments can be brought against the fanatic exclusivity of certain Freudians. The first is that it is false that Freud and psychoanalysis furnish us with a totality. Need we recall all the texts where Freud declares, without any ambiguity whatsoever, that he has clarified only a single group of instincts, those which were accessible to his practice, and that the realm of the ego, in particular, is only partly explored by the specific ego instincts which belong to the same cycle as the object libido? Psychoanalysis is only one beam among others projected upon human experience. But above all—and this argument is drawn from analytical practice itself—we must consider the doctrine as an ordering of a very specific experience by the use of concepts which have been constructed and coherently linked together. This is the analytical experience, and we must hold strictly to the point that, in the end, Freudian concepts come into play (that is, mimic and confirm one another) within its circumference. There are more things in heaven and on earth than in all our psychoanalysis. I just said that this experience can be understood and is homogeneous with human experience as a totality, but it is so precisely as one part in a whole. The vocation of philosophy is to arbitrate between not only the plurality of interpretations but, as I will try to say in conclusion, the plurality of experiences as well.

That is not all. Not only are analytical doctrine and experience partial; both also involve a dissonance and a breach which calls for philosophical interpretation. I am thinking here of the shift which occurs between Freud's discovery and the concepts at work in his system. This is, of course, true of all works. Eugen Fink recently pointed it out about Husserl. The concepts with which a theory operates are not all objectified in the fields which that theory thematizes. Thus, a new philosophy expresses itself partly in the language of preceding philosophies, which is the source of doubtless inevitable misunderstandings. In Freud's case the shift is manifest. His discovery operates on the level of effects on meaning, but he continues to express it in the language and through the concepts of energetics of his masters in Vienna and Berlin. It could be argued that this dissonance calls, not for a philosophical reconsideration, but for a clarification of the grammar of our language—as the English say, a recognition of the rules of this language game. But this anomaly on the part of Freudian discourse requires a more radical treatment. It is not simply a matter of a shift between the discovery and the available vocabulary, for this anomaly in Freudian discourse goes to the very nature of things. If it is true that psychoanalysis applies to the inflection between desire and culture, we can expect that it operates with notions which belong to two different levels of coherence and two universes of discourse, that of force and that of meaning. The language of force is all the vocabulary which designates the conflictual dynamics whose result, repression, is the best known and most studied of these mechanisms, but it is also the entire economic vocabulary, such as cathexis, decathexis, overcathexis, etc.

Thus, all the vocabulary about the absurdity or significance of symptoms and dream thoughts, about their overdetermination and the word plays which take place there, is the language of meaning. It is this sort of relation between meanings which is disentangled in interpretation. Between the apparent and the hidden meaning there is the relation between an intelligible and an unintelligible text. These meaning relations are thus entangled with force relations. Everything in "dream work" is stated in this mixed discourse. Force relations are enunciated and dissimulated in meaning relations at the same time that meaning relations express and represent force relations. This mixed discourse is not, in my opinion, equivocal in the sense of simply lacking clarity. It is not a "category mistake." It comes close to the very reality which our reading of Freud revealed and which we called the semantics of desire. All the philosophers who have reflected on the relations between desire and meaning have come across this problem. Plato, for example, balances the hierarchy of ideas by a hierarchy of love, and Spinoza binds the degrees of clarity of the idea to those of the assertion and action of the *conatus*, while Leibniz relates the monad's degrees of appetition and perception. "The action of the internal principle which brings about the change or passage from one perception to another may be called *appetition* . . ." (*Monadology*, §15). Freud can thus be relocated on a well-known trajectory. By the same token, however, an interpretation is imposed. The reading leads us to a critical point, "where one sees that the energetics implies a hermeneutics and the hermeneutics discloses an energetics. That point is where the positing or emergence of desire manifests itself in and through a process of symbolization."[2]

That is, moreover, what distinguishes the psychological concept of drive (*Trieb*) from the psychophysiological concept of instinct. Drives are accessible only in their psychic derivatives, their effects of meaning, and, more precisely, their distortions of meaning. Because drives occur in language in its psychic representing, one can interpret desire, although it may remain unspeakable as such. But if this mixed discourse prevents psychoanalysis from swinging toward the natural sciences, it prevents it from swinging toward semiology as well. The laws of meaning in psychoanalysis cannot be reduced to those of linguistics as inherited from Ferdinand de Saussure, Hjelmslev, or Jakobson. The ambiguity of the relation sustained by desire with language is irreducible to such an extent that, as Emile Benveniste has clearly shown, the symbolism of the unconscious is not a linguistic phenomenon *stricto sensu*. It is common to many cultures without a common language. It presents phenomena, such as displacement and condensation, which operate on the level of the image and not that of phonematic or semantic articulation. In Benveniste's terminology, dream mechanisms will appear sometimes as infra- and sometimes as supralinguistic. For our purposes, they manifest the confusion of the infra- and the supralinguistic. They are on an infralinguistic level in the sense that they mark the distortion of the distinctive function of language. They are on a supralinguistic level if we consider the dream, as Freud himself says, as finding its true relations in the great unities of discourse such as proverbs, maxims, folklore, and myths. From this point of view, it is rather on the level of rhetoric, with its metaphors, metonymy, synecdoche, euphemisms, allusions, antiphrases, and litotes that a comparison should be made. Rhetoric concerns not the phenomena of language but the procedures of subjectivity as manifested in discourse.[3] Furthermore, Freud always used the word *Vorstellung*— "representation"—to designate the effect of meaning to which drives are assigned. For him it is *Dingvorstellungen*—"thing representations" —which serve as models for *Wortvorstellungen* or "word representations." It is words that are treated as things and not the opposite. I included in *Freud and Philosophy*[4] Freud's important texts in this respect.

The representing of instincts (*Trieben*) is thus at the center of our problem. It is neither biological nor semantic. It is delegated by the instincts and promised to language and reveals instincts only in their derivatives while gaining access to language only by the twisted combinations of object cathexes which precede verbal representation. We must invoke an irreducible type of relationship between signifiers and signifieds. These signs and meaning effects have a linguistic vocation but are not, in their specific texture, of the order of language. This is what Freud indicates by the word *Vorstellung,* or representation, and it is what keeps the level of fantasy distinct from that of speech. Leibniz said as much in the text from which I just quoted a short passage: "The action of the internal principle which brings about the change or passage from one perception to another may be called *appetition.* It is true that appetite may not always entirely attain the whole perception toward which it tends, but it always obtains something of it and arrives at new perceptions" (*Monadology,* §15).

And so, there we are—with Leibniz's transposition of the Freudian problem of libido and symbol—at the threshold of the philosophical problem.

I am not saying that a single philosophy is capable of furnishing the vehicle in which relations between force and meaning can be explained. I believe that *the* correct reading of Freud is possible, while only *a* correct philosophical interpretation is possible. The one I propose is connected with reflective philosophy and is related to the work of Jean Nabert, to whom I long ago dedicated my *Symbolism of Evil.* It is in Nabert that I found the best formulation of the close relationship between the desire to be and the signs in which desire is expressed, projected, and explained. I stand fast with Nabert in saying that understanding is inseparable from self-understanding and that the symbolic universe is the milieu of self-explanation. This means that there is no longer a problem of meaning unless signs are the means, the milieu, and the medium thanks to which a human existent seeks to situate, project, and understand himself. In contrast, however, there is no direct apprehension of the self by the self, no internal apperception or appropriation of the self's desire to exist through the short cut of consciousness but only by the long road of the interpretation of signs. In short, my philosophical working hypothesis is concrete reflection, i.e., the *cogito* as mediated by the whole universe of signs.

I do not deny that this working hypothesis does not come from the reading of Freud. The reading of Freud encounters it only as something problematic. It encounters it exactly at the point where Freud also poses the question of the subject. Indeed, how can the sequence Unc., Pcs., Cs. and the sequence ego, id, superego even be stated, without posing the question of the subject? And how can the question of desire and meaning be posed without at the same time asking, "Whose desire?" and, "Whose meaning?" But if the question of the subject is implied problematically by psychoanalysis, it is not posed thematically. Even less is the subject posed apodictically. The act by which the subject is posited can be generated only out of itself. It is Fichte's thetic judgment. In this judgment, existence is posited as thought and thought as existence: I think, I am. With respect to this position and this apodictic proposition, all the "places" of the first topography and the "roles" of the second Freudian sequence are objectifications. The entire question will be one of justifying and legitimizing these objectifications as the privileged path toward a less abstract *cogito* and as the necessary way of concrete reflection.

I would like to emphasize, therefore, that there is a *gap* between the problematic implications of the question of the subject in psychoanalysis and its apodictic position in reflective philosophy. It is this gap which is responsible for the distance between *the* reading and *a* philosophical interpretation.

I cannot be accused of confusing Freud with reflective philosophy, because I am developing the reading of psychoanalysis without presupposing the *cogito*. The reading of Freud rests on a Platonic *hypotheton* which we have called the relation between desire and meaning, the semantics of desire. For psychoanalysts, it is a *ti hikanon,* "something sufficient," in the sense of sufficient for an understanding of all that takes place in the field of experience and theory. In constituting the question of the subject from the position "I think, I am," philosophy asks for the condition of the condition and turns toward the *anhypotheton* of this *hypotheton.* We must not, therefore, confuse the objections that can be made to the reading of Freud and those that can be brought against my philosophical interpretation.

A second misunderstanding occurs if we leap over this philosophical moment, omit the initial philosophical act, and bring ourselves directly to the furthest consequences of such a philosophical choice. This is what happens when one grabs hold of reflective conclusions on faith and religion and short-circuits them into the Freudian critique of religion. There is a necessary progression in the succession of steps which I posit: *the positing of the subject, the renewal of psychoanalysis as an archaeology of the subject, the dialectical positioning of archaeology and teleology, and the vertical irruption of the Wholly Other,* as the alpha and the omega in the twofold question of archaeology and teleology. We can, of course, separate these theses, which have indeed appeared in different orders and different places in other philosophies. But philosophy is not a puzzle of ideas or a heap of scattered themes which can be arranged in just any order. The way that philosophy proceeds and makes connections is all that is pertinent. Its architecture commands its theses. This is why my "ideas" on religion and faith are less important philosophically than the way in which they interact with the dialectic of archaeology and teleology. This dialectic in turn is of value only insofar as it articulates concrete reflection internally. And, finally, this concrete reflection makes sense only insofar as it succeeds in asking anew the Freudian question of the unconscious, the id, of instincts and meaning, in the promotion of the subject of reflection.

We must hold onto this, for it is the bolt which keeps everything together and by which this interpretation stands or falls.

I would like to explain now this reflective renewal of Freudian concepts. My question is the following: What happens to a philosophy of reflection when it allows itself to be instructed by Freud?

This question has two sides. First, it means, how can Freud's mixed discourse on desire and meaning be taken into reflective philosophy? But it also means, what happens to the subject of reflection when the guile of consciousness is taken seriously and consciousness is discovered as false-consciousness, which says something other than it says or believes it says? These two sides of the question are as inseparable as those of a coin or a cloth. For at the same time that I say that the philosophical location of analytical discourse is defined by the concept of the archaeology of the subject, I also followed Freud to say that one can no longer establish the philosophy of the subject as a philosophy of consciousness. Reflection and consciousness no longer coincide. Consciousness must be lost in order that the subject may be found. The subject is not what we think it is. There can be evidence for the apodicticity of the *cogito* only if the inadequacy of consciousness is recognized at the same time. Like the meaning of the thing, the meaning of my own existence is itself either presumed or presumptive, although the reasons for this are different. It is thus possible to repeat Freudianism, make a reflective repetition of it, which will also be an adventure of reflection. I called dispossession or disappropriation this movement to which I am constrained by Freudian systematics. It is the necessity of this dispossession which justifies Freudian naturalism. I would adopt what is more shocking, more philosophically insupportable in the Freudian realism of psychic "places." I would adopt its decided antiphenomenology and its dynamics and economics as the instruments of a suit which is filed against the illusory *cogito* which first occupies the place of the founding act of the *I think, I am.* In short, I make use of psychoanalysis just as Descartes made use of skeptical arguments against the *cogito* itself—or rather at the heart of the *cogito*—that psychoanalysis splits the ego's claims to apodicticity and the illusions of consciousness.

In an essay written in 1917, Freud speaks of psychoanalysis as a wound and humiliation to narcissism analogous to the discoveries of Copernicus and Darwin when, in their own way, they decentered the world and life with respect to the claims of consciousness. Psychoanalysis decenters in the same way the constitution of the world of fantasy with respect to consciousness. At the end of this dispossession, consciousness has switched philosophical signs. It is no longer a given. There are no longer "immediate givens of consciousness." There is, rather, a task, the task of becoming-consciousness. Where there had been *Bewusstsein,* or being-consciousness, there is now *Bewusstwerden,* or becoming-consciousness. Thus, the dynamic and economic side of Freudianism was asserted twice. First, in the reading of Freud, against all semiological reduction and in order to rescue the very specificity of psychoanalysis and hold it at the junction between force and meaning, and second, in the philosophical interpretation, in order to guarantee the authenticity of the ascesis and deprivation through which reflection must pass in order to remain authentic. At the same time, what is the enigma of Freudian discourse—an enigma at least for a pure epistemological consideration—becomes a paradox of reflection. As you will remember, the enigma of Freudian discourse was the intertwining of dynamic and hermeneutical language. Transcribed into reflective language, that gives the reality of the id and the ideality of meaning: reality of the id in the act of disappropriation and the regression of effects of meaning, appearing on the conscious level, to the point of instinct on the level of the unconscious; ideality of meaning in reappropriating and in the movement of interpretation which initiates the movement of becoming-conscious. It is thus that our reading of Freud itself becomes an adventure of reflection. What emerges from this reflection is a wounded *cogito,* which posits but does not possess itself, which understands its originary truth only in and by the confession of the inadequacy, the illusion, and the lie of existing consciousness.

The second stage of the philosophical interpretation which I propose is characterized by the dialectic between archaeology and teleology. This advance in reflection indeed represents something new, a polarity between the reflective *archē* and *telos.* I reach this stage by a reappropriation of the temporal aspects of Freudianism which are precisely bound to the Freudian realism of the unconscious and the id. Furthermore, they pertain to Freudian economics rather than Freudian topography. There is, indeed, in the positing of desire an *anteriority* which is both phylogenetic and ontogenetic, historical and symbolic. Desire is in every respect prior; it is anticipatory. The theme of anteriority pervades Freudianism. I would defend it against all the culturalisms which have tried to extract its fangs and pull its claws by reducing to defects of our current relationship to the environment the savage side of our instinctual existence, this prior desire, which pulls us backwards and insinuates the whole backward drift of affectivity on the level of family relationships, fantasies and works of art, ethics and guilt, religion and the fear of punishment, and the infantile wish for consolation. Freud is on secure ground when he speaks of the unconscious as *timeless,* i.e., as rebellious to the temporalization which is linked to becoming-conscious. This is what I call archaeology, the restrained archaeology of instincts and narcissism, the generalized archaeology of the superego and idols, the hyperbolic archaeology of the war of the giants Eros and Thanatos. But we must see that the concept of archaeology is itself a reflective concept. Archaeology is the archaeology of the subject. This is what Merleau-Ponty saw and said clearly in his introduction to the work of Dr. Hesnard, *L'Oeuvre de Freud.*

Because the concept of archaeology is a philosophical concept—a concept of reflective philosophy—the articulation between archaeology and teleology is also an articulation of and in reflection. It is reflective thought which says that only a subject which has an *archē* has a *telos;* for the appropriation of a meaning constituted prior to me presupposes the movement of a subject drawn ahead of itself by a succession of "figures," each of which finds its meaning in the ones which follow it.

This new advance on the part of thought surely constitutes a problem; this is why I propose to comment upon it by a few remarks of a more problematic nature. First, it is quite true that psychoanalysis is analysis, i.e., in Freud's own rigorous terms, a regressive decomposition. According to Freud, there is no psychosynthesis, or, at least, psychoanalysis as such need not propose any synthesis. This is why the teleology of the subject is not a Freudian idea but rather a philosophical notion which the reader of Freud forms at his own risk. Still, this notion of the teleology of the subject is not without support in Freud himself, who hinted at its equivalent or its beginning in a certain number of experiences and theoretical concepts set into motion by the practice of analysis. But these experiences and concepts do not find their place in the Freudian schema of the psychic apparatus. This is why they remain in the air, as I tried to show for the concepts of *identification* and *sublimation,* for which Freud said expressly that he had found no satisfactory explanation.

Second remark: I attached the idea of a teleology of the subject to Hegel's *Phenomenology of Mind.* This example is not restrictive, only illuminating, in that teleology—or, to cite Jean Hyppolite exactly, "dialectical teleology"—is the only law for the construction of the figures of the spirit. It is illuminating also in that the dialectic of the figures gives philosophical sense to all psychological maturation and to man's growth out of childhood. Psychology asks how man leaves his childhood. Indeed, he does so by becoming capable of a certain meaningful itinerary which has been illustrated by a certain number of cultural configurations which themselves draw their sense from their prospective arrangement. The example of Hegel is again illuminating in the sense that it allows us to dissociate teleology and finality, at least in the sense of final causes criticized by Spinoza and Bergson. Teleology is not finality. The figures in a dialectical teleology are not final causes but meanings which draw their sense from the movement of totalization which carries them along and pushes them ahead of themselves. The Hegelian example is illuminating, last of all, in that it allows us to give content to the empty idea of an existential project which would continually remain its own project and determine itself only in contingency, despair, or simply the flattest conformism.

If the Hegelian example is indeed exemplary, however, it is not restrictive. For my part, I tried to outline the sequence of cultural spheres, from economic possession (*avoir*) to political power (*pouvoir*) and personal values (*valoir*), all of whose contents are quite different, even though their general orientation is the same. In all of this our problem is the passage, not to consciousness, but from consciousness to self-consciousness. What is at stake is the Self or Spirit.

It is not unimportant to discover that pretensions of consciousness are no less humiliated in the ascending dialectic of figures of the spirit than they are in the regressive decomposition of fantasies of desire. Concrete reflection consists in this twofold self-dispossession and decentering of meaning. But reflection is still what holds together regression and progression. It is in reflection that the relationship between what Freud calls the unconscious and Hegel Spirit, between the primordial and the terminal, fate and history, functions.

You will allow me to stop here and not delve into the final circle of concrete reflection. I say in my synopsis, "This dialectic is the philosophical ground on which the complementarity of rival hermeneutics of art, morality, and religion can be established." I intentionally did not consecrate a special paragraph to this question of rival hermeneutics. The dialectical solution which I attempt to apply to this problem has no autonomy whatsoever with respect to what I called the dialectic of progression and regression, teleology and archaeology. I wish to apply a determinate philosophical method to a determinate problem, that of the constitution of the symbol, which I described as an expression with a double meaning. I had already applied this method to the symbols of art and the ethics of religion. But the reason behind it is neither in the domains considered nor in the objects which are proper to them. It resides in the overdetermination of the symbol, which cannot be understood outside the dialecticism of the reflection which I propose. This is why all discussion which treats my double interpretation of religious symbols as an isolated theme necessarily retrogresses to a philosophy of compromise from which the incentive for struggle has been withdrawn. In this terrible battle for meaning, nothing and no one comes out unscathed. The "timid" hope must cross the desert of the path of mourning. This is why I will stop on the threshold of the struggle of interpretations and do so by giving myself this warning: outside the dialectic of archaeology and teleology, these interpretations confront one another without possible arbitration, or are juxtaposed in lazy eclecticisms which are the caricature of thought.

CHAPTER 13

The Question of Proof in Freud's

Psychoanalytic Writings

The question of proof in psychoanalysis is as old as psychoanalysis itself.[1] And even before being an inquiry addressed to psychoanalysis by epistemologists, it is an internal exigency of psychoanalysis itself. The 1895 "Project" aims at being a project of scientific psychology. *The Interpretation of Dreams* purports to be a science and not a fantastic construction, a "fine fairy tale," to use Krafft-Ebing's remark, hurled at Freud at the close of one public presentation. All of Freud's didactic works—the *Introductory Lectures on Psychoanalysis,* the *New Introductory Lectures on Psychoanalysis,* and *An Outline of Psychoanalysis*—represent in each instance a new effort to communicate to the layman the conviction that psychoanalysis is genuinely related to what is intelligible and what claims to be true. And yet, psychoanalysis has never quite succeeded in stating how its assertions are justified, how its interpretations are authenticated, how its theory is verified.[2] This relative unsuccess of psychoanalysis to be recognized as a science results, I think, from a failure to ask certain preliminary questions which I will attempt to raise in the first two parts of this essay, before attempting to reply directly to the original question in the third part.

The first question concerns what is relevant as a *fact* in psychoanalysis. The second concerns the type of *relation* which obtains between the theory and analytic experience, under its double aspect of being both a method of investigation and of therapeutic treatment. Hence, my contention is that the question of proof in psychoanalysis can be validly raised only when these preliminary questions have been answered.

I. THE CRITERIA FOR FACTS IN PSYCHOANALYSIS

As regards the first question, we may begin by noting that traditional discussions about the epistemological status of analytic theory take it for granted that theories consist of propositions whose role is to systemize, explain, and predict phenomena comparable to those which verify or falsify theories in the natural sciences or in those human sciences which, like academic psychology, themselves adopt the epistemology of the natural sciences. Even when we are not dealing with a narrow empiricism which does not require a theory to be directly validated by observables, we nevertheless continue to ask the same questions we would put to an observational science. In this way, we ask by what specific procedures psychoanalysis connects this or that theoretical notion to definite and unambiguous facts. However indirect the verification process may be, definitions must become operational, that is, they must be shown to generate procedures for verification and falsification.[3]

But this is precisely what is in question: What in psychoanalysis merits being considered as a verifiable fact?

My thesis is that psychoanalytic theory—in a certain sense which will be described in the second part of this paper—is the codification of what takes place in the analytic situation and, more precisely, in the analytic relationship. It is there that something happens which merits being called the *analytic experience.* In other words, the equivalent of what the epistemology of logical empiricism calls "observables" is to be sought first in the analytic situation, in the analytic relationship.

Our first task, therefore, will be to show in what way the analytic relationship brings about a selection among the facts that are likely to be taken into account by the theory. I will propose four criteria of this process of selection as useful for our discussion.

First criterion: To begin, there enters into the field of investigation and treatment only that part of experience which is capable of *being said.* There is no need to insist here on the *talk-cure* character of psychoanalysis. This restriction of language is first of all an inherent restriction on the analytic technique; it is the particular context of uninvolvement with reality belonging to the analytic situation that forces desire to speak, to pass through the defile of words, excluding substitute satisfactions as well as any regression toward acting out. This screening through speech in the analytic situation also functions as a criterion for what will be held to be the object of this science: not instinct as a physiological phenomenon, not even desire as energy, but desire as a meaning capable of being deciphered, translated, and interpreted.

Hence, the theory necessarily has to account for what we may call the semantic dimension of desire.

We can already see the misunderstanding that prevails in ordinary epistemological discussions: facts in psychoanalysis are in no way facts of observable behavior. They are "reports." We know dreams only as told upon awakening, and even symptoms, although they are partially observable, enter into the field of analysis only in relation to other factors verbalized in the "report." It is this selective restriction which forces us to situate the facts of psychoanalysis inside a sphere of motivation and meaning.[4]

Second criterion: The analytic situation singles out not only what is sayable, but what is said *to another person.* Here again, the epistemological criterion is guided by something absolutely central to the analytic technique. The transference stage, in this regard, is highly significant, for we might be tempted to confine the discussion of transference to the sphere of psychoanalytic technique and thereby overlook its epistemological implications for the search for relevant criteria. To see this, let us consider just one text crucial for analytic technique, the 1914 essay entitled "Remembering, Repeating, and Working-Through" (*Durcharbeiten*).

In this essay, Freud begins with the precise moment in the cure when the memory of traumatic events is replaced by the compulsion to repeat which blocks remembering. Focusing on the relation between this compulsion to repeat, resistance, and transference, he writes, "The greater the resistance, the more extensively will acting out (repetition) replace remembering" (S.E., 12, 151). And he adds, "the analysee repeats himself rather than remember and does this by means of resistance. Then he introduces transference, which he describes as "the main instrument . . . for curbing the patient's compulsions to repeat and for turning it into a motive for remembering" (ibid., p. 154). Why does transference have this effect? The reply to this question leads to epistemological considerations directly grafted onto what appears to be a strictly technical matter. If the resistance can be cleared away and remembering made free to occur, it is because the transference constitutes something like "a playground in which [the patient's compulsion to repeat] is allowed to expand in almost complete freedom" (ibid.). Extending this analogy of the playground, Freud more specifically says: "The transference thus creates an intermediate region between illness and real life through which the transition from one to the other is made" (ibid.).

It is this notion of transference as a "playground" or "intermediate region" which guides my remarks on the second criterion for what is psychoanalytically relevant as a fact. *In this "playground," this "inter-*

mediate region," in effect, we can read the relationship with the other constitutive of the erotic demand addressed to another person. It is in this regard that "transference" has its place not only in a study of analytic technique, but also in an epistemological inquiry about criteria. It reveals this constitutive trait of human desire: not only is it able to be spoken, to be brought to language, but it is addressed to another; more specifically, it is addressed to another desire which is capable of denying its request. What is thereby singled out or sifted out from human experience is the immediately intersubjective dimension of desire.

We should, therefore, not overlook the fact that if we speak of objects, of "wish objects"—and we cannot fail to speak of them in such contexts as the object-choice, the lost object, and the substitute object, which we will return to below—this object is another desire. In other words, the relationship to the other is not something added on to desire. And in this respect Freud's discovery of the Oedipus complex in the course of his self-analysis is to be included within the very structure of desire seen as a triangular structure bringing into play two sexes and three persons. It follows from this that what the theory will articulate as symbolic castration is not an additional, extrinsic factor, but something which attests to the initial relation of desire to an agency of prohibition and imposition of standards lived out in fantasies by the child as a paternal threat directed against his sexual activities. Therefore, from the outset, all that might be considered a solipsism of desire is eliminated, in spite of what a definition of desire simply in terms of energy as tension and release might lead us to believe. The mediation of the other is constitutive of human desire as addressed to. . . . This other can be someone who responds or who refuses to respond, someone who gratifies or someone who threatens. He may be, above all, real or a fantasy, present or lost, a source of anguish or the object of a successful mourning. Through transference, psychoanalysis controls and examines these alternative possibilities by transposing the drama involving several actors which generated the neurotic situation onto a sort of miniature artificial stage. Thus, it is analytic experience itself which forces the theory to include intersubjectivity within the very constitution of the libido and to conceive of it less as a need than as an other-directed wish.

Third criterion: The third criterion introduced by the analytic situation concerns the coherence and the resistance of certain manifestations of the unconscious which led Freud to speak of *psychical reality* in contrast to material reality. It is the differential traits of this psychical reality which are psychoanalytically relevant. And this criterion is paradoxical to the extent that what common sense sets in opposition to reality is what constitutes this psychical reality.

In the *Introductory Lectures on Psychoanalysis,* for example, Freud writes, "fantasies possess a psychical reality opposed to material reality . . . ; in the world of neurosis, this psychical reality plays the dominant role." Symptoms and fantasies "abstract from the object and thus renounce every relation with external reality." He then goes on to refer to infantile scenes which themselves "are not always true." This is an especially important admission when we remember how difficult it was for Freud to give up his initial hypothesis of the father's real seduction of the child. More than fifteen years later he remarked how disturbing this discovery remained for him.[5] What is so disturbing about it? Precisely that it is not clinically relevant whether the infantile scenes are true or false. And it does not matter, therefore, from an epistemological point of view either. This is just what is expressed by the phrase "psychical reality."

What is important here is that it is the analytic experience itself which necessitates the use of "psychical reality" to designate certain productions which fall under the opposition of the imaginary and the real, not just according to common sense, but also, in a way, in apparent contradiction with the fundamental opposition in psychoanalysis between the pleasure principle, to which the fantasy affixes itself, and the reality principle. This is why this concept meets resistance not only as induced by common sense or the attitude formed by the observational sciences, but also from psychoanalytic theory itself and its tenacious dichotomy between the imaginary and the real.

The epistemological consequences of this paradox from analytic experience are considerable: while academic psychology does not question the difference between the real and the imaginary, inasmuch as its theoretical entities are all said to refer to observable facts and ultimately to real movements in space and time, psychoanalysis deals only with psychical reality and not with material reality. So the criterion for this reality is no longer that it is observable, but that it presents a coherence and a resistance comparable to that of material reality.

The range of phenomena satisfying this criterion is wide. Fantasies deriving from infantile scenes (observing the parents' sexual relations, seduction, and above all castration) constitute the paradigmatic case to the extent that in spite of their fragile basis in the real history of the subject they present a highly structured organization and are inscribed in scenarios which are both typical and limited in number.

The notion of psychical reality is not exhausted by that of fantasy understood in terms of such archaic scenarios, however. The imaginary, in a broader sense, covers all the kinds of mediations implied in the unfolding of desire.

Close to the infantile scene, for example, we may put the whole domain of abandoned objects which continue to be represented as fantasies. Freud introduces this notion in connection with the problem of symptom formation. Objects abandoned by the libido provide the missing link between the libido and its points of fixation in the symptom.[6]

And from the notion of abandoned objects, the transition to that of the substituted object, which places us at the very heart of the analytic experience, is easy. *Three Essays on the Theory of Sexuality* starts from the variability of the object in contrast to the stability of the aim or goal of the libido and derives from it the substitutability of love-objects. And in *Instincts and Their Vicissitudes,* Freud goes on to construe on this basis, in a systematic fashion, the typical configurations arising from the crisscrossing of substitutions—through inversion, reversal, etc., the ego is capable of putting itself in the place of the object, as in the case of narcissism.

Substitutability, in turn, is the key to still another set of phenomena central to the analytic experience. From the time of *The Interpretation of Dreams,* Freud perceived the remarkable ability of dreams to be substituted for a myth, a folktale theme, or for a symptom, a hallucination, or an illusion. In effect, the entire reality of these psychic formations consists in the thematic unity which serves as a basis for the interplay of their substitutions. Their reality is their meaning, and their meaning is their capability of mutually replacing one another. It is in this sense that the notions of the lost object and the substitute object—cardinal notions for analytic experience—deserve to occupy a key position in the epistemological discussion as well. Put quite simply, they forbid our speaking of a "fact" in psychoanalysis in the same way as in the observational sciences.

I do not want to leave this criterion of psychical reality without adding a final link to the chain of examples which has led us from fantasy to the lost object, then to the substitute object. This final link will assure us that the entire chain is placed fully within analytic experience. This example is the work of mourning.

Mourning, as such, is a remarkable case of reacting to the loss of an object.[7] It is, of course, reality which imposes the work of mourning, but a reality which includes the loss of the object, therefore a reality signified as the verdict of absence.[8] Consequently, mourning consists in "the step-by-step realization of each of the orders proclaimed by reality." But this realization consists precisely in the interiorization of the lost object, concerning which Freud says, "its existence continues psychically."

If I conclude this examination of the criterion of psychical reality with the work of mourning, this is not only to emphasize the wide range of phenomena arising out of the abandonment of the object, but to show at what point the phenomenon of mourning is close to the very core of psychoanalysis. Psychoanalysis begins by acknowledging the fantasy as the paradigm of what for it represents psychical reality, but it continues by means of a labor that may itself be understood as a work of mourning, that is, as an internalization of the lost objects of instinctual desires. Far from restricting itself to vanquishing the fantasy to the benefit of reality, the cure also recovers it as fantasy in order to situate it, without confusing it with what is real, on the level of the imaginary. This kinship between the cure and the work of mourning confirms, if any further confirmation is needed, that it is the analytic experience which requires that we add the reference to fantasies to the two preceding criteria; for what has been said (the first criterion) and what is demanded of the other person (the second criterion) bear the mark of the particular imaginary formations which Freud brings together under the term *phantasieren*. It follows that what is relevant for the analyst is not observable facts or observable reactions to environmental variables, but the meaning which the same events that the behavioral psychologist considers as an observer assume for a subject. I will venture to say, in summation, that *what is psychoanalytically relevant is what a subject makes of his fantasies.*

Fourth criterion: The analytic situation selects from a subject's experience what is capable of entering into a story or narrative. In this sense, "case histories," as histories, constitute the primary texts of psychoanalysis.[9] This narrative character of the psychoanalytic experience is never directly discussed by Freud, at least to my knowledge. But he refers to it indirectly in his considerations about memory. We may recall the famous declaration in *Studies on Hysteria* that "hysterical patients suffer principally from reminiscences." Of course memories will appear to be merely screen-memories and fantasies rather than real memories when Freud seeks the real origin of neurotic suffering, but such fantasies in turn will always be considered in their relation to forgetting and remembering due to their relation to resistance and the connection between resistance and repetition. Remembering, then, is what has to replace repetition. The struggle against resistance—which Freud calls "working-through"—has no other aim than to reopen the path of memory.

But what is it to remember? It is not just to recall certain isolated events, but to become capable of forming meaningful sequences and ordered connections. In short, it is to be able to constitute one's own existence in the form of a story where a memory as such is only a fragment of the story. It is the narrative structure of such life-stories that makes a case a case history.

That such an ordering of one's life episodes in the form of a story

constitutes a kind of work—and even a working-through—is attested
to by the role of one fundamental phenomenon of fantasy life, namely,
the after-the-event phenomenon (*Nachträglichkeit*) which has been
brought out so well by Jacques Lacan. It is the fact that "expressions,
impressions, mnesic traces, are recast later in function of new experience, of the access to a new stage of development, and that they may
assume, not only a new meaning, but a new efficiency" (*Vocabulary
of Psychoanalysis*, p. 33). Before raising a theoretical problem, this
phenomenon is implied in the work of psychoanalysis itself. It is in
the process of working-through just mentioned that Freud discovers
that the subject's history does not conform to a linear determinism
which would place the present in the firm grasp of the past in a univocal fashion. On the contrary, recovering traumatic events through
the work of analysis reveals that "at the time they were experiences
they could not be fully integrated in a meaningful context." It is only
the arrival of new events and new situations that precipitates the subsequent reworking of these earlier events. Thus, in the "wolf-man,"
it is a second, sexually significant scene which, after the event, confers
upon the first scene its effectiveness. And, generally speaking, numerous repressed memories only become traumas after the event. It is a
question of more than just a delay or a deferred action. Here we see
that we are far removed from the notion of a memory which would
simply reproduce real events in a sort of perception of the past; this
is, instead, a work which goes over and over extremely complex struc-
turations. It is this work of memory that is implied, among other
things, by the notion of the story or narrative structure of existence.

For the fourth time, then, a vicissitude of the analytic experience
reveals a pertinent trait of what, psychoanalytically, counts as a "fact."

II. INVESTIGATORY PROCEDURE, METHOD OF TREATMENT, AND THEORETICAL TERMS

The second preliminary question concerning proof in psychoanalysis
is that of the nature of the relation which can be found between theory
and what counts as a fact in psychoanalysis.

From the perspective of operational analysis, the theoretical terms
of an observational science must be capable of being connected to observables by way of rules of interpretation or translation which assure
the indirect verification of these terms. The question here is: How do
we know whether the operative procedures which allow the transition
from the level of theoretical entities to that of facts have the same
structure and the same meaning in psychoanalysis as in the observational sciences? To reply to this question, I would like to return to one

of Freud's statements which deals precisely with the epistemological status of theory in psychoanalysis. We read in "Psychoanalysis and Libido Theory" that

> Psychoanalysis is the name (1) of a procedure (*Verfahren*) for the investigation of mental processes; (2) of a method (based upon that investigation) for the treatment (*Behandlungsmethode*) of neurotic disorders; and (3) of a collection of psychological information (*Einsichten*) attained along those lines, which is gradually being accumulated into a new scientific discipline (S.E., 18, 235).

It is this triangular relation between a procedure of investigation, a method of treatment, and a theory which will hold our attention because it takes the place of the theory-fact relation in the observational sciences. Not only does psychoanalysis deal with "facts" of a special nature, as has just been stated, but what takes the place of the operative procedures at work in the natural sciences is a unique type of relation between the investigatory procedure and the method of treatment. It is this relation which mediates between the theory and the facts.

Now, before anything can be said about the role of the third term, theory, in relation to the other two terms, the relation between the investigatory procedure and the method of treatment is itself not easy to grasp. If this relation may appear unproblematical for a practice which has little concern for theoretical speculations, it does raise difficulties for epistemological reflection. Broadly speaking, we may say that the investigatory procedure tends to give preference to relations of *meaning* between mental productions, while the method of treatment tends to give preference to relations of *force* between systems. The function of the theory will be precisely to integrate these two aspects of psychical reality.

The investigatory procedure has, in effect, a strong affinity with the disciplines of textual interpretation. We read, for example, in *The Interpretation of Dreams*—the title of which is itself revealing: *Traumdeutung*—that

> The aim which I have set before myself is to show that dreams are capable of being interpreted. . . . My presumption that dreams can be interpreted at once puts me in opposition to the ruling theory of dreams and in fact to every theory of dreams with the exception of Scherner's; for "interpreting" a dream implies assigning a "meaning" to it—that is, replacing it by something which fits into the chain of our mental acts as a link having a validity and importance equal to the rest (S.E., 4, 96).

In this regard, interpretation is often compared to the translation from one language into another or to the solution of a rebus (see, for example, S.E., 4, 277–278).[10] Freud never doubted that, however inaccessible the unconscious might be, it still participates in the same psychic structures as does consciousness. It is this common structure which allows us "to interpolate" unconscious acts into the text of conscious acts. This trait belonging to the method of investigation coheres with the criteria for "facts" in psychoanalysis discussed above, in particular with the criteria of sayability and substitutability (considered under criteria one and three). If the investigatory procedure may be applied to both neurotic symptoms and dreams, it may be done because "dream-formation (*Traumbildung*) and symptom-formation (*Symptombildung*) are homogeneous and substitutable" (S.E., 5, 605–608). This was recognized as early as *Studies on Hysteria*, where the "Preliminary Communication" already treats the relation between the determining cause and the hysterical symptom as a "symbolic tie," akin to the dream process. *This deep kinship among all the compromise formations allows us to speak of the psyche as a text to be deciphered.*

This broadly inclusive notion of a text encompasses the profound unity not only of dreams and symptoms, but also of these two taken together with daydreams, myths, folktales, sayings, proverbs, puns, and jokes. And the gradual extension of this method of investigation is assured by the special kinship which exists between, on the one hand, the group of fantasies referred to earlier as infantile scenes (classed in *The Interpretation of Dreams* along with typical dreams: dreams of nudity, of the death of someone dear, etc.), and, on the other hand, the most highly organized and most permanent mythical structures of humanity. Under the same investigatory procedure comes most notably the "textual" structure common to the Oedipus complex discovered by Freud in his self-analysis and the Greek tragedy of Oedipus carried down to us in literature. There is, thus, a correspondence between the extension of the investigatory procedure and what could be termed *the space of fantasy in general* in which psychic productions as diverse as daydreams, children's games, psychological novels, and other poetic creations are set out. In the same way, the psychic conflicts portrayed in stone by Michelangelo's Moses lend themselves to interpretation in virtue of the figurable and substitutable nature of all the sign systems which are included within the same investigatory procedure.

But if we were only to follow the suggestion of the concepts of the text and interpretation, we would arrive at an entirely erroneous notion of psychoanalysis. Psychoanalysis would be purely and simply subsumed under the aegis of the historico-hermeneutical sciences, alongside philology and exegesis. And we would overlook the very features of interpretation which are only grasped when the investigatory procedure is joined to the method of treatment. Why, in effect, are the meaning of the symptom and the meaning of the dream so difficult to decipher, if not because between the manifest and the hidden meaning are interposed distortion mechanisms (*Entstellung*), the same mechanisms which Freud listed under the term "dream work" in *The Interpretation of Dreams*? (The various forms of this work are well known: condensation, displacement, etc.; we are not concerned here, therefore, with the theory of dreams, but with the relation between interpretation and the method of treatment.)

This "distortion" is indeed a strange sort of phenomenon,[11] and Freud employs all sorts of quasi-physical metaphors to render this transformation which he says, "does not think, calculate, or judge in any way at all." We have already mentioned condensation and displacement, which are quasi-physical metaphors for the dream work. But it is the central metaphor of *repression* that orders all the others to the point of becoming a theoretical concept whose metaphorical origin is forgotten (as, moreover, is that of the concept of distortion itself, which literally signifies a violent displacement as well as a deformation). And the semimetaphor of regression belongs to the same cycle.[12]

Another quasi-physical metaphor of equal importance is that of *cathexis,* concerning which Freud does not conceal the kinship with the operation of a capitalist entrepreneur who invests his money in something. This metaphor allows regression to acquire not only a topographic signification, but also a dynamic one, to the extent that regression to an image proceeds from "changes in the cathexes of energy attaching to the different systems" (S.E., 5, 543). This play of metaphors becomes extremely complex because Freud goes on to interweave textual metaphors (translation, substitution, overdetermination, etc.) and energy metaphors, producing mixed metaphors such as disguise, censorship, etc.

Now, why does Freud get himself into such difficult straits with concepts which remain semimetaphors and, in particular, with inconsistent metaphors which tend toward the polarity of, on the one hand, the *textual* concept of translation and, on the other hand, the *mechanical* concept of compromise, itself understood in the sense of a result of various forces interacting? I suggest that it is the conjunction of the investigatory procedure with the method of treatment which compels the theory to operate in this way, using semimetaphorical concepts which lack coherence.

I would like to pause here to consider the word "treatment" (*Behandlung*) which we earlier distinguished from the method of investigation. The notion of a method of treatment must be understood in a sense that extends far beyond its strictly medical sense of "cure" to designate the whole analytic procedure insofar as analysis itself is a sort of work. This work is both the inverse of what we just described as the dream work and the correlative of what earlier was termed the work of mourning. To the question of how analysis is a work, Freud gives a constant reply: Psychoanalysis is essentially *a struggle against resistances.*[13] And it is this notion of resistance that prevents us from identifying the investigatory procedure with a simple interpretation, with an entirely intellectual understanding of the meaning of symptoms. Interpretation, seen as translation, or as deciphering, as the substitution of an intelligible meaning for an absurd one, is only the intellectual segment of the analytic procedure. Even transference (which appeared earlier as an intersubjective criterion of desire) must be treated as one aspect of the handling of resistances (as is apparent in the essay "Remembering, Repeating, and Working-Through," S.E., 12, 147–156). Hence, the three themes of compulsion to repeat, transference, and resistance are found to be connected at the level of analytic praxis.

What does this mean for our epistemological inquiry? Essentially the following: the pair formed by the investigatory procedure and the method of treatment takes exactly the same place as the operative procedures in the observational sciences which connect the level of theoretical entities to that of observable data. This pair constitutes the specific mediation between theory and "fact" in psychoanalysis. And this mediation operates in the following manner: by coordinating interpretation and the handling of resistances, analytic praxis calls for a theory in which the psyche will be represented both as a text to be interpreted and as a system of forces to be manipulated. In other words, it is the complex character of actual practice which forces the theory to overcome the apparent contradiction between the metaphor of the *text* to be interpreted and that of the *forces* to be regulated; in short, practice forces us to think of meaning and force together in a comprehensive theory. It is through the practical coordination of interpretation and the handling of resistances that the theory is given the task of forming a model capable of articulating the facts acknowledged as relevant in analytic experience. It is in this way that the relations between the investigatory procedure and the method of treatment constitutes the necessary mediation between theory and "facts."

Now, does psychoanalysis possess a *theory* which satisfies these requirements, that is, which takes into account both the criteria for "facts" in psychoanalysis and the cohesion between the theory and the pair formed by the investigatory procedure, and the method of treatment (to the extent that in analysis this pair takes the place of mediation between theory and experiments)?

It seems to me that it is in light of such questions that Freud's theoretical work—that is, essentially, his "metapsychology"—should be examined today. If Freud's metapsychology has been turned into a fetish by some and scorned as marginal by others, it is because it was treated as an independent construction. Too many epistemological works examine the great theoretical texts—from the "Project" of 1895 and chapter 7 of the *Traumdeutung* to *The Ego and the Id*—outside the total context of experience and practice. Isolated in this way, the body of doctrine can only lead to premature and truncated evaluations. The theory must therefore be relativized, by which I mean it must be placed back into the complex network of relations which encompass it.

For my part, I should like to submit two theses, apparently opposed to each other, but which taken together in their unstable equilibrium, attempt to consider Freud's theoretical work as the imperfect yet indispensable starting point for any reformulation of this theory.

On the one hand, I am prepared to acknowledge that Freud's theoretical model (or models) is (or are) not adequate to analytic experience and practice as these are formulated in his other writings (i.e., the case histories, the writings on psychoanalytic technique, and the so-called essays on applied psychoanalysis). More specifically, Freud's metapsychology does not succeed in codifying and integrating into a single unified structure meaning and force, textual interpretation and the handling of resistances.

In the first place, Freud always tends to reverse the relations between theory, on the one hand, and experience and practice, on the other, and to reconstruct the work of interpretation on the basis of theoretical models which have become autonomous. He thus loses sight of the fact that the language of the theory is narrower than that in which the technique is described. Next, he tends to construct his theoretical models in the positivist, naturalistic, and materialist spirit of the sciences of his day. There are many texts which assert the exclusive kinship of psychoanalysis with the natural sciences and even with physics, or which announce that in the future psychoanalysis will be replaced by a more refined pharmacology.

In this respect, Jürgen Habermas, in the extensive study dealing with psychoanalysis in his *Erkenntniss und Interesse,* is correct in speaking of the "self-misunderstanding of psychoanalysis as a natural science" (translated by Jerome T. Shapiro: *Knowledge and Human Interests,* Boston: Beacon Press, 1971, p. 247). According to Habermas, technique and experience call for a structural model which is betrayed by the preferred model of energy distribution. This latter model is superimposed upon analytic experience ignoring its derivation from the work of reconstructing an individual history on the basis of scattered fragments. Most seriously, this model is in many ways antecedent to analytic experience, as we see in the 1895 "Project," and it imposes its reference system on this experience: quantifiable energy, stimulation, tension, discharge, inhibitions, cathexis, etc. Even when the psychical apparatus includes only "psychical localities" which are not anatomically localizable (as is the case in chapter 7 of the *Traumdeutung*), the spatial arrangement and the temporal sequence of the systems continue to lend support to the energy distribution model. The great article, "The Unconscious," is the principal witness to its sovereignty.

What is lost from sight in a model like this, however, is the very specificity of the psychoanalytic "fact," with its fourfold nature of being able to be said, to be addressed to another person, to be fantasized, figured, or symbolized, and to be recounted in the story of a life. This set of criteria requires that elements be introduced in a suitable manner at the theoretical level which are capable of accounting for what occurs in the analytic relation. This is why I can adopt, up to a certain point, the suggestions which Habermas offers in light of the work of Lorenzer in his *Uber den Gegenstand der Psychoanalyse* (Frankfurt, 1973). (I will state my reservations below when I present my second thesis concerning the status of theory in Freud.)

These authors assume as their framework of reference the symbolizing process at work in human communication and, in general, in human interaction. The disturbances which give rise to psychoanalytic interventions are then considered as the pathology of our linguistic competence and are placed alongside the distortions uncovered, on another level, by the Marxist and post-Marxist critique of ideologies. Psychoanalysis and the critique of ideologies, in effect, share a common obligation to explain and interpret these distortions, which are not accidental but systematic in the sense that they are organized systematically in the text of interhuman communication. These distortions are the occasion of a subject's self-misunderstanding. This is why, in order to account for this, we need a theory which is not limited to restoring the integral, unmutilated, and unfalsified text, but one which takes as its object the very mechanisms which distort the text. And this explains why, in turn, the interpretative decoding of symptoms and dreams goes beyond a simply philological hermeneutics insofar as it is the very meaning of the mechanisms which distort the texts that must be explained. This is also why the economic metaphors (resistance, repression, compromise, etc.) cannot be replaced by the philological metaphors (text, meaning, interpretation, etc.).

But the opposite is no less true: neither can the economic metaphors replace their complements. They cannot lose their metaphorical character and set themselves up as an energetic theory to be taken literally. It is basically against this reduction to the literal nature of the energy distribution model that our authors formulate their own theories in terms of communication and symbolic interaction. According to these alternative models, the mechanisms of the unconscious are no longer held to be things, they are "split-off symbols," "delinguisticized" or "degrammaticized motives." Like banishment or political ostracism, repression banishes a part of language from the public sphere of communication and condemns it to the exile of a "privatized" language. This is how mental functioning simulates a natural process. But only to the extent that it has been objectified and reified. If, therefore, we forget that this reification results from a process of desymbolization, hence from *a specific self-alienation,* we end up constructing a model where the unconscious is literally a thing. But, at the same time, we are then unable to understand how resymbolization is possible, that is, how analytic experience itself is possible. We can understand this only if we interpret the phenomena revealed by this experience in terms of *communication disturbances* and analytic experience as a reappropriation which *inverts the process of splitting-off symbols.*[14]

To the extent that I take up this critique of the energetic model of Freudian metapsychology, I accept classing psychoanalysis along with the critical social sciences, which are guided by the interest in emancipation and motivated in the final analysis by the wish to recover the force of *Selbstreflexion.*

Yet, in return, I would not want this rapprochement with the critical social sciences and this ultimate reference to self-reflection to go beyond the goal of placing the theory back into the complex network of psychoanalytic experience and practice. This is why I want to defend with equal vigor the complementary thesis which holds that we must always start from the Freudian system in spite of its faults, even— I would venture to say—because of its deficiencies. Indeed, as Habermas himself has remarked, the self-misunderstanding of psychoanalysis is not entirely unfounded. The economic model, in particular, even in its literal energetism, preserves something essential which a theorizing introduced from outside the system is always in danger of losing sight of, namely, that man's alienation from himself is such that mental functioning does actually resemble the functioning of a thing. This simulation keeps psychoanalysis from constituting itself as a province of the exegetical disciplines applied to texts—as a hermeneutics, in other words—and requires that psychoanalysis include in the process of self-understanding operations which were originally reserved for the natural sciences.

This requirement may be illustrated through a brief critique of those efforts at reformulating the theory which immediately exclude in principle this simulation of the thing. I am thinking here especially of those reformulations which borrow from phenomenology, from ordinary language analysis, or from linguistics. All these reformulations omit the task of integrating an explanatory stage into the process of desymbolization and resymbolization.

I will limit myself here to those efforts which arise from consideration of the semantics of action in the school of linguistic analysis. (I discussed the phenomenological interpretation at length in *Freud and Philosophy*, pp. 375ff., and I treat the properly linguistic reformulations elsewhere.[15])

Under the name of the philosophy of action, an autonomous discipline has been constituted, one influenced by Austin, Wittgenstein, and the philosophy of ordinary language, which assigns itself the task of describing the logic implicit in our discourse on action when it uses terms designating actions, intentions, motives, individual or collective agents, etc. Some of the analysts who practice this discipline—although less numerous today, it is true, and subjected to increasingly rigorous criticism by other semanticists—have maintained the thesis that discourse on action brings into play criteria of intelligibility distinct from and different than the criteria for physical movement or observable behavior. One of the implications of this dichotomy between the two "language games" of action and movement bears directly on the point at issue in our discussion: according to these analysts, our motives for acting can in no way be assimilated to the causes by which we explain natural events. Motives are reasons for our action, while causes are the constant antecedents of other events from which they are logically distinct.

Can psychoanalytic theory be reformulated on the basis of this distinction? Some authors have thought so and have interpreted psychoanalysis as an extension of the vocabulary of action (intentions, motives, etc.) beyond the sphere where we are aware of what we do. Psychoanalysis on this interpretation adds nothing to ordinary conceptuality except the use of the same concepts of ordinary language in a new domain characterized as "unconscious." In this way, for example, it is said of the "rat-man" analyzed by Freud that he experienced a feeling of hostility toward his father without being aware of it. Understanding this assertion rests on the ordinary meaning we give to this sort of hostility in situations where the agent is able to recognize such a feeling as his own. The only novelty here is the use of clauses such as "without being aware," "unknowingly," "unconsciously," etc.

In a sense this is true. Freud himself declares that in the unconscious we do find representations and affects to which we can give the same name as their conscious counterparts and which lack only the property of being conscious. But what is completely omitted in this reformulation is the very paradox of psychoanalytic theory, namely, that it is the becoming unconscious as such which requires a specific explanation so that the kinship of meaning between conscious and unconscious contents may be recognized. Now, the explanatory schema capable of accounting for the mechanisms of exclusion, banishment, reification, etc., completely challenges the separation of the domains of action and movement, along with the dichotomy between motive and cause. And in this regard, Michael Sherwood's demonstration in the critical part of his *Logic of Explanation in Psychoanalysis* (New York: Academic Press, 1969) is entirely convincing. What is remarkable about psychoanalytic explanation is that it brings into view motives which are causes and which require an explanation of their autonomous functioning. Besides, Freud could not oppose motive to cause by giving motives the sense of reason for . . . , inasmuch as rationalization (a term which he borrowed from Ernest Jones) is itself a process which calls for an explanation and which, by this very fact, does not permit us to accept an alleged reason as the true cause.

As a result, Freud is correct in completely ignoring the distinction between motive and cause and in making even its theoretical formulation impossible. In many ways his explanation refers to "causally relevant" factors, whether this is in terms of the initial phenomenon (the *origin* of a neurosis, etc.), the intermediate stages (the *genesis* of a symptom, of a libidinal structure, etc.), its *function* (compromise-formation, etc.), or, finally, its *significance* (substitution or symbolic value, etc.). These are the four modes of explanation retained by Sherwood, not only in Freud, but in general as well. Freud's use of the idea of cause and of causal explanation is perhaps both complex and flexible —Sherwood (p. 172) quotes a text from Freud which also distinguishes between preconditions, specific causes, and concurrent causes—but he leaves no room for an opposition between cause and motive. All that is important to him is to explain through one or another of the explanatory modes just mentioned, or through an "overdetermined" use of several of them, what in behavior are "the incongruities" in relation to the expected course of a human agent's action.

It is the attempt to reduce these "incongruities" that forbids distinguishing between motives and causes because it calls for an *explanation* by means of causes in order to reach an *understanding* in terms of motives. And this is what I try to express in my own terms by saying that the facts of psychoanalysis arise from the category of the text, and hence of meaning, as well as from the categories of energy and resistance, and hence of force. To say, for example, that a feeling is unconscious is not just to say that it resembles conscious motives occurring in other circumstances; rather, it is to say that it is to be inserted as a causally relevant factor in order to explain the incongruities of an act of behavior, and that this explanation is itself a causally relevant factor in the work—the working-through—of analysis.

From this brief discussion it follows that psychoanalytic theory cannot be reformulated from the outside, on the basis of an alien conceptuality, if we are not to mistake the initial situation in psychoanalysis, namely, that the human psyche under certain conditions of self-alienation is unable to understand itself by simply expanding its immediate interpretive capacities, but instead requires that the hermeneutics of self-understanding take the detour of causal explanation.

If Freud's economic model can therefore legitimately be accused of generating misunderstanding concerning the relation between theory and the analytic situation, it must also be said, with equal force and in the opposite direction, that a model of understanding—be it phenomenological, linguistic, or symbolic—which does not integrate some explanatory segment, some economic phase, misunderstands the very facts that are brought to light by analytic experience.

This is why today we can neither be satisfied with the Freudian metapsychology, nor find another starting point to rectify and enrich the theoretical model to the extent that it is true that "the misunderstanding of psychoanalysis as a natural science is not without basis."[16]

III. TRUTH AND VERIFICATION

I will now attempt to deal directly with the specific question of proof in Freud's psychoanalytic writings.

As I stated in my introduction, we cannot pose this question in a useful way until two preliminary questions have been resolved, that of the criteria which determine what counts as a *fact* in psychoanalysis, and that of the relation which is established between the theory and analytic experience through the *double mediation* of the investigatory procedure and the method of treatment. Having considered these two preliminary questions, it is now a matter of showing how our response to these questions affects our response to the question of proof.

To inquire about proof in psychoanalysis is to ask two separate questions: (1) What truth-claim is made by the statements of psychoanalysis? and (2) What sort of verification or falsification are these statements capable of?

What truth-claim is made by psychoanalytic statements? This question is not only one of degree, but also of the nature of truth, not only a question of quantity, but also of the quality of truth. Or to put it another way, the degree of exactitude which can be expected of psychoanalytic statements depends on the sort of truth which can be expected in this domain.[17] For lack of an exact view of the qualitative diversity of the types of truth in relation to the types of facts, verificational criteria appropriate to the sciences in which facts are empirically given to one or more external observers have been repeatedly applied to psychoanalysis. Then the conclusion has been either that

psychoanalysis does not in any way satisfy these criteria or that it satisfies them only if they are weakened. Now, the question is not how to
loosely use strict criteria and so place psychoanalysis higher or lower on
a single scale of verifiability (and undoubtedly quite low on the scale),
but how to specify the truth-claim appropriate to the facts in the psychoanalytic domain?

Let us return to our enumeration of the criteria for facts in psychoanalysis and ask ourselves what sort of adequacy of statements is appropriate to them?

First, if analytic experience is desire coming to discourse, the sort of
truth that best answers to it is that of a saying-true rather than a being-
true. This saying-true is negatively intended in the characterization of
the mechanisms of distortion as disguise, falsification, illusion, and in
general as forms of misunderstanding. Truth here is closer to that of
Greek tragedy than to that of modern physics. *Pathei-mathos,* learn
through suffering, says the chorus in Aeschylus' *Agamemnon.* And
indeed, what is truth for Oedipus, if not the recognition of himself as
he who . . . , he who has already killed his father and married his
mother? Recognition is accepting instead of denigrating and accusing
oneself, and this is the truth befitting saying-true according to
Sophocles.

This movement from misunderstanding to recognition is also the
standard itinerary of analytic experience, and it designates what might
be called the veracity threshold of truth in psychoanalysis.[18] And
with certain reservations which will be introduced below, we may
say along with Habermas that this sort of truth involves above all the
capacity for *Selbstreflexion* belonging to a subject. The truth-claim of
psychoanalysis is primarily its claim to increase this capacity by helping
the subject to overcome the distortions which are the source of self-
misunderstanding.

Second, if the analytic situation elicits—principally by means of the
act of transference—what is said *to the other,* the truth-claim of psychoanalysis can legitimately be placed within the field of intersubjective
communication.[19] Everything Freud says about self-misunderstanding
can, in fact, be carried over into misunderstanding the other. All his
analyses concerning the object choice, the lost object, substitutions
for the lost object, mourning, and melancholia suggest that the place
of misunderstanding is the other person.

This second feature of the truth-claim of psychoanalytic statements
is thereby characterized in a negative manner, namely, that of pursuing
self-recognition through the restoration and extension of the symbolic
process in the public sphere of communication. In this sense, psychoanalysis pursues in its own way the project of recognition which Hegel
placed at the summit of ethical life in his Jena philosophy. This thesis

will seem less banal if we see its critical point in relation to the danger of manipulation which seems to me implicit in any reduction of the historical sphere of communication to the empirical sphere of observable facts. If it is true that the sphere of empirically verifiable statements coincides with that which governs our interest for control and domination, then reducing the historical to the empirical would entail the danger of placing the order of symbolic communication under the same system for controlling results as our instrumental action.[20] This warning is not empty in light of a certain tendency of psychoanalysis to take the process of self-recognition and of recognizing the other as an "adjustment" to the objective conditions of a society which is itself diseased.

With the third criterion for psychoanalytic facts we encounter the major difficulty facing the truth-claims of psychoanalysis. We concluded from the study of the third criterion that what is psychoanalytically relevant is what a subject makes of his fantasies. What becomes of the truth-claim of psychoanalysis when it is set within the framework of a more positive recognition of fantasy than Freud himself allowed?[21] By losing its reference to actual reality and by giving wider rein to the liberation of fantasizing, to emotional development, and to enjoyment than Freud wanted to do, are we not breaking the bond between veracity and truth? This is undoubtedly so. Nevertheless, I think that there is still something to be sought in the truth-claim made from the perspective of the proper use of fantasies. In thinking this, I base myself on texts from Freud himself, such as "Dissolution of the Oedipus Complex" and "Analysis Terminable and Interminable." From such texts arises the notion that the analytic cure may be understood as a work of mourning which, far from striking down the fantasy, recovers it as a fantasy in order to situate it clearly with the real on the plane of the imaginary in the strong sense of *Einbildungskraft* used by Kant and the great post-Kantians.[22] And in the same sense, I suggested in *Freud and Philosophy* that analytic experience aims at articulating several prime signifiers of existence (phallus, father, mother, death, etc.) in order to make their structuring function appear.

Here the truth-claim would concern the passage from the fantasy as alienating to the symbolic as founding both individual and collective identity.[23]

The fourth criterion for psychoanalytic facts—the criterion of narrativity—will perhaps rid us of some of the difficulties raised by the preceding criterion. One could, in effect, raise the objection to the preceding analysis that by introducing something like a "reasoned mythology" in the recognition process—self-recognition as well as the recognition of the other—we also introduce fiction into the circumference of truth. How can *Dichtung und Wahrheit* be reconciled, to borrow

Goethe's title? If we remember that fiction is pretending and that pretending is doing, are we not substituting doing-true, i.e., make-believe, for saying-true? Perhaps. But are not saying-true and doing-true reconciled in the idea of constructing or reconstructing a *coherent story or account* from the tattered remains of our experience? Let us follow this pathway opened up by the narrative character of psychoanalytic facts. Here the truth-claim is tied to what Michael Sherwood calls the "narrative commitment of psychoanalytic explanation." It seems to me that this author has shown in a clearly relevant manner that ultimately what is at issue in psychoanalysis is giving "a single extended explanation of an individual patient's entire case history" (op. cit., p. 4).[24] Hence, to explain here is to reorganize facts into a meaningful whole which constitutes a single and continuous history (even if it does not cover an entire life span).

I think it is wise to approach things in this way, for the narrative interest or involvement at issue here has no parallel in an observational science where we speak of "cases" but not of "case histories." The psychoanalytic explanation of a case is a narrative explanation in the sense that the generalizations or lawlike statements which are implied by the explanatory segments referred to in the second part of our study contribute to the *understandable narrative* toward which each individual case study leads. If we stated earlier that causal connections are explanatory segments in a process of understanding, even of self-reflection in Habermas's sense, this is because understanding is narrative and because the partial explanatory segments of this or that fragment of behavior are integrated in a narrative structure.[25] So the validation of analytic statements draws its specific nature from this ultimate reference to a *narrative commitment* in the name of which we try to integrate isolated or alien phenomena in "a single unified process or sequence of events" (ibid., p. 169).

We are thus invited to reflect upon the concept of narrative intelligibility which psychoanalysis has in common with the historical sciences.[26] Now, it is difficult to define this concept inasmuch as the criteria for adequacy are difficult to handle on this level. Indeed, it is precisely in psychoanalysis that reduction of the "incongruities" raises the question of knowing what is meant by an intelligible account. A history which would remain inconsistent, incoherent, incomplete, or partial would clearly resemble what we know of the course of life in ordinary experience, namely, that a human life as a whole remains strange, disconnected, incomplete, and fragmented.

We might be tempted, therefore, to give up any attempt to tie a truth-claim to the idea of the intelligible accounts of an existence. But I do not think it would be correct to give in to this epistemological defeatism, for we would thereby turn psychoanalytic statements into the rhetoric of persuasion under the pretext that it is the account's acceptability to the patient which is therapeutically effective. Then, besides the renewed suspicion of suggestion by the analyst—which Freud never ceased to combat—a more serious suspicion is insinuated, namely, that the criterion of therapeutic success is exclusively the patient's ability to adapt to a given social milieu. And this suspicion leads in turn to the suspicion that the psychoanalyst finally represents, with regard to the patient, only the point of view of society and that he imposes this on his patient by subtly involving him in a strategy of capitulation to which he alone holds the key. This is why we must not give up our efforts to link a truth-claim with the narrativity criterion, even if this claim is validated on a basis other than that of narrativity itself.[27] In other words, we must maintain the critical dimension of narrativity, which is just that of self-recognition, of recognition of the other, and of recognition of the fantasy. We may even say, then, that the patient is both the actor and the critic of a history which he is at first unable to recount. The problem of recognizing oneself is the problem of recovering the ability to recount one's own history, to endlessly continue to give the form of a story to reflections on oneself. And working-through is nothing other than this continuous narration.

We can now turn to the second half of our question: What sort of verification or falsification are the statements of psychoanalysis capable of? To ask about the procedures of verification and falsification is to ask which *means of proof* are appropriate to the truth-claims of psychoanalysis. My thesis here is as follows: *If the ultimate truth-claim resides in the case histories, the means of proof reside in the articulation of the entire network: theory, hermeneutics, therapeutics, and narration.*

The preceding discussion on narrativity is a good introduction to this final stage of our investigation. We have assumed that all truth-claims of psychoanalysis are ultimately summed up in the narrative structure of psychoanalytic facts. But it does not follow that the means of proof are contained in the narrative structure itself, and the question remains whether the means of truth relevant to narrative explanation are not carried by the nonnarrative statements of psychoanalysis.[28]

To prove this point, it will suffice to think about what makes a narration an explanation in the psychoanalytic sense of the term. It is the possibility of inserting several stages of causal explanation into the process of self-understanding in narrative terms. And it is this explanatory detour which entails recourse to nonnarrative means of proof. These are spread over three levels: (1) the level of generalizations resulting from comparison with the rest of the clinical explanation; (2) the level of lawlike propositions applied to typical segments of behavior (symptoms, for example), which are, as Sherwood has shown, themselves divided into explanations in terms of origin, explanations in terms of genesis, others in terms of function, and still others in terms of significance; finally (3) the level of *very general hypotheses* concerning the functioning of the psychic apparatus, which could be considered as axiomatic. This last level is divided into the topography, the theory of agencies, and the successive theories of instinctual drives, including the death instinct. Generalizations, laws, and axioms, therefore, constitute the nonnarrative structure of psychoanalytic explanation.

At its first level, that of generalizations, this nonnarrative structure of explanation is already present in the ordinary explanations of individual behavior; alleged motives—for example, hate or jealousy—are not particular events, but classes of inclinations under which a particular action is placed in order to make it intelligible. To say that someone acted out of jealousy is to invoke in the case of his particular action a feature which is grasped from the outset as repeatable and common to an indeterminate variety of individuals. Such a motive draws its explanatory value from its power to place a particular action in a meaningful context characterized from the start by a certain universality of significance. So to explain is to characterize a given action by ascribing to it as its cause a motive which exemplifies a class. This is all the more true when we are dealing not with classes of motives, identifiable as the general features of human experience, but with fantasies which present organized, stable, and eminently typical scenes, or with stages—oral, anal, genital, etc.—which themselves are also typical organizations of libidinal development. And taking the next step, we are ready to understand that excommunication, on the basis of which an unconscious ensemble is autonomously structured, tends to produce the stereotyped incongruities which are the very object of analytic explanation.

The transition from generalities to lawlike statements broadly corresponds to the explanation not only in terms of unconscious motives, but also in terms of the mechanisms of distortion which render the motivational process unrecognizable. And above these lawlike statements we still have the propositions concerning the theoretical entities posed by psychoanalysis; these statements constitute the metapsychology as such, which can be considered from the point of view of the structure of these statements as the metalanguage of psychoanalysis—all that can be said regarding instinct, the representatives of instinct, the destiny of instinct, etc. At this level, every narrative feature, by which I mean the reference to a case history, is erased, at least at the manifest level of the statements.[29]

This style of explanation has as its consequence that in Freud what Sherwood calls *narrative commitment* and *explanatory commitment* continually split apart, only to merge together again in the case histories—again we must note that even in the case histories, including the "rat-man," Freud juxtaposes the case study as such and theoretical considerations. In the other writings, which are far more numerous, however, they diverge again. We could even say that in these writings the relation between "narrative commitment" and "explanatory commitment" is reversed. Thus, case histories constitute just one pole of a very wide range of writings for which the essays on metapsychology constitute the other pole, which is basically nonnarrative.[30]

Such is the way in which it may be said that in psychoanalysis the means of proof reside in the very articulation of the entire network constituted by the theory, the interpretive procedures, the therapeutic treatment, and the narrative structure of the analytic experience.

I am not unaware that this assertion leads to the most formidable objection of all against psychoanalysis, namely, that these statements are irrefutable and therefore unverifiable if the theory, method, treatment, and interpretation of a particular case are all to be verified at once. If this entire investigation of mine does nothing more than formulate this objection correctly and assemble the means to reply to it, it will have attained its goal.

I will leave aside the crude form of this objection, namely, that the analyst *suggests* to his patient that he accept the interpretation which verifies the theory. I am taking for granted the replies which Freud opposes to this accusation of suggestibility. They are worth what the measures taken at the level of the professional code and the analytic technique itself against the suspicion of suggestion are worth. I grant that these measures define a good analyst and that there are good analysts.

It is more interesting to take Freud at his word and to contend with a subtler form of the accusation of self-confirmation, that is, that validation in psychoanalysis is condemned to remain circular since everything is verified at once. Let us consider this argument. It is all the more important to do so since the notion of a circle is not foreign to all the historico-interpretive disciplines, in which a "case" is not only an example to be placed under a law, but something which possesses its own dramatic structure which makes it a "case history." The problem, Heidegger says with reference to the hermeneutical circle, is not avoiding the circle but properly entering into it. This means: taking measures so that the circle is not a vicious circle. Now, a circle is vicious if it takes the form of begging the question, that is, if the verification in each of the areas considered is the condition for verification in another area. The circle of verification will not be vicious, however, if validation proceeds in a cumulative fashion through the mutual reinforcement of criteria which taken in isolation would not be decisive, but whose convergence makes them plausible and, in the best cases, probable and even convincing.

I will say, therefore, that the validation apt to confirm the truth-claim belonging to the domain of psychoanalytic facts is an extremely complex process which is based on the synergy of partial and heterogeneous criteria. If we take as our guideline the idea of a constellation formed by the theory, the investigatory procedure, the treatment technique, and the reconstruction of a case history, we can then say the following:

1. A good psychoanalytic explanation must be coherent with the theory, or, if one prefers, it must conform to Freud's psychoanalytic system, or to the system by which this or that school claiming his name is identified—recall, however, that I have limited my consideration in this essay to Freud's writings.

This first criterion is not peculiar to psychoanalysis. In every field of inquiry explanation establishes a connection of this kind between a theoretical apparatus of concepts and an array of facts relevant to this theoretical style. In this sense, all explanations are limited by their own conceptual framework. Their validity extends as far as the correlation between theory and facts works. For the same reason, any theory is questionable. A new theory is required, as Kuhn has argued, as soon as new facts are recognized which can no longer be "covered" by the ruling paradigm. And something like this is happening today in psychoanalysis, perhaps. The theoretical model of energy distribution appears more and more inadequate, but no alternative model seems to be powerful enough to "cover" all the accepted facts relevant to psychoanalysis or their paradoxical nature.

2. A good psychoanalytic explanation must satisfy the universalizable rules set up by the procedures of interpretation for the sake of decoding the text of the unconscious. This second criterion is relatively independent from the preceding one to the extent that it relies on the *inner* consistency of the new text substituted by means of translation for the unreadable text of symptoms and dreams. In this respect, the model of the rebus is quite appropriate. It shows that the character of intelligibility of the substituted text resides in its capacity to take into account as many scattered elements as possible from those provided by the analytic process itself, especially as a result of the technique of free association.

A corollary of this second criterion deserves attention. It concerns the expansion of the procedures of interpretation beyond the native domain of psychoanalysis, i.e., symptoms and dreams, along the analogical lines which connect tales, puns, jokes, etc. to the first analogon of this series, the dream. A new kind of coherence is implied here which concerns not only the inner intelligibility of the translated text, but also the analogy of structure which obtains between all the members of the series of psychic productions. This second criterion of validation may be formulated accordingly in two complementary ways as a criterion of intratextual consistency and a criterion of intertextual consistency. The second formulation may even be the more decisive one to the extent that the universalization of the rules of decoding relies on the soundness of the analogical extrapolation from symptoms and dreams to other cultural expressions. At the same time, the merely analogical character of this extrapolation reminds us of the problematic value of this means of proof. But even the limitation resulting from the analogical structure of this criterion of validation proceeds from structural reasons distinct from those which impose a limitation on the first criterion. The second criterion is not only relatively independent from the first one, but it may correct and even shatter it inasmuch as it is under the guidance of these procedures of investigation that new facts are released which may defeat the claim of the theoretical framework to "cover" them. This is what happens, for example, to the energy distribution model when it is confronted with the facts yielded by the procedures of interpretation in conjunction with the methods of treatment.

3. A good psychoanalytic explanation must be satisfactory in economic terms; in other words, it must be able to be incorporated into the work of the analysand, into his "working-through," and so become a therapeutic factor of amelioration. This third criterion, too, is relatively independent of the first one since it implies something which *happens to* the analysand under the condition of his own "work" (hence the substitution of the term analysand for that of patient and even of client). And it is relatively independent of the second one, to the extent that an interpretation which is only understood, i.e., intellectually grasped, remains ineffective and may even be harmful so long as a new pattern of energies has not emerged from the "handling" of resistances. The therapeutic success resulting from this new energetical configuration constitutes, in this way, an autonomous criterion of validation.

4. Finally, a good psychoanalytic explanation must raise a particular case history to the sort of narrative intelligibility which we ordinarily expect from a story. This fourth criterion should not be overemphasized as would be the case in a purely "narrative" account of psychoanalytic theory. But the relative autonomy of this criterion must not be overlooked either, because narrative intelligibility implies something more than the subjective acceptability of one's own life-story. It comes to terms with the general condition of acceptability that we apply when we read any story, be it historical or fictional. In the terms of W. B.

Gallie, a story has to be "followable," and in that sense, "self-explanatory." We interpolate explanation when the narrative process is blocked and in order to "follow-further." These explanations are acceptable to the extent that they may be grafted upon the archetypes of storytelling which have been culturally developed and which rule our actual competence to follow new stories. Here psychoanalysis is not an exception. Psychoanalytic reports are kinds of biographies and autobiographies whose literary history is a part of the long tradition emerging from the oral epic tradition of the Greeks, the Celts, and the Germans. It is this whole tradition of storytelling which provides a relative autonomy to the criterion of narrative intelligibility, as regards not only the consistency of the interpretive procedures, but also the efficacity of the change in the balance of libidinal energies.

Consequently, when these criteria of validation do not derive from one another, but mutually reinforce one another, they constitute the proof apparatus in psychoanalysis. It may be granted that this apparatus is extremely complex, very difficult to handle, and highly problematical. But it can at least be assumed that this cumulative character of the validation criteria is the only one suited to both the criteria for psychoanalytic facts which specify the truth-claim in psychoanalysis, and the complex relations between the theory, the investigatory procedure, and the method of treatment which govern the means of proof in psychoanalysis.

V. RELIGION AND FAITH

The first article in this section examines the nature of religion in the aftermath of its critique by Marx, Nietzsche, and Freud. Ricoeur argues that their "external" critique must be met by an "internal" critique, which gives rise to a hermeneutics of the text itself. Interpretation, in turn, raises the problem of communication, which is the concern of the second essay, "The Language of Faith." The problem of communicating the kerygma is, among other things, that of overcoming the cultural distance that separates us from the originators of the text. Ricoeur explores this as the problem of "how to restore meaning, how to return to contemporary discourse a language which does not pertain to the same cultural circle as mine." We finally see Ricoeur attempting to do precisely this by recapturing the meaning of a biblical text in "Listening to the Parables of Jesus."

SOURCES

"The Critique of Religion" and "The Language of Faith," translated by R. Bradley DeFord, *Union Seminary Quarterly Review* 28 (1973):205–12; 213–24. Used by permission.

"Listening to the Parables of Jesus," *Criterion* 13 (1974):18–22. Used by permission.

CHAPTER 14

The Critique of Religion

I. DEMYSTIFICATION

Christianity presents itself as a kerygma, that is to say a proclamation, a discourse *addressed to*. The Greek word "kerygma" has an exact meaning: announcement, proclamation, message—demystification deals precisely with this address, with this discourse *addressed to*. . . .

We say that we have been victims of a mystification when, having received a letter, we discover that it was not sent by whom we believed. The problem of demystification interests us in this very precise sense, that it is not so much a critique of the content—it is not that we have not received the letter—but of the origin: it did not come from whom we thought.

It is just the problem of an illusion about the origin which is here posed; I would enter into this critique by the analysis of the function of *suspicion*, inasmuch as it is the critical instrument of demystification, and attempt to understand what it signifies at the heart of our culture.

I am therefore constrained to speak of the impact, which seems to me to be irreversible, of three masters of suspicion—Marx, Nietzsche, and Freud, who belong to our culture and with whom we are bound to converse.

I want to make it understood that they make sense only if we take them together, or if we understand them as a unity, for it is at the moment when their critiques converge that they become significant. If the place of Marx, Nietzsche, and Freud as phenomena of culture, as cultural events, still remains uncertain, it is because they truly have still not been brought together in their joint impact on our culture. Taken separately, we cannot really understand them, for we are at once sensitive to their narrowness, and we miss their significance for us when we concern ourselves only with their individual historical limitations.

Marx appears to us at first as a critic of the economic world to whom we could be indebted for an anatomy and physiology of capitalism in the mid-19th century. And we extricate ourselves quickly from his message by proclaiming this political economics out of date, nonscientific, etc.

In the same way, we elude the blow that Nietzsche struck at us when we take him by the limitation of the romanticism of the will to power which seems in line with the philosophies of life; we say, "This is not scientific biology any more than Marxism is scientific economics."

In the same way, we would confine Freud in a purely psychiatric theory, in order to abandon to him the neurotic or psychotic side of man; but we then miss his impact on our culture insofar as he instituted a fundamental critique of modern culture.

If we are to succeed in understanding as a unity the theory of ideologies in Marx, the genealogies of ethics in Nietzsche, and the theory of ideas and illusions in Freud, we will see the configuration of a problem—hereafter posed before the modern mind—the problem of *false-consciousness.* Therefore, it is to illuminate this problem of false-consciousness that we engage in a common rereading of Marx, Nietzsche, and Freud. The term "false-consciousness" appears especially in Marx. But I think that it can be applied usefully to Nietzsche and Freud, for it is a specific problem. It is a problem which is not concerned as such only with the individual as if he were in error in a purely epistemological sense, or a falsehood in a purely ethical sense; illusion is a cultural structure, a dimension of our social discourse.

From here on, with Marx, Nietzsche, and Freud, a new type of critique of culture appears.

To be sure, Marx could not conceive of this illusion other than as a reflection of the class struggle. Nietzsche could not grasp false-consciousness other than as vengeance, or the resentment of the weak against the strong. And Freud could not experience this same problem apart from what I will call a semantics of desire, a history of human desire entrapped by cultural prohibitions.

These are the reasons why the approach to the problem of false-consciousness differs from one to the other; but each of them, disengaged from his narrowness, cooperates in a *general exegesis* of false-consciousness and belongs by this fact in a *hermeneutics,* in a theory of interpretation, under the negative form of demystification. But with Marx, Nietzsche, and Freud, beyond their economism, biologism, and psychiatrism respectively, demystification is characterized in the first place as the exercise of *suspicion.* I call suspicion the act of dispute exactly proportional to the expressions of false-consciousness. The problem of false-consciousness is the object, the correlative of the act of suspicion. Out of it is born the quality of doubt, a type of doubt which is totally new and different from Cartesian doubt.

Descartes doubts things but leans on the fortress of consciousness. Consciousness is what it is, it is what it says, it says what it is. Consciousness is, therefore, equal to itself. Only things are doubtable, only things can have appearance dissociated from their reality. It is the very heart of Cartesian doubt that the more I doubt things, the more I attest to the coincidence in being itself which constitutes the very act of *cogito.*

The problem of false-consciousness could only appear by way of a critique of culture where consciousness appears in itself as a doubtful consciousness. But—and this is a second trait—this doubt can only work through a totally new technique which is a new method of deciphering appearances. This deciphering will enable us to grasp what we have to say on demystification. What distinguishes false-consciousness from error or falsehood, and what motivates a particular type of critique, of denunciation, is the possibility of signifying another thing than what one believes was signified, that is, the possibility of the masked consciousness. These two words, "false consciousness," pertain usually to Marx. The metaphor of the mask is essentially Nietzschean. Consciousness, far from being transparent to itself, is at the same time what reveals and what conceals; it is this relation of conceal/reveal which calls for a specific reading, a *hermeneutics.* The task of hermeneutics (I will come to this particularly in the second part) has always been to read a text and to distinguish the true sense from the apparent sense, to search for the sense under the sense, to search for the intelligible text under the unintelligible text. There is, then, a proper manner of uncovering what was covered, of unveiling what was veiled, of removing the mask.

It is with this relation between the concealed and the revealed, the veiled and the unveiled, that a method of destruction of a totally new type is built: in this respect, the fundamental contribution of Marx will not remain his theory of class struggle, but the discernment of the hidden relation which connects ideology to the phenomena of domination. This reading of ideology as a symptom of the phenomena of domination will be the durable contribution of Marxism beyond its political applications. From this point of view Marx does not belong solely to the Communists. Marxism, let it never be forgotten, appeared in Germany in the middle of the last century at the heart of the departments of Protestant theology. It is, therefore, an event of western culture, and I would even say, of western theology.

Therefore, this relation between ideology on the one hand, and domination on the other, and finally submission, authorizes an interpretation of the phenomenon of religion as a sort of coded language of domination and submission. Substitute paradise for the submissive, ideological justification for the powerful, and you have a perfectly valid and legitimate reading of religion and a kind of denunciation of what religion falsely proclaims in ignorance of its economic *motivation*.

I insist again on the fact that the critique of Marx is interesting only in the degree to which it is not the critique of a moralist. Very often people have tried to retrieve Marx by saying, "But there is a moralist in him, not simply a scientist." To my mind, what is interesting in Marx is neither his science, which seems to me suspect, in any case uncertain, nor what could remain of moralism, even if it is to see an ethic reminiscent of the Prophets; but it is this art of deciphering applied to certain structures. Marx is interesting, not when he accuses the capitalists as men, but capital as a structure which is ignorant of itself as a false creation of values. It is this history of the great money fetish which is the most important work of Marx. The denunciation of the religious implications of the great fetish is the point of the Marxist critique of religion. We can surely apply this critique to ourselves; we must appropriate it to ourselves as a task of truth and authenticity.

In the same manner, the Nietzschean genealogy of morals must, I believe, be understood as a certain hermeneutics of our will—the willing will that Nietzsche tried to look for behind the "willed" will in its limited objectives. This great deciphering of the will in its significations, in its projections of value, requires of him also a very particular technique; this is more evident in Nietzsche than in Marx. Nietzsche is a "hermeneut"; it was he who first had the insight that philosophy, as philosophy of culture, was a hermeneutics, an analysis of significations. Nietzsche was the first to see that hermeneutics is not simply a reflection on the rules of exegesis—exegesis limited to texts whether the texts be texts of classical antiquity or of biblical antiquity—because culture itself is a text; consequently, philosophy is exegetical in the degree to which it is the deciphering—behind the masked signs—of the intentions and the implied significations in a strong will and in a weak will. That surpasses considerably the apparent biologism.

And in order to speak of Freud in a few words—I will have the occasion of returning to this in treating our second topic—I think he would be much better understood if we would discern his place in a critique of culture. It is through psychiatry that he exercises his critique, but at the bottom it is a critique of the ideals and of the values of this culture, to the extent that they no longer pertain to a genealogy of the will, as in Nietzsche, but a genealogy of desire. The interest of Freud is always to wonder, faced with a cultural phenomenon, how this cultural phenomenon pertains to the history of human desire, be it as a substituted object for lost primitive objects, be it as a factor of prohibition, of inhibition, of frustration, of fear. And in this sense, his critique of religion is perfectly legitimate. Any dispute with this critique can be made only on its own terms. It is necessary to accept these terms as they have been designated and marked off in the great books by Freud on the origins of morals and religion, namely, *Totem and Taboo, Moses and Monotheism,* and *The Future of an Illusion.* This critique concerns religion as far as it is effectively for us a compensation stemming from fear or a substitute for prohibited pleasures. It is obviously this "as far as" which will be the object of our study in the second essay.

Beyond this suspicion, beyond this work of deciphering, we have finally come to the third trait, to discern a common power of affirmation: we have thus to struggle in ourselves not only with suspicion, with this deciphering, but also with the affirmation. For all three of these men, finally, are positive thinkers, in the sense that they have pressed fundamentally for the restoration of man's positivity.

It is at this point that it would be necessary to relate these three, Marx, Nietzsche, and Freud, to Feuerbach. It was Feuerbach in the first place who said, and saw, that man was emptying himself into the absolute—that the absolute is a loss of substance. The task of man is to reappropriate his own substance, to stop this bleeding of substance into the sacred.

This hermeneutics was, as I just described it, a movement which sets out from an original negation, advances through a work of deciphering and a struggle against masks, and finally is put in the quest of a new affirmation. But what kind of affirmation?

You doubtless know how the *young* Marx, when he was more a philosopher than an economist, had reinterpreted the words of Feuerbach. Man, he said, in producing riches and in reproducing his existence, determines man. Ultimate affirmation, according to Marx, is this engendering of man by man through a biology of reproduction and an economy of production. What is at stake, therefore, is that man posits man. It is in this sense that man is a god for man, to take a phrase of Spinoza. I think that one would understand this discourse of the young Marx if one could align with it the themes of the old Marx, speaking of the leap from necessity to freedom. This leap from necessity to freedom by the knowledge of necessity, and by the mastery exercised on all the alienated forces, is finally the arrival of the kingdom of man. Then man enters into transparency. This is the end of false-consciousness—to know the moment when what man says is equal to what man does, and when his work is truly equal to his being. And in this kind of equation between being human, doing, praxis, and speaking, there is no longer ideology; such is the eschatology of Marxism, his true affirmative content.

Let us return to this idea of the "understood necessity"; we would do well to reappropriate this positive thrust of Marxism within the same positive thrusts in Nietzsche and Freud.

I think that one would understand the affirmations of Marxism if one also understood the affirmation which inhabits the great enterprise of Nietzschean destruction. Because the great problem of Nietzsche, and in this sense he was less naïve than Marx, if I can say so, is that God is dead, and since He is dead, culturally, man cannot survive. This is why the problem of Nietzsche concerns itself with the afterman, the superman. And Nietzsche saw very well that the great *affirmation,* which Marx believed attainable by revolution through a political-social process, demands in truth a veritable new birth of man. One can only attain and anticipate this rebirth through three broken myths: the Superman, the Eternal Return, and Dionysus—triple myths of the future and of the will to power.

To tell the truth, and Nietzsche knew it well, we do not have, we no longer have, we do not yet have the key to decipher this new myth. But perhaps this is the myth of modernity par excellence. Modernity is becoming its own myth. What Marx called "understood necessity" moving to the transparency of consciousness to itself, becomes with Nietzsche the innocence of becoming—*Unschuld des Werdens;* this innocence of becoming would ultimately be the kingdom of necessity having become freedom.

Such is the key also to the work of Freud. You know how at the end of his life Freud had remythologized, remythized all of his work; the great problem of man, in effect, is to pass from the pleasure principle into the reality principle, thereby making the sacrifice and bereavement of infantile desire. But this kingdom of necessity, this *ananké* as it is called in his last works, can be understood only in the struggle between Eros and death, between the life and death instincts. One would understand the one work by the other if one could understand that this relation, this wager for Eros against Thanatos, has with Freud the same meaning as the myth of Dionysus for the late Nietzsche. It is difficult to understand fully these three myths of the classless society or the understood necessity, of the eternal return, and of the reality principle. What they have in common, perhaps, is a certain way of blessing reality for what it is, a sort of celebration of the liberating power of necessity.

It is necessary to go this far in order to understand fundamental acquisitions that I have just placed under the theme of demystification. It is at this point that we can appropriate what Jaspers called a combat of lovers. It is a battle of lovers that we must mediate, not simply with the brute negations of one or the other, but rather with their enterprise of deciphering, and finally with their fundamental affirmation. If we can follow them this far, we will understand the positive function of the dispute with religion by all three. Because what they have in common first of all is iconoclasm, the fight against idols, that is, against the gods or the God of men.

I will try to show in the next essay that to smash the idols is also to let symbols speak. But today I do not wish to assure a good outcome in the face of so great and respectable a critique. I think with Bonhoeffer, and others, that hereafter a critique of religion, nourished by Feuerbach and these masters of suspicion pertains to the mature faith of modern man. In this sense, one can say that *this* atheism concerning the gods of men, pertains hereafter to any possible faith. What we have therefore appropriated to ourselves is first, the critique of religion as a mask, a mask of fear, a mask of domination, a mask of hate. A Marxist critique of ideology, a Nietzschean critique of resentment and a Freudian critique of infantile distress, are hereafter the views through which any kind of mediation of faith must pass.

II. DEMYTHOLOGIZATION

In this second part, I want to show how we can extend this external critique of religion into an internal critique; in the same way that I have tried to locate the place of demystification in a modern hermeneutics, I want to situate demythologization.

Whatever we may think of Bultmann's solution to the hermeneutical problem, his question is in any case unavoidable and urgent.

The question which Bultmann has posed from the interior is for me only completely understood when it is placed in relation with the question posed from the exterior by Feuerbach, Marx, Nietzsche, etc.: that of our *cultural estrangement,* of the cultural distance between, on the one hand, our world and our discourse of modern man and, on the other, the cultural expressions and the cultural world of the Gospel.

In order to understand this problem adequately, it is necessary to understand the paradoxical relationship, from the beginning of preaching, between the kernel of the preaching of the Gospel and the culture. This relationship, it seems to me, is a double one. On the one side, it is certain that the kerygma, the primitive proclamation, performs a sort of rupture in the discourse of ancient man. The preaching of the Cross, as St. Paul said, is a folly for the world (we who have read Marx and Nietzsche understand better now the notion of folly). It is a folly in this sense—and here I feel myself thoroughly faithful to Karl Barth— that this preaching is not fundamentally rooted in our experience, has no correspondence in our experience; it cannot justify itself, prove itself by something about which we could say we truthfully await; it is the eruption of something from the other side, from the totally other into our culture.

But it is necessary at once to add that this kerygma has only become visible by becoming itself a fact of culture. Not only has it ruptured into our culture, but it has appeared as a fact of culture. It has created new words, new affirmations, including an art, a philosophy, which Hegel may have been the first to think through systematically as Christology. Consequently, a double relationship is instituted with culture, a relationship of discontinuity and a relationship of continuity.

Relationship of discontinuity: This means that the Gospel will always be carried by an extraordinarily fragile testimony, that of the preacher, that of personal life, that of community. There is no proof which can support either the experience or the rationale. In this sense, the Cross *remains* a folly for the intelligent, a scandal for the wise.

But at the same time a new structure of communication, a new discourse appears which is of cultural importance, and which happens through what one could call an "available believable" (*croyable disponible*). That is what we learned first from the school of form criticism, then from Bultmann. I must say that we are today in theology doubly debtors: to Barth and to Bultmann.

Each epoch permits a believable and an unbelievable. So it is certain that the language in which "those things" have been spoken, in order to return to the expression of the beginning, is folly; but, at the same time, it is folly which speaks into a certain available believable at a given time.

In the preceding century, one was particularly concerned with the contaminations of the Gospel by Orientalism, Hellenism, etc. Think of the work of Harnack, trying to rediscover an "essence," as he said, the essence of Christianity, uncontaminated by Hellenism. Our generation has discovered something more important than these additions of Hellenism and Orientalism—something which pertains even to the composition of the text we now read: to know that the cultural vehicle has imposed its own law, that it is present in the expressions of the text. This presence first manifests itself under the form of a conception of the world which one could call mythological in the sense that it represents the world as a system of regions and of localities where the destiny of beings is deployed; it is, therefore, by a sort of eschatological cosmology, with its hell and heaven, that the cultural vehicle first becomes evident. This mythological view in itself did not constitute a scandal for ancient man. It has become a scandal for modern man, *but this scandal is not that of the Cross;* it is the *false scandal* of a cultural vehicle which is no longer ours.

But it is not only this mythological framework which falsely provokes the scandal. There is also the framework which I would call natural believable, to know that the folly of the Cross will be said within the available credible of a given culture: the signs will become miracles, the divine origin of Christ is going to be expressed by way of the virgin birth; victory over death, the Resurrection, is going to be told in statements on the empty tomb, the miraculous apparitions. But now that long and durable coalescence between the folly of the message and what has been the believable of an epoch has been broken before our eyes, and it is this dissociation between the cultural believable on the one hand, and the folly and the scandal of the Cross and the Resurrection on the other which to me constitutes the problem of demythologization. This problem is not only legitimate, but urgent and unavoidable, to such an extent that it has become the central event in our culture.

If we are always equally far from the folly of the Cross, if it is no more believable today than it was for ancient man, what has become irreversible is our cultural estrangement from a cultural vehicle which is, for us, to a great extent mythological. In this regard the work of Bultmann is perfectly legitimate, to dissociate the true scandal from the false scandal. To demythologize is to dissolve the false scandal in order to have the true scandal, the original scandal, revealed to all.

Thus, we are now in a hermeneutical age: on the one hand, the deciphering of illusions of religious consciousness belongs hereafter to the attestation of the faith of modern man; and yet, we know now that in deciphering the cultural vehicle of the text, we have to discover what is more than text, what is the preaching of the Person and of the event of Christ. To put it another way, it is a proclamation purified of its mythological vestments with which Christian preaching is confronted today.

It is true that there has always been a hermeneutics, in the sense that the Fathers of the Church posed the problem in the manner of St. Paul,[1] how can one interpret the Old Testament in terms of the New? In another sense, there has always been a hermeneutical problem. Not only was it necessary to decipher the images of the Old Testament into the New, but it was also always necessary to decipher the New Testament into life. St. Paul is the founder of this second signification of Christian hermeneutics when he showed that the relationship of the Cross to the Resurrection of Christ has its analogy in the relationship of the death of the old man and the birth of the new. Therefore, this analogical relationship, this analogy of faith between Christ and ourselves, duplicates the typological relationship between the figures of the Old Testament and the New Testament. Such was the kernel of what one could call the ancient hermeneutics. But we modern men are confronted with a totally new necessity: to know, to decipher scripture itself as a text which at the same time reveals and conceals. For the first Christians, it is certain that the kerygma was not a text. On the contrary, it was a living Word which showed the way to read a text. There was only one text, the Old Testament, and what they preached was Christ as a living Word in relationship to a text that had become, accordingly, an obsolete letter, an old letter, the *Old* Testament. But caught in its own cultural trap, the New Testament became, it also, a testament—it became a letter. And our hermeneutical problem is then the following: what to do so that the New Testament will not be a second Old Testament? What to do so that it will not be a letter? We have thus entered into an age when it is in interpreting, consequently in trying to discern what is announced through what has been said in a certain cultural language, that the faith of modern man is possible.

We are, therefore, today in a situation where it is in reinterpreting that we can believe. And I am not afraid to say that we are in a "circle" in the sense that Bultmann, taking an expression of Heidegger, speaks of the "hermeneutical circle." I can only, in effect, approach a text if I hear it as it speaks to me, if I am seized by what is said through the text. It is in this sense that it is necessary to believe in order to understand, but I cannot grasp what it has told me unless I first decipher the text.

Bultmann has forcefully understood the true nature of this circle, which is not only a *psychological* circle (to know that it is necessary to have within oneself the emotion or the experience of faith in order to approach a text), but also a *methodological* one, to know that it is the object of faith that rules the reading, but that it is also the *method* of decipherment which rules the comprehension, the comprehension itself being ruled in the *Worauf hin*, that is, in the "toward which" of the looking and the hearing.[2]

The exegete is not his own master; to understand is to place himself under the object which is at stake in the text; thus, the Christian hermeneutics must be placed in motion by the Announcement which is at stake.

There is a circle because in order to understand the text, it is necessary to believe what the text announces. But what the text announces is given nowhere else than in the deciphering of the text and in this kind of struggle between the false and the true scandal in the heart of the text itself.

I will say, then, that this circle can only be broken by the believer in the hermeneutics when he is faithful to the community, and by the "hermeneut" in the believer when he does his scientific work of exegesis. This is today the dual condition of modern man in whom struggles both a believer and an atheist; in the believer himself there confront one another an adult critic and a naïve child who listen to the Word.

I have by design *juxtaposed* the external critique and the internal critique, demystification and demythologization. We learn their organic connection when in the following essay, we incorporate them together in the struggle for the language of faith.

CHAPTER 15　　　The Language of Faith

As my title, "The Language of Faith" suggests, the subject of this essay involves an explicit limit—the problem of communication.

How can one communicate to another and to oneself the meaning of the kerygma in such a way as to develop something approaching a comprehensible discourse?

Why approach things this way? Because we are in a cultural epoch when we meet people who do not reject the faith by an explicit decision, but who do not encounter the subject matter at all; who ask, instead, "What does it mean to me when one speaks of being lost or being saved?"

In order to discuss this question, I will depart from the given which the previous essay had assumed: the distance between our culture and the one in which the proclamation, the kerygma, was written. We understand more about this cultural distance because we understand better today that it is not only a distance in relation to some very elaborated theological theories, but that it is in the Gospel itself that we now find a cultural framework of categories, of notions, to which our culture renders us strangers. How can we make ours something to which we have become strangers?

In this sense, we said before, the hermeneutical task is always to overcome a cultural distance. It is this problem which, in one way, Kierkegaard posed when he asked, "How does one become contemporaneous with Christ?" But this problem of contemporaneity which Kierkegaard posed on the level of individual affirmation, at the root of faith, is a problem which I am not going to treat at present—we are going to attack it at the center of understanding, of language, of the articulation of Christian discourse.

What we understood in the first essay as a fact, we will now treat as a *question*. In effect, this cultural distance can be surmounted in two ways. One is what we considered in the first essay and which consists of demythologizing the cultural categories of the ancient message. Only, in this work of putting into question, we are ourselves secure *in the certitude of our own culture* in saying: we, modern men, now have a certain standard of what is physical, historical, true, false, believable and unbelievable. To put it another way, before we took as a norm the believable and the unbelievable of our time. I want to show now that the task of the "hermeneut," of him who searches in order to interpret, is not simply to surrender before the standard of believable and unbelievable of his time, but also to question it. Furthermore, another way of making us contemporaneous with the text of another time is opened to us; it consists of transferring ourselves into another universe of meaning and thereby putting ourselves at a kind of distance with regard to *our* actual discourse.

Our proper task, then, is to open up our present discourse—to allow what I will call an interval of discourse in which the question of being created, the question of being lost or saved, the question of being condemned or justified, of being destroyed or glorified, a sort of preliminary to the question of faith, can make sense.[1] That will be the object of our first part.

I.

We have to struggle with the believable and the unbelievable of our time in order to make a place for intelligent discourse.

Cultural distance is not only the altering of the vehicle, but also the forgetting[2] of the radical question conveyed by the language of another time. It is necessary to undertake, therefore, a struggle against the *forgetting* of the question, that is, a struggle against our own alienation in relation to what operates in the question. And this struggle against the forgetting of the question itself is going to constitute the turning point, in the proper sense of the word, between the de-construction of which I spoke yesterday and the reinterpretation of which I will speak in the second part.

This is a turning point, because it is again a destruction, but a destruction of what destroys, a de-construction of the assurances of modern man. But this de-construction already belongs to the positive about which I want to talk in the second part, in what I will call the recollection of meaning, which is the positive task of hermeneutics.

To put it another way, we are again going to use another kind of suspicion, but a suspicion with respect to ourselves, with respect to those who suspect what is suspected. In order to do that I will begin with what seems to me to constitute the two fundamental traits of the process of secularization, which does not happen outside of us but within ourselves, at the heart of our culture, which it fundamentally defines.

The first trait—more evident than the second—is the *extension of rationality* to all areas and all levels of reality. Nature and man are involved in a process of universal objectification. This produces a reduction from the mysterious to the problematic—to use the language of Gabriel Marcel. There are, hereafter, problems to resolve, as opposed to mysteries to decipher and to contemplate. There is, therefore, in the name of this conquest of rationality, the expulsion, out of our consideration and out of our language, of the cosmic sacred, of the psychic sacred, in favor of a sort of transparency of the object. But this process can only be named secularization because it is accompanied by a second process which will finally give it its true character. At the same time that the totality of the world, with man understood as part of nature, appears to us as an object susceptible of being explained, this same man comes of age as a being responsible for his destiny. Paralleling the objectification of the world, there is set up the *autonomy of man* as an agent of his own history.

But the counterpart is this: what we have called *objectification* on the plane of knowledge becomes, in the order of the practical, of human praxis, the realm of the manageable, of the *universally available.* The world in which we live is not only a spectacle for the regard which considers it; it is the world in which we exercise domination: in this way, it is the universal order of the available.

The age of science appears to us not only as a consequence of science, but also as a new way of existing. If there has always been technology, more or less, today technology is no longer an accessory of our existence; it is the axis of it. Technology is a way of viewing the world, a means to practice it, as a universal manifestation of the available. In this sense, technology represents a new ontological regime.

Take a phenomenon of the culture as important as birth control. In affirming that the birth of a being is no longer an act of fate, but an event one can "plan," we treat life as a segment of the available, with all the ambiguity that that entails. It is at the same time the conquest of a responsibility and the elimination of a certain experience of destiny. We try to treat death in the same way, be it in seeking to hide it, as death, under euthanasia of which we all more or less dream, or be it in eluding it and in a general way treating it as the loss of a tool grown useless; death is no more than an accidental rupture which happens to the available. Birth and death are eliminated as significant experiences and as instructive destiny.

This available extends, therefore, from the realm of things to the human realm. One can certainly foresee experimentation in human biology; it extends to human economy: planned economy and reasonable politics.

This new regime is a given in the culture and, as such, unimpeachable, and at the same time a problem of existence and consequently questionable. An immense fact is now transformed into a great question.

It is an immense fact because it is not possible for us to dream of drawing back, of returning to another age. Those nostalgias are assuredly meaningless. In a certain way, it is the destiny of man to dominate over all things and perhaps even over his life; this great enterprise seeking to desacralize, to profane the universe, in its cosmic, biological, and psychic aspects, is in line with a certain destiny proclaimed in the Old Testament. Man is called to dominate over all beings—Psalm 8 mentions it, as does the first chapter of Genesis, provided that he holds love of neighbor as the limit and the rule of all usage. There is nothing, as it were, sacred, and the Old Testament already announces this possibility, this profound theological signification of desacralization.

It is not, therefore, *against* this given of culture, but in its very heart that we have to rediscover the question of "to be lost" or "to be saved." The very disconcerting paradox of this great conquest of rationality and of responsibility is that it commands simultaneously the *forgetting* of the question of the origin and the meaning of our life. A forgetting which we all feel and whose symptoms overrun us. We well know the way of life that conforms to this rationality, conforms to this universal available, is a way of life entirely on the surface of ourselves. Words like "inwardness" are in the process of losing their meaning. This hollowness of our existence is portrayed vividly in the novel, the film, and the contemporary theatre, revealing from every angle the kind of existential senselessness which is the sly counterpart of the universal available, universal objectivity.

The loss of meanings affects levels of our existence as fundamental as sexuality, which in becoming available, also became senseless, meaningless in the true sense of the word: to the degree that sexuality becomes more available, it loses its value as an expression, as an engagement of the entire person. Some psychoanalytical friends of mine have often told me how much the clientele of the analyst has changed, even since the time of Freud. One observes much less obsession due to prohibition than people who, for lack of prohibition, suffer from the loss of affectionate contact, from impotence to love or to hate. This sly and diffuse nonsense affects equally our language, and it is this, surely, that I want to go into, since it is there that we are going to choose our field of battle.

That is why I say that the loss of the question of origin and of meaning must be treated prior to the question of preaching, because it is the restoration of this ground and this kind of humus of meaning which appears to me to be one of the tasks of Christian preaching. Christian preaching not only has to continue the language of Scripture, but to restore a signifying language, a language of being and of existence, in order to find a cultural expression.

I see this task, therefore, at the turning point of destruction and re-interpretation, because it is the calling into question of the process of secularization, of the process which has instituted the distance, not only between us and the culture in which the kerygma was expressed, but between us and what is at stake in the kerygma. Also, we cannot content ourselves with a task such as we have defined it in the first essay under the title of demythologization, which would consist in re-pudiating the cultural tools of that age which is no longer our own. It is necessary for us to struggle also with the presuppositions of modern man himself, with the presupposition of his modernity.

Here I will say: to preach is not to capitulate before the believable and the unbelievable of modern man, but to struggle with the presup-positions of his culture, in order *to restore this interval of interrogation* in which the question can have meaning. If we consider the problem of secularization no longer only as the end of mythology and the religious era, as we did in the previous essay, but as an estrangement from the kerygmatic situation itself, then the whole problem of myth will from this point of view become immediately changed.

I would, in the context of the first analysis, simply place a few sign-posts in the direction that I have called preunderstanding. I see three directions in which, according to the taste and competence of each individual, it would be possible to conquer or reconquer this preunder-standing.

1. There is first the line which one could very generally call *a philo-sophic anthropology;* for my part, I understand it, I practice it in the style of phenomenology or the existential tradition; assuredly, it can be used in very different perspectives (for example, that of Teilhard de Chardin, etc.). I will speak, therefore, of the one which is most familiar to me, and I will say how a description of human existence, of the human condition, has value as *prediscourse* with respect to preaching and how preaching is responsible always for reconstructing this prediscourse.

The description of man as a being who is born into a world, bound to a body which is both himself and his aperture to the world, his fini-tude and his openness, concerns fundamentally the signification of our culture. Why? Because it is the only philosophical critique of science. A philosophical critique of science, it seems to me, does not at all consist of criticizing the results or the methods of science. There the scientist has nothing to learn uniquely from the philosopher. Scientific knowledge is a proper mode of knowledge and a proper mode of results, principles, laws, etc. But the task for which the philosopher is responsible is to understand how scientific understanding takes place within the comprehension of my existence in the world. In questioning the place and function of scientific knowledge, I happen upon the question that I have designated previously as that of objectification. What is the place of objectification, that is, of a grasp of reality according to the facts articulated in laws, elaborated in theories, and formalized in axioms according to fundamental principles? How does this articulate itself in an *existence* in which things *appear* and *disappear?* What is the relationship of objectification to the surgings of existence which constitute me?

Here, it seems to me, the task of comprehension is to show that in proportion to the progress of our objective knowledge, the condition of existing hides and conceals itself to itself. Comprehension is, then, a struggle against the deceit which progresses along with our knowledge and action, a step toward the primitive, the primordial, the original. What is there under this layer of objective knowledge? What is this way of manifesting in a world of appearances and apparitions? As Merleau-Ponty said, perception is not only one function among others which serves to prepare scientific knowledge, but it is an access to the manifestation of the world.

I would like to show the theological weight of such a reflection with respect to a text like the first chapter of Genesis. There is no possibility of squaring this account of creation with a scientifically organized universe. But if we understand that the first account of creation is actually *the theological reading of a phenomenology of perception,* everything has meaning; this account is the progressive portrayal of the theatre of our existence. Light appears here as the medium of visibility; with the progressive portrayal of the world of plants and animals intrudes what is manifested in this light; thus is articulated the original theatre of our existence, for which we moderns fashion a scientific explanation.

Consequently, it is not with a scientific discourse that we can recover the meaning of this construction, which certain scholars have presented as the building of a temple, but which is rather the setting up of a world in which man is placed at the center. Be it that this construction is cosmologically out of date, it remains existentially true. Existentially, I am born *here,* and as Valéry said: the entire universe trembles on my stalk. And this universe which trembles on my stalk is what is posited as a structure of existence about me, as *Umwelt,* as the surrounding world. Therefore, it is not a cosmological nature which is posited here, but actually an *Umwelt* of existence at the center of which man is placed as a being who will have to decide, to choose, and in which a destiny will develop. It is, therefore, the field of existence, the territory of an existential drama which is thus portrayed.

I think that everything which awakens this kind of primordial reading of our "birth-death-existence-decision-communication with others," in sum all that restores the primordial, the primitive existential, belongs in the domain of preunderstanding. To this primordial reading I will attach the comprehension of time, no longer as the objective time of the world, but as that time about which St. Augustine spoke in the eleventh book of the *Confessions,* that time which is the distension and intension of our existence, which deploys itself only from a lived present by retention of a past and anticipation of a future. All that restores the primordial tissue of existential comprehension reestablishes the first soil in which the question of the meaning, of being created, lost, and saved, can be found.

Here is a first direction which will be more familiar to those who have a knowledge of phenomenology or of philosophy of existence.

2. But I also propose another direction which seems to me a very good approach. *All that reestablishes the question of humanity taken as a whole, as a totality,* has a value of preunderstanding for preaching.

One cannot elude the fact that a consideration of totality has no other support than the singular subjects which live historically and whose existence the previous analysis has recognized. But it remains that the question which we are able to raise concerning humanity as a whole, concerning the aim of the total human adventure, is equally legitimate. It is not doubted that Christians have, in the course of history, bit by bit, abandoned this domain which was once very familiar to the Fathers of the Church, to Tertullian, and to Augustine, when he wrote the *City of God,* and that we have narrowed somewhat our vision of salvation to the isolated individual; the confrontation of theology with Marxism in particular will bring us to rediscover the question of evil and the question of salvation in a reading of the great forces which regulate our economic life, our political life, and our cultural life. We would not be going very far in an understanding of *being lost* or *being saved* if we could not read this condition in the great stories told by institutions and by structures.

I will use three examples drawn from the anthropology of Kant; great human passions, he says, revolve around three main themes: having, power, and worth. Therefore, a critique of man as being possessive will not be possible if we do not discern the meaning of having, the question of property, of money; it is in our experience with property, with money, that we learn that man is not only being, but having, and that the dialectic of being and having happens within the great institutions of property. In the same way, without reading Plato, Machiavelli, or Hobbes, we would not know what power is, our being as power; it is on this level that we discern the philosophical and theological question of the state as the titulary of power, as claiming power. And consequently it is surely on the scale of this adventure of power in the history of man that we can rediscover the question of being lost or saved. Recall how Plato opposed the philosopher to the tyrant—the tyrant, personifying power in the face of the truth—and how he established a connection between power and falsehood. Here is a problematic which is always to be raised beyond any science of politics.

Similarly, if the question of having must be deciphered in the economic world and the question of power in the political world, that of worth must be deciphered in all images of man which are born not in a singular imagination but by the means of literature and the arts. When van Gogh paints a chair, it is a figure of man; which is to say that this tableau on which man is not represented is a view of the world which denounces a certain man, which dismisses a certain man capable of inhabiting this world. When I speak of the images of man it is not simply a question of the expressed representations of man, but of imaginative projections of creation in which is implied, as from behind, as a virtual image, man himself. It is evident that it is not only through a critique of man as an economic being or as a political being, but of man as the carrier of culture and inventor of the signs of culture that this preunderstanding can be exercised in which the fundamental question of man, of a destiny or of one destined, can be raised.

3. As for the third direction in which the understanding preliminary to preaching could be explored, it is *on the level of language.* In effect, the two preceding analyses lead to this. We are responsible for conserving, to rediscover or to recreate a language which is convenient to these two themes: to exist in the world as an individual being, to pursue a historical adventure in a humanity that seeks to become whole. Language is not one power or one faculty among others. When I have said, with Kant, that there are three powers of man: having, power, worth, I cannot say there is in him a fourth which would be language. Language is not one function among others, but the semantic aspect of all functions. That is why Humboldt said that man *is* language.

I believe that here our task, in preunderstanding, is to maintain as completely open as possible the fan of our language which tends to narrow itself down to technical language, that is, to some languages which establish, describe, and order facts: factual language, language of the experimental sciences; or at the other extreme, to a perfectly formalized language, what some Anglo-Saxon philosophers now call the "metalanguages" of mathematical and symbolic logic. And assuredly our cultural discourse tends to polarize on the one hand toward some practical signals and on the other toward a symbolic language, in the sense of symbolic logic. I would be tempted to say that the focus of the process of secularization is here. If man is language, it is therefore in this *being-language* that we are really fundamentally questioned. A struggle is to be waged not only for an existential and historic fusion, as I have said, but for the language of the existential and historic.

The forgetting of which I spoke earlier is precisely a fundamental forgetting when it is a forgetting of the dimensions of language in which is expressed the possibility to exist as man, the possibility of displaying a history. It is the struggle against this central, nuclear forgetting which gives me the task of preserving beside scientific language, which objectifies, the language which understands; beside technological language, which disposes, the language which awakens possibilities. It is this language which it is now necessary to try to qualify, in appealing to a reflection on the relation between sign and symbol.

We are in quest of a language which would be appropriate to the kind of *imagination* which expresses most characteristic existential possibilities. Yes, it is necessary *to say;* it is this opening of human possibility, this *attempt* of my projects by which I advance toward my being.

In order to have this understood, I would say that it is this that happens when we go to the theatre and we understand a tragic hero, for example, Shakespeare's Richard III or Iago. It is evident that by understanding them, we certainly do not rediscover something similar in ourselves; all the less, I hope. In the theatre I can understand perfectly extreme jealousy, even in being totally estranged from this base sentiment. But I can participate imaginatively in the meaning deployed through the tragic character, by deciphering it in the signs deployed before me by the character of the play. There is a sort of reading, of existential decipherment, by the center of my existence which is imaginary, as Schelling said; imagination, here, is the organ of a veritable ontological exploration. It is this ontological exploration which in turn requires the language of accurate conceptualization.

We see now why this reflection on the language of comprehension prepares a new approach to the problem of demythologization, about which I will now speak in the second part.

II.

The dominant theme of this second part is this: how to restore meaning, how to return to contemporary discourse a language which does not pertain to the same cultural circle as mine? This is the inverse problem of demythologization, for which it was a question of eliminating an inadequate discourse which is no longer our own. Now it is a question of knowing how I can recover it, how I can express it in modern speech.

It is in order to confront this problem, in order to try to resolve it, that I pose the question of philosophy as a hermeneutics; our philosophical task, it seems to me, is to elaborate a general theory of interpretation, to do in the light of Marx, Nietzsche, and Freud what Schleiermacher had begun and Dilthey continued. It is a question of extending the problem of the understanding of texts, which has been the problem of exegesis, to the understanding of all susceptible signs as being considered as texts. It seeks, therefore, to make hermeneutics not simply a reflection on the rules of exegesis, but a sort of generalized exegesis.

I see two tasks for this discipline: for the first, a task of *validation*, of justification, and for the second, a task of *arbitration.*

The task of validation or of justification of symbolic language. It seems to me that the dimension of language in which preaching is deployed, in which therefore the kerygma is able to be spoken and myth able to be preserved, is from end to end a symbolic dimension. And I believe that the philosopher can contribute to the debate over demythologization, eventually preventing some confusions or some false alternatives, by elaborating something like a critique, in the Kantian sense of the word, of symbolic language, that is, a study of its structures, of its functioning, and a justification of its validity in relation to a certain sphere of objects. Such a critique of symbolic language must precede the discussion on myth and perhaps renew it.

The symbolic activity of thought and of language appears in the prolonging of a part of my power to dream—this is the oneiric side of the symbol—but it appears also outside of me, bound to the countenance of my universe, to the appearances of the universe such as water, fire, earth, wind, and sky. This is the approach of Eliade, in his great *Treatise of the History of Religions;* one sees there how representations of the divine have been attached to physiognomic values, for example, those of the sky; this is what we continue to do when we say, "Our Father who art in heaven"; we see in the word "sky" a sort of double meaning of the firmament sky, in which the characteristics of elevation, distance, and inaccessibility are dominating. Consequently, a certain number of physiognomic values are chosen as functions of their analogy with the dimension of existence and being which one wants to signify. There is, therefore, a sort of double essence, a double meaning of the cosmic representation, which is the movement itself of the symbol.

In short, other symbols—occasionally the same symbols—are bound to language by the power of the creation of poetic activity in the milieu of sensory images (visual, tactile, etc.). Thus the symbol has a triple root: a basically psychic root—of desire, of the libido as Freud said—

and therefore in the archaeology of human desire which comes to the surface in oneiric language; a cosmic root, by its liaison to appearances (or apparitions) of the universe; and finally it is born in the relation of image to language in the words of the poet.

I only resume this analysis[3] in order to enunciate on this basis what I will call the task of validation of symbolic language.

I believe that here the responsibility of the philosopher is to show that symbolism is not a deficient language, but that it is an appropriate language, a correct, pertinent, adequate language. To show this is the first task of general hermeneutics; what gives this language value, validity, is its overdetermination. All symbolic language is a language which says something other than what it seems to say, and by its double meaning, releases meaning, releases signification. And in the same way, it plays the role of an exploratory instrument of my existential possibilities, of my situation in being.

What is remarkable is that under its three aspects, oneiric, cosmic, or poetic, the symbol presents the following semantic structure: Through a first sense, an immediate sense which is often material and physical, an existential sense is intended; thus, in our language concerning the confession of sins (our symbols of evil have borrowed sensible representations such as stain, deviation from orientation in space, burden and weight), the power of the double-meaning operates in such a way that we do not dispose of this language, but that this is a language which disposes of us.

I believe that the great difference between logical or technical language and the above language is that a logical or technical language signifies very precisely what we have decided and posited. The fundamental task of the logician is, then, to struggle against equivocation, to struggle against double meaning, in a way that perfects a language which is perfectly univocal. Univocality is presupposed by any argumentation; it is necessary that a meaning remain identical all the time that it is carried through an argument. Consequently, the coherence of an argument depends on the unity of meaning.

With symbolic language, we are in turn faced with a language which says more than what it says, which says something other than what it says and which, consequently, grasps me because it has in its meaning created a new meaning. Here the words I use have a semantic charge which is, properly speaking, inexhaustible. To put it another way, a univocal signification is a signification in a single ray of meaning such that it is the meaning of something. In symbolic language, I find myself faced with multivocal significations in which one meaning leads to another meaning; the word "allegory," in its origin, did not mean anything different.

This double-meaning is very clear in the analysis of dreams. There is the manifest meaning, and then there is the other meaning, which one finds through analysis. There is a relationship from one text to another, and this relationship from meaning to meaning constitutes the proper semantics of this domain. We are faced with some significations which do not speak of facts but which point indirectly, by means of the meaning of the meaning, to existential and ontological possibilities.

I am persuaded that there is a profound connection between the domain of understanding, what I have described as the domain of the existential and historical, and a certain language which has a great cultural continuity and which conveys this power of the double-meaning; by the meaning of the meaning I can learn something other than facts, something other than the describable and the available.

The task of a general theory of interpretation is, therefore, to give foundation to the transcendental deduction. Kant called transcendental deduction the work of the philosopher which consists of showing that categories are justified by their power to organize a given domain of experience. Kant has done this in the order of physical knowledge, in showing that a certain number of categories like substance, causality, reciprocal action, etc., render the organization of the domain of Newtonian physics possible; similarly, to justify, to validate in its semantic structure, this symbolic language consists in showing that it remains articulate, that it articulates the domain of experience which belongs to the *preunderstanding*.

That is why I would say that there are two kinds of equivocations in our language. There is an equivocation by default, by vacillation of the meaning. It is this that the logician must eliminate if we wish to construct a scientific language, a formalizable language, a language susceptible of supporting a technology. In symbolism we are faced with languages which are equivocal not by default of univocation, but by an excess of meaning. The task of hermeneutics is, then, to struggle against forgetting (about which I have spoken above) in returning to language a richness of meaning; only these overdetermined languages, which say more than what they say, conceal an exploratory equivocation; it is this superabundance of meaning which can be relevant, revealing a ground of existence.

I would like, in finishing my analysis, to evoke the second task of a generalized hermeneutics, what I have called the task of *arbitration*. I believe that the goal—which I can only catch a glimpse of—is to attain a point where we will understand that there is a profound unity between *destroying* and *interpreting*. I think that any modern hermeneutics is a hermeneutics with a double edge and a double function. It is an effort to struggle against idols, and, consequently, it is destructive. It is a critique of ideologies in the sense of Marx; it is a critique of all flights and evasions into otherworlds in the sense of Nietzsche; a struggle against childhood fables and against securing illusions in the sense of psychoanalysis. In this sense, any hermeneutics must be disalienating, aimed at disalienation, at demystification. Long ago this was the task of second Isaiah when he tied the preaching of Yahweh to the fight against the Baals, and consequently joined iconoclasm to preaching.

But we understand better that this task of destruction pertains also to the act of listening, which is finally the positive aspect of hermeneutics. What we wish is to hear through this destruction a more original and primal word, that is, to let speak a language which though addressed to us we no longer hear, which though spoken to us we can no longer speak. It is this access to interpretation which is the driving force of hermeneutics. It is the expectation and hearing of a kerygma which is the incentive even of the enterprise of demythologization. What I have called the function of recollection, of recapitulation, which I would illustrate in the example of myth, I have left suspended until the present. I think that what we have labelled demythologization is actually the negative and, in the end, the less important side of this understanding. It seems to me that demythologization pertains only to the etiological function of myth, that is, to the rational function of explication, to the extent that each myth relates how an institution has been built, how a rite has been begun, how things have begun, how they will end.

But I believe that the semantics of symbol that I have just tried to develop shows us that the explicative function of myth is a secondary function and that in reality myth has a function that is itself symbolic. That is why I subordinate entirely the problem of myth to the problem of symbol. It is the semantics of symbol which regulates that of myth, which permits us to discern in myth what is explication and false rationality, as distinct from what is symbolic expression.

I will say, therefore, that demythologization works in reality on the level of the false rationality of myth in its explicative pretention. It is just in this fact that modern thought exercises its power of demythologization, in the degree to which it has complied with true rationality, which expels this false rationality. But I also think that having eliminated this explicative function, we must liberate the symbolic function of myth; this is what I have called "saving the myth." I have tried to show this in the domain of myths concerning the origin and the destination of evil. These myths elaborate, besides the primarily symbolic (stain, deviation, burden) a symbolism of the second degree, a symbolism from which it is necessary to free the meaning. For example, the Adamic account has a function of existential exploration since it permits us, through a sort of great hero of culpability resembling the hero of a tragedy, to read all of human history. One could say that the figure of Adam represents what Hegel called a concrete universal; it means that I read in a psychological frame, the significance of the human adventure; a singular experience, that of the Exile of Israel, becomes a universal experience by way of myths. There is a sort of universalization by means of myth—universalization on the level of imaginative exploration, of symbolic exploration. But at the same time this story, in relating events and by its very structure, gives an orientation to history and consequently introduces a temporality, held between the *Exile* and the *Kingdom.* Finally, more fundamentally, this myth of Paradise Lost tries to relate, by a past event, disruption in human experience: on the one hand I confess that I am a good creature, and on the other hand I confess that evil is already there. The myth here explores the confrontation of the two discourses, the discourse of creation related later in the first chapter of Genesis, and also the confession of sins; I am radically evil but fundamentally good. It is this confrontation of the originally good and the radically evil which is explored by means of a story, which attempts to catch that moment on which Kierkegaard has meditated in the *Concept of Dread,* that moment of slipping where innocence is no longer and where evil is not yet there, and yet where everything has already occurred; this is what the myth says of an ancestor whom I could never recover in any history and who figures the priority of evil in relation to each man.

I do not think that to break the cultural framework of a myth is the fundamental act of hermeneutics. I think that, on the contrary, the fundamental act of hermeneutics is the liberation of the significant potential held in suspense in the myth and which consequently constitutes its symbolic content.

It is in this framework that one could try to show the validity and the limits of a Marxist approach and of an approach by psychoanalysis. Each of these approaches is not limited because something is prohibited to it (as if one could say to the iconoclast: up to here but no farther!), but because each approach is limited by the structure of its own theory. The task of arbitration that I evoke here would consist of a reflection of the Kantian type on the legitimacy, or the limit of legitimacy, of each particular hermeneutics.

I think that this is a task, a program, and that the modesty of philosophic reflection when faced by the theologian and the exegete consists in admitting that it is the exegete who has taught us what it is to read a text. If we succeed in understanding that the entirety of human existence is a text to be read, we will be at the threshold of that general hermeneutics, by means of which I have tried to define the task of the next philosophy.

Have I responded to all the questions raised? Certainly not. I want at least to make it understood how the conception of hermeneutics which

I have just outlined permits confrontation with the fundamental atheism of our contemporary culture.

In conceiving hermeneutics as a hermeneutics with a *double edge,* I bind in an indivisible way the de-construction of religious language and the restoration of a meaning capable of giving a language to faith.

For what I have prepared myself to confront is the ultimate core of the destructive hermeneutic; this core, one discovers, is not *suspicion,* the *reduction* of ideologies and illusions, but the affirmation of man in the recognition of necessity; *amor fati!* love of fate, said Nietzsche. We are thus brought to say that the stake of any discernment, at the heart of ourselves, between the authentic and the inauthentic, is the meaning that we give to the *affirmation.* What do we affirm? What is our source, our resource of affirmation? It is at this ultimate level that I confront the three princes of necessity: man, they say, must come to love necessity—to love fate—to love things as they are and accept the fact that his life disappears, that reality continues, anonymous and silent. Such is the atheistic *affirmation* of my culture.

But the question that I pose to myself, then, is this: What are the place and origin of *possibility?* Faced with this ascetics of necessity, I see the moment in the other hermeneutics when I encounter the problem of what I will call the grace of imagination, the surging up of the possible: how is man a possible, not a necessary, reality?

It is here that I would like to respond with the Kierkegaardian part of myself to this Spinozic myth of totality and necessity. As I understand it, man is always sustained by his mythicopoetic core; he is always created and recreated by a generative word.

I believe that the fundamental theme of Revelation is this awakening and this call, into the heart of existence, of the imagination of the possible. The possibilities are opened before man which fundamentally constitute what is revealed. The revealed as such is an opening to existence, a possibility of existence. Consequently, the circle of the atheistic hermeneutics recloses on the necessary, but the circle of the kerygmatic hermeneutics opens on the generation of possibility in the heart of imagination of our language.

Therefore, the ultimate stake is what I have just called the mythicopoetic center of imagination and which is at the same time the point of origin of the word—of man as word. Feuerbach, the common master of all atheism, tells us: let us return to man what he has given to God, so that man reappropriates what he has poured into the sacred by emptying himself. But I think that our question—and we understand it better after Marx, Nietzsche, and Freud—is: what is man? Do we know man better than we know God? In the end, I do not know what man is. My confession to myself is that man is instituted by the word, that is, by a language which is less spoken *by* man than spoken *to* man.

Finally, what constitutes our answer to the apology of Necessity and resignation is the faith that man is founded, at the heart of his mythico-poetic power, by a creative word. Is not The Good News the instigation of the *possibility* of man by a creative word?

CHAPTER 16

Listening to the Parables of Jesus

To preach today on the Parables of Jesus looks like a lost cause. Have we not already heard these stories at Sunday School? Are they not childish stories, unworthy of our claims to scientific knowledge, in particular in a University Chapel? Are not the situations which they evoke typical of a rural existence which our urban civilization has made nearly ununderstandable? And the symbols, which in the old days awakened the imagination of simple-minded people, have not these symbols become dead metaphors, as dead as the leg of the chair? More than that, is not the wearing out of these images, borrowed from the agricultural life, the most convincing proof of the general erosion of Christian symbols in our modern culture?

To preach today on the Parables of Jesus—or rather to preach the Parables—is indeed a wager: the wager that in spite of all contrary arguments, it is still possible to listen to the Parables of Jesus in such a way that we are once more astonished, struck, renewed, and put in motion. It is this wager which led me to try to preach the Parables and not only to study them in a *scholarly* way, as a text among other texts.

The first thing that may strike us is that the Parables are radically profane stories. There are no gods, no demons, no angels, no miracles, no time before time, as in the creation stories, not even founding events as in the Exodus account. Nothing like that, but precisely people like us: Palestinian landlords traveling and renting their fields, stewards and workers, sowers and fishers, fathers and sons; in a word, ordinary people doing ordinary things: selling and buying, letting down a net into the sea, and so on. Here resides the initial paradox: on the one hand, these stories are—as a critic said—narratives of normalcy—but on the other hand, it is the Kingdom of God that is said to be like this. The paradox is that the *extraordinary* is *like* the *ordinary*.

Some other sayings of Jesus speak of the Kingdom of Heaven: among them, the eschatological sayings, and they seem to point toward something Wholly-Other, to something beyond, as different from our history as heaven is from earth. Therefore, the first thing which may amaze us is that at the very moment we were expecting the language of the myth, the language of the sacred, the language of mysteries, we receive the language of our history, the language of the profane, the language of open drama.

And it is this contrast between the kind of thing *about* which it is spoken—the Kingdom of Heaven—and the kind of thing *to* which it is compared which may put in motion our search. It is not the religious man in us, it is not the sacred man in us, but precisely the profane man, the secular man who is summoned.

The second step, beyond this first shock, will be to ask what makes sense in the Parables. If it is true—as contemporary exegesis shows—that the Kingdom of God is not compared to the man who . . . to the woman who . . . to the yeast which . . . but to *what happens* in the story, we have to look more closely at the short story itself, to identify what may be paradigmatic in it. It is here that we run the risk of sticking too closely to the sociological aspects which I evoked at the beginning when I said that the situations described in the Parables are those of agricultural activity and of rural life. What makes sense is not the situations as such, but, as a recent critique has shown, it is the *plot,* it is the structure of the drama, its composition, its culmination, its denouement.

If we follow this suggestion, we are immediately led to look at the critical moments, at the decisive turning points in the short dramas. And what do we find? Let us read once more the shortest, the most condensed of all the Parables: Matthew 13, verse 44. Three critical moments emerge: *finding* the treasure, *selling* everything else, *buying* the field. The same threefold division may be found in the two following Parables: Matthew 13:45–46, 47–49.

If we attempt, now, to let these three critical moments expand, so to say, in our imagination, in our feeling, in our thought, they begin to *mean much more* than the apparent practical, professional, economical, commercial transactions told by the story. *Finding* something . . . This simple expression encompasses all the kinds of *encounters* which make of our life the contrary of an acquisition by skill or by violence, by work or by cunning. Encounter of people, encounter of death, encounter of tragic situations, encounter of joyful events. Finding the other, finding ourselves, finding the world, recognizing those whom we had not even noticed, and those whom we don't know too well and whom we don't know at all. Unifying all these kinds of finding, does not the parable point toward a certain fundamental relation to time? Toward a fundamental way of being in time? I mean, this mode which deserves to be called the Event par excellence. Something happens. Let us be prepared for the newness of what is new. Then we shall "find."

But the art of the parable is to link dialectically *finding* to two other critical turning points. The man who found the treasure went and sold everything he had and *bought* it. Two new critical points, which we could call after a modern commentator, himself taught by Heidegger: Reversal and Decision. Decision does not even come second. Before Decision; Reversal. And all those who have read some religious texts other than biblical, and even some texts other than religious, know how much has been invested in this word "conversion," which means much more than making a new choice, but which implies a shift in the direction of the look, a reversal in the vision, in the imagination, in the heart, before all kinds of good intentions and all kinds of good decisions and good actions. Doing appears as the conclusive act, engendered by the Event and by the Reversal. First, encountering the Event, then changing one's heart, then doing accordingly. This succession is full of sense: the Kingdom of God is compared to the chain of these three acts: letting the Event blossom, looking in another direction, and doing with all one's strength in accordance with the new vision.

Of course, all the Parables are not built in a mechanical way along the same pattern. If this were the case, they would lose for that very reason the power of surprise. But each of them develops and, so to say, dramatizes one of the other of these three critical terms.

Look at the so-called parables of Growth: Matthew 13:31-33. This unexpected growth of the mustard seed, this growth beyond all proportion, draws our attention in the same direction as finding. The natural growth of the seed and the unnatural size of the growth speak of something which happens to us, invades us, overwhelms us, beyond our control and our grasp, beyond our willing and our planning. Once more the Event comes as a gift.

Some other Parables which have not been read this morning will lay the stress on the Reversal. Thus the Prodigal Son changes his mind, reverts his glance, his regard, whereas it is the father who waits, who expects, who welcomes, and the Event of the encounter proceeds from the conjunction of this Reversal and this Waiting.

In some other Parables, the emphasis will fall on the decision, on the doing, even on the good deed, as in the Parable of the Good Samaritan. But, reduced to the last critical turn, the Parable seems to be nothing more than a moral fable, a mere call to "do the same." Thus reduced to a moral teaching, the Parable ceases to be a Parable of the Kingdom to become an allegory of charitable action. We have to replace it within the inclusion of the Parables of Event, Reversal, and Decision, if the moral fable is to speak once more as a Parable.

Having made, in that way, this second step and recognized the dramatic structure, the articulation of the plot which makes sense, we are ready for a new discovery, for a new surprise. If we ask: "And finally, what is the Kingdom of Heaven," we must be prepared to receive the following answer. The Gospel says nothing about the Kingdom of Heaven, except that it is *like* . . . It does not say what it *is,* but what it *looks like.* This is hard to hear. Because all our scientific training tends to use images only as provisory devices and to replace *images* by *concepts.* We are invited here to proceed the other way. And to think according to a mode of thought which is not metaphorical for the sake of rhetoric, but for the sake of what it has to say. Only *analogy* approximates what is wholly practical. The Gospel is not alone to speak in that way. We have elsewhere heard Hosea speaking of Yahweh as the Husband, of Israel as the Wife, of the Idols as the Lovers. No translation in abstract language is offered, only the violence of a language which, from the beginning to the end, *thinks through* the Metaphor and never *beyond.* The power of this language is that it abides to the end *within* the tension created by the images.

What are the implications of this disquieting discovery that Parables allow no translation in conceptual language? At first sight, this state of affairs exposes the weakness of this mode of discourse. But for a second glance, it reveals the unique strength of it. How is it possible? Let us consider that with the Parables we have not to do with a unique story dramatically expanded in a long discourse, but with a full range of short Parables gathered together in the Unifying form of the Gospel. This fact means something. It means that the Parables make a whole, that we have to grasp them as a whole and to understand each one in the light of the other. The Parables make sense together. They constitute a network of intersignification, if I dare say so. If we assume this hypothesis, then our disappointment—the disappointment which a scientific mind perceives when it fails to draw a coherent idea, an equivocal concept from this bundle of metaphors—our disappointment may become amazement. Because there is now more in the Parables taken together than in any conceptual system about God and his action among us. There is more to *think through* the richness of the images than in the coherence of a simple concept. What confirms this feeling is the fact that we can draw from the Parables nearly all the kinds of theologies which have divided Christianity through the centuries. If you isolate the Parable of the Lost Coin, if you interrupt the dynamism of the story and extract from it a frozen concept, then you get the kind of doctrine of predestination which pure Calvinism advocated. But if you pick the Parable of the Prodigal Son and extract from it the frozen concept of personal conversion, then you get a theology based on the absolutely free will of man, as in the doctrine that the Jesuits opposed to the Calvinists, or the Protestant Liberals to the Orthodox Protestants.

Therefore, it is not enough to say that the Parables say nothing directly concerning the Kingdom of God. *We must say in more positive terms, that taken all together, they say more than any rational theology.* At the very moment that they call for theological clarification, they start shattering the theological simplifications which we attempt to put in their place. This challenge to rational theology is nowhere more obvious than in the Parable of the Good Seed spoiled by the darnel sowed among the wheat. The farmer's servants went to their master and said, "Sir, was it not good seed that you sowed in your field? Then where has the darnel come from?" Such is the question of the philosopher when he discusses theoretically the so-called problem of evil. But the only answer which we get is itself metaphorical: "This is an enemy's doing." And you may come through several kinds of theologies in agreement with that enigmatic answer. Because there is more to think about in the answer said in a parabolic way than any kind of theory.

Let me propose one more step, a step which I hope will increase our surprise, our amazement. Many people will be tempted to say, "Well, we have no difficulty dropping all systems, including rational or rationalizing theologies." Then, if all theories are wrong, let us look at the Parables as mere practical teaching, as moral or maybe political teaching. If Parables are not pieces of dogmatic theology, let us look at them as pieces of practical theology. This proposal sounds better at first sight than the first one. Is it not said that to listen to the word is to put it into practice? This obviously is true. But what does that mean, to put in practice the Parables?

I fear that a too-zealous attempt to draw immediate application from the Parables for private ethics or for political morality must necessarily miss the target. We immediately surmise that such an indiscreet zeal quickly transposes the Parables into trivial advice, into moral platitudes. And we kill them more surely by trivial moralizing than by transcendent theologizing.

The Parables obviously teach, but they don't teach in an ordinary way. There is, indeed, something in the Parables which we have as yet overlooked and which they have in common with the Proverbs used by Jesus according to the Synoptics. This trait is easy to identify in the Proverbs. It is the use of paradox and hyperbole, in such aphorism and antithetical formulae as: "Whoever seeks to gain his life will lose it, but whoever loses his life will preserve it." As one commentator says, the paradox is so acute in this overturning of fates that it jolts the imagination from its vision of a continuous sequence between one situation and another. Our project of making a totality continuous with our own existence is defeated. For who can plan his future according to the project of losing "in order to win"? Nevertheless, these are not ironical nor skeptical words of wisdom. In spite of everything, life is granted by the very means of this paradoxical path. The same has to be said of hyperbolic orders like: "Love your enemies, do good to those who hate you." Like paradox, hyperbole is intended to jolt the hearer from the project of making his life something continuous. But whereas humor or detachment would remove us from reality entirely, hyperbole leads back to the heart of existence. The challenge to the conventional wisdom is at the same time a way of life. We are first disoriented before being reoriented.

Does not the same happen with the Parables? Is their way of teaching different from that of reorientation by disorientation? We have not been aware enough of the paradoxes and the hyperbole implied in those short stories. In most of them there is an element of extravagance which alerts us and summons our attention.

Consider the extravagance of the landlord in the Parable of the Wicked Husbandman, who after having sent his servants, sent his son. What Palestinian property owner living abroad would be foolish enough to act like this landlord? Or what can we say about the host in the Parable of the Great Feast who looks for substitute guests in the streets? Would we not say that he was unusual? And in the Parable of the Prodigal Son, does not the father overstep all bounds in greeting his son? What employer would pay the employees of the eleventh hour the same wages as those hired first?

The Parables of Growth are no less implausible. Here it is the hyperbole of the proverb that is at work. What small seed would yield a huge tree where birds can nest? The contrast is hardly less in the Parable of the Leaven. As to the Parable of the Sower, it is constructed on the same contrast. If it points to eschatological plenitude, it is because the yield of grain in the story surpasses by far all reality.

The most paradoxical and most outlandish Parables, as far as their realism is concerned, are those which Joachim Jeremias has grouped under the titles "The Imminence of Catastrophe" and "It may be Too Late." The schema of *occasion,* which only presents itself *one time* and after which it is *too late,* includes a dramatization of what in ordinary experience we call seizing the occasion, but this dramatization is both paradoxical and hyperbolic; paradoxical because it runs counter to actual experience where there will always be another chance, and hyperbolic because it exaggerates the experience of the unique character of the momentous decisions of existence.

At what village wedding has anyone slammed the door on the frivolous maidens who do not consider the future (and who are, after all, as carefree as the lilies of the field)? It is said that "these are Parables of Crisis." Of course, but the hour of testing and the "selective sorting" is signified by a crisis in the story which intensifies the surprise, the scandal, and sometimes provokes disapproval as when the denouement is "unavoidably tragic."

Let me draw the conclusion which seems to emerge from this surprising strategy of discourse used by Jesus when he told the Parables to the disciples and to the mob. To listen to the Parables of Jesus, it seems to me, is to let one's imagination be opened to the new possibilities disclosed by the extravagance of these short dramas. If we look at the Parables as at a word addressed first to our imagination rather than to our will, we shall not be tempted to reduce them to mere didactic devices, to moralizing allegories. We will let their poetic power display itself within us.

But, was not this poetic discussion already at work, when we read the Parable of the Pearl and the Parable of Event, Reversal, and Decision? Decision, we said, moral decision comes third. Reversal precedes. But the Event opens the path. The poetic power of the Parable is the power of the Event. Poetic means more than poetry as a literary genre. Poetic means creative. And it is in the heart of our imagination that we let the Event happen, before we may convert our heart and tighten our will.

Listen, therefore, to the Parables of Jesus (Matthew 13:31–32 and 45–46):

> And another parable he put before them, saying, "The Kingdom of heaven is like a grain of mustard seed which a man took and sowed in his field; it is the smallest of all seeds, but when it has grown it is the greatest of shrubs and becomes a tree, so that the birds of the air come and make nests in its branches.
>
> "Again, the kingdom of heaven is like a merchant in search of fine pearls, who, on finding one pearl of great value, went and sold all that he had and bought it."

Notes

CHAPTER 3, THE HERMENEUTICS OF SYMBOLS AND PHILOSOPHICAL REFLECTION

1. The first part of this study disengages the methodological implications of *Finitude et Culpabilité*: Vol. II, *La symbolique du mal* (Aubier, 1960). Extracts of it were published in the review *Esprit* (July–August, 1959) under the title "Le symbole donne à penser." In the second and third parts I sketch out some of the themes to which will be devoted Vol. III of *Finitude et Culpabilité*.

2. The long way seems to me all the more necessary when I confront my interpretation with that of psychoanalysis. An introspective psychology does not hold up in face of the Freudian or Jungian hermeneutics; whereas a reflective approach, by the detour of a hermeneutics of cultural symbols, not only holds up but also opens a true debate of one hermeneutics with another. The regressive movement to the archaic, the infantile, the instinctual, must be confronted with the progressive movement of an ascending synthesis, of the symbolism of confession.

3. Augustine *Contra Secundinum*, nn. 11–12; *De libero arbitrio*, I, 16, 35; II, 19, 53–54.

4. Augustine *Contra Felicem*, n. 8.

5. Plato *Republic*, bk. IV.

6. The *Treatise to Simplician* of the year 397 is interesting in this regard, for it precedes the first anti-Pelagian treatise by fourteen years; it already contains the essence of the Augustinian argumentation.

7. "Essai sur le mal radical" (in *La religion dans les limites de la simple raison*, p. 56).

8. Ibid., p. 60, note 1.

9. "By tendency (*propensio*) I understand the subjective ground of the possibility of an inclination (habitual appetite, *concupiscentia*) as contingent for humanity in general" (*La religion* . . . , p. 48).

10. Ibid., p. 63.

11. Ibid., p. 65.

CHAPTER 6, FROM EXISTENTIALISM TO THE
PHILOSOPHY OF LANGUAGE

1. Ricoeur here is referring to volume 1 of *Philosophie de la volonté,* published
in French as *Le volontaire et l'involontaire* (Paris: Aubier, 1950) and in English
translation as *Freedom and Nature: The Voluntary and the Involuntary,* trans.
Erazim V. Kohák (Evanston: Northwestern University Press, 1966), [Ed.].

2. Ricoeur is here referring to his study with Mikel Dufrenne, *Karl Jaspers et
la philosophie de l'existence* (Paris: Seuil, 1947) and to his own work, *Gabriel
Marcel et Karl Jaspers* (Paris: Temps Présent, 1947), [Ed.].

3. Ricoeur translated volume 1 of Husserl's *Ideen* into French under the title
Idées directrices pour une phénoménologie (Paris: Gallimard, 1950), which also
offered Ricoeur's copious notes and commentary on Husserl's work. Ricoeur
also supplied an appendix dealing with Husserlian phenomenology to E. Bréhier,
Histoire de la philosophie allemande, 3rd ed. (Paris: Vrin, 1954), [Ed.].

4. See "The Model of the Text: Meaningful Action Considered as a Text,"
Social Research 38 (1971): pp. 529–562, [Ed.].

CHAPTER 10, METAPHOR AND THE MAIN PROBLEM
OF HERMENEUTICS

1. My main disagreement concerns their use of the "field of associated commonplaces" or of the "potential range of connotations" which concerns more
trivial metaphors than genuine metaphors. In that case, which is a lone paradigmatic, the contextual effect goes further than mere actualization of the potential
range of commonplaces or connotations. I shall return to this point in the second
part. The theory of metaphor must address itself directly to novel metaphor and
not proceed through an expansion from flat metaphors to novel metaphors.

2. Max Black, *Models and Metaphors: Studies in Language and Philosophy*
(Ithaca: Cornell University Press, 1962), page references included in text.

3. Monroe C. Beardsley, *Aesthetics: Problems in the Philosophy of Criticism*
(New York: Harcourt, 1958), page references included in text.

CHAPTER 11, EXPLANATION AND UNDERSTANDING

1. "Introduction à l'analyse structurale du récit," *Communication* 8, p. 19.
2. Ithaca: Cornell University Press, 1971.
3. Ithaca: Cornell University Press, 1957.

CHAPTER 12, A PHILOSOPHICAL INTERPRETATION
OF FREUD

1. Paul Ricoeur, *Freud and Philosophy: An Essay on Interpretation,* trans.
Denis Savage (New Haven: Yale University Press, 1970).
2. Ibid., p. 65.
3. Ibid., p. 395.
4. Ibid., footnote 69, p. 398.

CHAPTER 13, THE QUESTION OF PROOF IN FREUD'S
PSYCHOANALYTIC WRITINGS

1. My presentation is limited in two ways. First, I am restricting myself to Freud's work, and I will refrain from making any judgment concerning developments in psychoanalysis' problematic or its epistemology after Freud. Second, I am limiting myself to Freud's written work, not having had access to his oral teaching, his working notes, or any information apart from his published works.

2. Cf., for example, the discussion that followed Heinz Hartmann's study, "Psychoanalysis as a Scientific Method," at the Washington symposium in 1958, and recall Ernest Nagel's biting comments published under the title "Methodological Issues in Psychoanalytic Theory," in the volume *Psychoanalysis, Scientific Method and Philosophy*, edited by Sidney Hook (1959).

3. Despite efforts as remarkable as those of Rapaport in *The Structure of Psychoanalytic Theory*, psychoanalysts have not managed to convince epistemologists that psychoanalysis is capable of satisfying the requirements of operational analysis as it is defined, for example, by P. W. Bridgman. We need only recall here B. F. Skinner's strident criticism in the volume on psychoanalysis of the *Minnesota Studies in the Philosophy of Science* (ed. by Feigel and Scriven, 1956). For him, Freud's mental entities are the same sort of thing as phlogiston or ether are in physical theory; the forces alleged by psychoanalysis cannot be quantified, so they cannot be integrated into an empirical science worthy of the name. Moreover, it is doubtful whether reformulations of psychoanalysis to a modified or revised form of operationalism would meet the requirements of operational analysis any better than did Freud's own presentation in the *Outline of Psychoanalysis*. In order to assimilate psychoanalytic entities to operationalism's "intervening variables" and "dispositional concepts," they would have to refer to facts which were themselves observables in the sense that this term is used in logical empiricism.

4. I will leave until later a discussion of whether in saying this motive is to be opposed to cause, meaning to energy, and understanding to explanation. This may be too hasty a conclusion which does not take into account as yet unexamined facts and which, at first glance, is not in line with the semantic, signifying, and sayable trait singled out by the analytic situation and relationship.

5. Confronted with a patient who takes no account of the difference which exists between reality and imagination, "we are tempted to bear a grudge against the patient because he bores us with his imaginary stories. Reality seems to us to be separated from the imagination by an unbridgeable gap and we take it in a totally different way. This is, by the way, also the patient's point of view when he is thinking normally." Here, then, is the paradox: in what follows, Freud says that the administration of the cure forbids us either to rid the patient of his illusions or to take him at his word, that is, to consider the difference between the imaginary and the real as relevant.

6. "These objects and directions, or their derivatives, still persist with a certain intensity in the representations of the fantasy. Hence it suffices for the libido to return to its representations to find the pathway which must lead to all its repressed fixations. . . . The libido's regression toward its imaginary objects or fantasies constitutes one intermediary step along the path which leads to the formation of symptoms."

7. Freud defines it specifically as follows: "Mourning is regularly the reaction to the loss of a loved person, or to the loss of some abstraction which has taken the place of one, such as one's country, liberty, an ideal and so on" ("Mourning and Melancholia," S.E., 14, 243).

8. The "experience of reality has shown that the loved object has ceased to exist and the whole libido is called upon to renounce the tie which bound it to this object. It is against this fact that an understandable revolt is produced."

9. There are other senses in which psychoanalysis displays historical features. If, for example, we emphasize the first term of the expression "case-histories," we may characterize the analytic situation as historical in the sense that what unfolds itself there occurs only once. Even if a typology may serve as a guide in the diversity of individual situations, types remain the intellectual instruments of an understanding governed by singular instances. The type is not a law for which the individual would be only an example. On the contrary, it is in the service of the "case" that the type offers the mediation of its intelligibility. In this sense the word "case" does not have the same sense in psychoanalysis as in the observational sciences due to this inverse relation of the type to the case. Later on we will see what difficulties this specific relation raises for the question of proof in psychoanalysis. The analytic experience also has many other historical features. It will suffice here to recall the archaism of the unconscious, the stages of the libido, the genesis of the object-choice, the history of the substitute objects, the relation between primary and secondary processes, etc. All these traits in one way or another contribute to the narrative structure of the analytic experience.

10. In the essay entitled "The Unconscious," Freud will again say, "It is of course only as something conscious that we know it, after it has undergone transformation (*Umsetzung*) or translation (*Übersetzung*) into something conscious" (S.E., 14, 166). And in the same sense, "it may be pointed out that the interpretations of psychoanalysis are primarily translations from a mode of expression that is alien to us into one with which our thought is familiar" ("The Claims of Psychoanalysis to Scientific Interest," S.E., 13, 176). Elsewhere Freud compares censorship to press censorship. "If the analogy is not pursued too strictly, we may say that repression has the same relation to other methods of defence as omission has to distortion of the text, and we may discover in the different forms of this falsification parallels to the variety of ways in which the *ego* is altered" (*Analysis Terminable and Interminable*, S.E., 23, 236).

11. Freud cautiously speaks of it in the following terms: "Two separate functions may be distinguished in mental activity during the construction of a dream: the production of the dream-thoughts, and their transformation into the content of the dream." This activity "is completely different (from waking thought) qualitatively and for that reason not immediately comparable to it. It does not think, calculate or judge in any way at all; it restricts itself to giving things a new form" (S.E., 5, 506–507).

12. Evidence of this can be found in chapter 7 of *The Interpretation of Dreams* to give a graphic representation of the above by means of the famous schema of the psychical apparatus which Freud calls an "auxiliary representation." Thanks to this topographic representation, regression acquires its properly topographic meaning in conjunction with the forces which compel this movement backwards.

13. As is well known, it is the acknowledgment of the strategic role of resistances and of the struggle against resistances which made Freud decide to abandon Breuer's cathartic method insofar as it was aimed at reaching an anamesis without work. Speaking in 1910 of "The Future Prospects of Psychoanalytic Therapy" (S.E., 11, 141–151), Freud described his technical innovations in these terms: "As you know, our technique has undergone a fundamental transformation. At the time of the cathartic treatment what we aimed at was the elucidation of the symptoms; we then turned away from the symptoms and devoted ourselves instead to uncovering the 'complexes,' to use a word which Jung has made indispensable; now, however, our work is aimed directly at finding out and overcoming the 'resistances,' and we can justifiably rely on the complexes coming to light without difficulty as soon as the resistances have been recognized and removed" (ibid., p. 144). This very struggle against resistances invites us to be forewarned against overestimating interpretation in its analytic form. It is completely ineffective for revealing to the patient the meaning of his symptoms so long as the entirely intellectual understanding of their meaning has not been incorporated into the work of analysis. Moreover, as Freud wrote in 1910 in " 'Wild' Psychoanalysis," "informing the patient of his unconscious regularly results in an intensification of the conflict in him and an exacerbation of his troubles" (S.E., 11, 225). Freud even goes so far as to warn beginners in analytic treatment against trying to make an exhaustive interpretation of dreams for this can be used by the resistance to delay the healing process (see "The Handling of Dream-Interpretation in Psychoanalysis," S.E., 12, 91–96).

14. Our authors concede that Freud's second topography—the ego, id, and superego—preserves more of the features of this twofold process of desymbolization and resymbolization than does the first topography (which alone, moreover, deserves to be called a topography). The three agencies, in effect, designate positions in relation to this twofold process: the neuter id designates the derivation of that part of ourselves which was banished from public communication; the *"über"* (super, over) of the superego designates the agency of interdiction, itself objectified and reified, which bars the way of the subject's becoming an ego. But it is in relation to the capacity to become an ego that there is an id and a superego, in accordance with Freud's own celebrated adage: *Wo es war, soll ich werden* ("Where id was, there shall ego be"). It is therefore necessary to give up the idea of an asymbolic unconscious, that is, one foreign to the very fate of desymbolization. If Freud nevertheless clung to this idea as, for example, in *The Ego and the Id,* it was doubtless for a lack of a suitable linguistic model, as Marshall Edelson has convincingly demonstrated in *Language and Interpretation in Psychoanalysis* (New Haven: Yale University Press, 1975). But it was also and especially because of an obstinate will to pattern psychoanalysis after the natural sciences and to maintain its discovery within the aura of the *Aufklärung* which presided over its birth.

15. See my "Language and Image in Psychoanalysis" appearing in *Psychiatry and the Humanities,* vol. III, edited by Joseph H. Smith (New Haven: Yale University Press).

16. I therefore find myself in agreement with some of Habermas's remarks concerning the incorporation of causal explanation into *Selbstreflexion.* But is this mixture of self-understanding and causal explanation clarified by a return to

the Hegelian theme from the Jena period of the "causality of destiny"? And is the process of resymbolization, to the extent that it intends to overcome causal connections in order to recover the current of personal motivations and public symbolization, capable of being assimilated to the Hegelian *Begreifen* which is precisely the counterpart of the causality of destiny? Already in *Freud and Philosophy* I noted this "fated" side of causality in Freudian explanation.

17. Aristotle already notes at the beginning of the *Nicomachean Ethics* that we cannot call for the same *acribie* in human things as in the natural sciences, and that it is always the nature of the things characteristic of an area of investigation which determines the type of adequation appropriate to that discipline.

18. This is the *Redlichkeit*—the intellectual probity—dear to Nietzsche. In my study on "Psychiatry and Moral Values" (in Silvano Arieti et al., *American Handbook of Psychiatry* [New York: Basic Books, 1974], 2nd. ed., vol. I, pp. 976–990), I suggest that *Redlichkeit* is the only ethical "value" which remains within the ethical neutrality of the analytic relationship.

19. We stated earlier in what way the incongruities of behavior giving rise to psychoanalysis could be considered as disturbances in communication, as modes of excommunication, due to the privatization of disconnected symbols.

20. It is, therefore, of fundamental importance to clearly distinguish the criteria for extending self-consciousness and for liberating our capacities for interaction and symbolic communication from the criteria for instrumental action.

21. Freud was not overly disturbed by his own discovery of the range and ramifications of the imaginary domain because he remained faithful to the threefold idea that fantasy was set in opposition to the real, that in the final analysis it derives from an actual experience either in the individual's childhood or in the archaic history of humanity, and that lastly it is something to be cleared away in favor of the reality principle (see the short paper of 1911, "Formulations on the Two Principles of Mental Functioning," S.E., 12, 218–226). In this way he was able to tie his truth principle in psychoanalysis to that of reality inasmuch as the real is the opposite of the fantasy, the origin of the fantasy, and the ultimate horizon beyond the death of the fantasy. And so, entering this foreign inner country he called "psychical reality," Freud never relinquished the stubborn conviction that the fantasy stood out against the background of a primordial contact with an undeceptive reality. This undeceptive reality, therefore, continued to be at once the measure of the fantasy's falsity, the real origin of the fantasy, and the principle which was to prevail over the pleasure principle under which the fantasy was classed and dismissed. We may say that it was on the basis of this concept of reality that Freud felt he was able to maintain the continuity between psychoanalysis and the sciences of physical and biological reality.

22. It is this hypothesis that the cure is itself a liberation of fantasies as much as a struggle against resistances which made me take the recognition of the fantasy as a criterion for deciding what counts as a fact in psychoanalysis. And it is because psychoanalysis is concerned with the fate of the fantasy that its domain cannot be reduced to that of physiology or psychophysiology.

In the same sense, I suggested in *Freud and Philosophy* that analytic experience aims at articulating several prime signifiers of existence (phallus, father, mother, death, etc.) in order to make their structuring function appear. And I

253   Notes

said, "What confronts us in this reasoned mythology is the problem of access to true discourse, which is something quite different from the adaptation that some appeal to in their haste to overcome the scandal of psychoanalysis and to render analysis socially acceptable. For who knows where a single true discourse might lead with respect to the established order, that is to say, with respect to the idealized discourse of the established disorder?" (pp. 372–373).

23. I offer a sample of this sort of analysis in my essay "Fatherhood: From Phantasm to Symbol," in *The Conflict of Interpretations* (Evanston: Northwestern University Press, 1974), pp. 468–497.

24. It is in a history like this that incongruities appear, that is, behaviors, experiences, and feelings which do not "fit together." This is why Sherwood chooses to pose the question of the logic of analytic explanation at the level of the case history. For the various reasons which he gives, he chooses Freud's "rat man" as his primary example and asks in this regard what is "the psychoanalytic explanation of an individual act of behavior?" By asking this question at this level, the narrative structure of psychoanalytic explanation is immediately evident.

25. Sherwood (p. 169) speaks of "a fairly unified narrative within which a great deal of previously unexplained material takes on comprehensible forms." From this point of view, the narrative property of statements in case histories encompasses their explanatory capacity. The explanation involves episodes— fragments initially isolated, then reorganized into a comprehensive whole—but the ultimate context is narrative. In the same sense, Habermas, basing himself on Arthur Danto's logic of narrative statements (in his *Analytic Philosophy of History* [New York: Cambridge University Press, 1965], pp. 143ff.), also develops a narrative theory of interpretation and of the "process of self-formation" (ibid., pp. 258–260).

26. Can we conclude from this narrative structure of psychoanalytic statements that "the logic of psychoanalytic explanation then resolves itself into the logic of psychoanalytic narratives" (Sherwood, p. 191)? I have certain reservations on this point for reasons which concern the very place of "case histories" in the constellation of psychoanalytic statements. Although I am prepared to say that the truth claim is related to the narrative character of the facts in psychoanalysis, I question the assertion that the logic of explanation resolves itself into that of narration. It will be precisely the object of the second part of our reply to consider the role of theory in the validation process. In return, it is perfectly legitimate to isolate the truth-claim which is tied to the narrative aspect of psychoanalytic facts.

27. Sherwood himself grants this (pp. 244–257) when he concedes that *adequacy* goes along with *accuracy,* which poses the problem of validation in terms other than those of acceptability to the patient, therapeutic effectiveness, or finally adjustment to one's surroundings. Habermas expresses this conjunction of narrative accuracy and reflection in the following terms: "Only the patient's recollection decides the accuracy of the construction. If it applies, then it must also 'restore' to the patient a portion of lost life-history: then it must be able to elicit a self-reflection" (ibid., p. 230).

28. If we consider the Freudian corpus—and this is all that we are considering

at this time—"case histories" account for only a small part of it. And in this corpus, as Sherwood has shown, only the "rat man" satisfies the criteria for a good analytic explanation. Besides the analogical applications of analytic explanation to works of art, and to cultural facts like morality and religion, the major part of Freud's written work concerns the theory, the investigatory procedure, and the analytic technique itself.

29. We may, of course, agree with Sherwood—to whom we are indebted for having challenged the dichotomy between cause and motive and to whom we owe the schema of fourfold explanation in Freud—that *in a case history* the explanatory segments are incorporated into the narrative structure which forms their enveloping structure and reference. But must we not say that the means of proof are carried by these explanatory segments themselves? Psychoanalysis is an analysis precisely because the meaning of the whole always proceeds from a decomposition into fragments and from an explanation in terms of details.

30. Of course, we could give preference to the case histories in all of Freud's writings and so emphasize the narrative commitment by subordinating the explanatory commitment to it. But then the great mass of Freudian writings would be arbitrarily directed against their dominant theoretical orientation. This strategy is not without certain advantages inasmuch as it cautions us against the hypostatization of the theoretical, but in return, its disadvantage is that it tends to misconstrue the epistemological problem posed by the entire constellation of Freud's writings, divided as they are among the theory, the investigatory procedure, the method of treatment, and the case histories.

CHAPTER 14, THE CRITIQUE OF RELIGION

1. The Old Testament has an allegorical relation to the New, as when St. Paul compares Hagar and Sarah to the two alliances of servitude and freedom (Gal. 4: 24–27). "Those things," he says, "have been told allegorically." In this respect, Origen only expanded and systematized a Pauline reading of the Old Testament.

2. See Bultmann, "The Problem of Hermeneutics," in *Essays Philosophical and Theological* (London: SCM Press, 1955), pp. 234–261. In that, Bultmann's hermeneutics is opposed to that of Dilthey, which wants to be a psychological comprehension of the author's intentions and of the life that has created all the cultural expressions.

CHAPTER 15, THE LANGUAGE OF FAITH

1. This is what Bultmann called preunderstanding.

2. This is a Heideggerian theme.

3. Cf. the excellent presentation of these topics in the preface of M. Javet to my philosophy of the will and my *The Symbolism of Evil*.

Selected Bibliography

This bibliography is limited to Ricoeur's major works in English and to book-length secondary sources. The three parts of Ricoeur's *Philosophie de la Volonté* are listed first; the remainder of his books and monographs are listed in the order of publication in English. For a complete bibliography of Ricoeur's numerous articles and works in all languages, see Vansina's comprehensive bibliography listed below. For secondary sources, see Lapointe's bibliography, also listed below.

BOOKS BY PAUL RICOEUR

Freedom and Nature: The Voluntary and the Involuntary, translated by Erazim V. Kohák (Evanston: Northwestern University Press, 1966).

Fallible Man, translated by Charles Kelbley (Chicago: Henry Regnery, 1965).

The Symbolism of Evil, translated by Emerson Buchanan (New York: Harper & Row, 1967); paperback edition (Boston: Beacon Press, 1969).

History and Truth, translated by Charles A. Kelbley (Evanston: Northwestern University Press, 1965).

Husserl: An Analysis of His Phenomenology, translated by Edward G. Ballard and Lester E. Embree (Evanston: Northwestern University Press, 1967).

The Religious Significance of Atheism, with Alasdair MacIntyre (New York: Columbia University Press, 1969).

Freud and Philosophy: An Essay on Interpretation, translated by Denis Savage (New Haven: Yale University Press, 1970).

The Conflict of Interpretations: Essays in Hermeneutics, edited by Don Ihde (Evanston: Northwestern University Press, 1974).

Political and Social Essays, collected and edited by David Stewart and Joseph Bien (Athens: Ohio University Press, 1974).

Biblical Hermeneutics. Semeia 4, edited by Dominic Crossan (Missoula, Montana: Scholars Press, 1975).

Interpretation Theory: Discourse and the Surplus of Meaning (Fort Worth: The Texas Christian University Press, 1976).

The Rule of Metaphor, translated by Robert Czerny (Toronto: The University of Toronto Press, 1977).

SECONDARY SOURCES

Bourgeois, Patrick L., *Extension of Ricoeur's Hermeneutic* (The Hague: Martinus Nijhoff, 1973).

Ihde, Don, *Hermeneutic Phenomenology: The Philosophy of Paul Ricoeur* (Evanston: Northwestern University Press, 1971).

Rasmussen, David M., *Mythic-Symbolic Language and Philosophical Anthropology: A Constructive Interpretation of the Thought of Paul Ricoeur* (The Hague: Martinus Nijhoff, 1971).

Reagan, Charles E., editor, *Studies in the Philosophy of Paul Ricoeur* (Athens: Ohio University Press, 1978).[1]

PUBLISHED BIBLIOGRAPHIES

Vansina, Dirk F., "Bibliographie de Paul Ricoeur," *Revue philosophique de Louvain* 60 (1962): 394–413; 66 (1968): 85–101; 71 (1974): 156–181.

Lapointe, François H., "A Bibliography of Paul Ricoeur," *Philosophy Today* 16 (1972):28–33; 17 (1973):176–182.

Revised and updated editions of both these bibliographies are found in Reagan, *Studies in the Philosophy of Paul Ricoeur.*

Index

Aesthetics: Problems in the Philosophy of Criticism: 248 *(Ch. 10) n.3*

Agamemnon: 202

Alain, Emile Chartier: 82

Analysis Terminable and Interminable: 250 *n.10*

Analytic Philosophy of History: 253 *n.25*

Anscombe, G. E.: 156-57

Anthropology from a Pragmatic Point of View: 32

Anthropology, philosophical: 20, 160; and Adam symbol, 52; conflict in, 34-35; examples of, 28, 227; and finitude, 21

Aquinas, Saint Thomas: 18

Aron, Raymond: 161

Aristotle: and causality, 156-57; on freedom, 49; on interpretation, 126; and metaphor, 135, 146; and motivation, 65; *Nichomachean Ethics,* 49-50, 61, 252 *n.17; Organon,* 26; *Poetics,* 146-48, 161; and tragedy, 155; and volition, 61-62, 69, 72

Augustine, Saint: 97; *City of God,* 229; *Confessions,* 229; *Contra Felicem,* 247 *n.4; Contra Secundinum,* 247 *n.3; De libero arbitrio,* 247 *n.3;* on evil, 48-49, 58, 62; and Kant, 55; on original sin, 52-53; *Treatise to Simplician* 247 *n.6;* and will, 69

Austin, J. L.: 93, 136, 155

Barth, Karl: 219-20

Barthes, Roland: 152, 154

Beardsley, Monroe: 130-31, 135, 138, 140–41, 143, 146, 248 *(Ch. 10) n.3*

Being and Nothingness: 83

Being and Time: 107

Benveniste, Emile: 114, 176; *Essays on General Linguistics,* 121

Berggren, Douglas: 130

Bergson, Henri: 28-29, 171, 181

Black, Max: 114, 130, 138, 140-41, 248 *(Ch. 10) n.2*

Body: in Marcel, 81; in Merleau-Ponty, 81, 84; and motivation, 73; as organ, 7-8, 18; "owned body," 81-82, 87; phenomenology of, 13; as totality of powers, 14; and the voluntary, 8, 12, 17; and will, 74

Bonhoeffer, Dietrich: 219

Bridgman, P. W.: 249 *n.3*

Brunschvicg, Leon: 82

Bultmann, Rudolf: 220, 254 *(Ch. 15) n.1;* and biblical exegesis, 100; demythologization, 219-221; hermeneutics, 222, 254 *(Ch. 14) n.2;* post-Bultmannian schools, 88, 91

Cartesian Linguistics: 117

Cartesian Meditations: 77, 101

Cassirer, Ernst: 98

Chomsky, Noam: 118; *Cartesian Linguistics,* 117; *Current Issues in Linguistic Theory,* 117

City of God: 229

Civilization and Its Discontents: 173

Cogito: 9, 170, 178, 180; as act, 16; Cartesian, 4, 179; and consciousness, 177, 179; and experience of the other, 10; false cogito, 104, 178; in Husserl, 101-102; and vital needs, 11

Collingwood, R. G.: 161-62

Concept of Dread: 79, 236

Confessions: 229

The Conflict of Interpretations: 253 *n.23*

Consciousness: false, 214, 217; intentionality of, 77; and perception, 82

Contra Felicem: 247 *n.4*

Contra Secundinum: 247 *n.3*

Copernicus: 179

Critique of Practical Reason: 50

Current Issues in Linguistic Theory: 116

Danto, Arthur: 159, 253 *n.25*

Darwin, Charles: 179

De libero arbitrio: 247 *n.3*

Demythologizing: 231-32; 235; of evil in Augustine, 48; reflection as, 47

Descartes, René: 150, 169, 171; and the *cogito,* 4, 179; and consciousness, 213; dialectic, 25; dualism, 3-4; on error, 62-63; on motivation, 65; starting point for philosophy, 37; *Treatise on the Passions,* 3, 13, 17; on will, 69

Dilthey, Wilhelm: 91, 102, 134, 151, 161, 232, 254 *(Ch. 14) n.2;* and discourse, 153; theory of *Verstehen,* 150-52, 155; on text, 97

Edelson, Marshall: 251 *n.14*

Ego: and id, 191; and libido, 173; and superego, 172, 177

Elaide, Mircea: 89, 98, 106, 232

Emotion: in Descartes, 18; power of, 14-15; psychology of, 12

Enuma Elish: 42

"Essay on Radical Evil": 21, 50, 54, 247 *n.7-11*

Essays on General Linguistics: 121

Essays Philosophical and Theological: 254 *(Ch. 14) n.2*

Ethics (Spinoza): 105

Evans, Donald: 92

Evil: ethical vision of, 48, 51; as involuntary, 53; problem of, 87

Explanation and Understanding: 155

Fallible Man: 20, 86

Feuerbach, Ludwig: 89, 217, 219

Fichte, Johann Gottlieb: 177

Finitude et Culpabilité. See *Freedom and Nature* and *The Symbolism of Evil*

Freedom: and the body, 82; and fate, 65; in Marcel, 83; phenomenology of, 83-84; ultimate nature of, 61

Freedom and Nature: The Voluntary and the Involuntary: 248 *(Ch. 6) n.1*

Frege, Gottlob: 114-15

Freud, Sigmund: 226, 232; *Analysis Terminable and Interminable,* 250 *n.10;* archeology, 106, 170, 180; *Civilization and Its Discontents,* 173; critique of religion, 178, 213; development of his work, 173, 253-254 *n.28;* on dreams, 99, 193, 208, 250 *n.11,* 251 *n.13; The Ego and the Id,* 196, 251 *n.14;* on false consciousness, 102, 104, 214; and fantasy, 252 *n.21-22; The Future of an Illusion,* 217; and hermeneutics, 89, 247 *n.2;* on the id, 169, 173, 177, 179, 251 *n.14; Instincts and Their Vicissitudes,* 189; and imagination, 249 *n.5; The Interpretation of Dreams,* 172, 184, 189, 192-94, 250 *n.12; Introductory Lectures on Psychoanalysis,* 184, 188; metapsychology, 99, 173, 196; and mixed discourse, 169; *Moses and Monotheism,* 217; and mythology, 15;

New Introductory Lectures on Psychoanalysis, 184; *An Outline of Psychoanalysis*, 184, 249 *n.3*; *The Papers on Metapsychology*, 173; Project of 1895, 184, 197; psychoanalytic method, 250 *n.10*, 251 *n.13*; *Studies on Hysteria*, 190; *Three Essays on the Theory of Sexuality*, 172, 189; *Totem and Taboo*, 217; and the unconsciousness, 250 *n.10*

Freud and Philosophy: 88, 89, 176, 199, 203, 248 *(Ch. 10) n.4, (Ch. 12) n.1-4*, 252 *n.16*

The Future of an Illusion: 217

Gabriel Marcel et Karl Jaspers: 248 *(Ch. 6) n.2*

Gadamer, Hans-Georg: 91, 144, 154

Galileo: 63, 77, 150

Geach, Peter: 114

Genealogy of Morals: 80

Gestalt psychology: 10

Gilkey, Langdon: 92

Guillaume, Gustave: 117-18

Habermas, Jürgen: 196-98, 202, 204, 251 *n.16*, 253 *n.25*

Habit: 12, 15; pacifying function of, 18; Ravaisson on, 14, 28

Harnack, Adolf von, 220

Hartmann, Heinz, 249 *n.2*

Hegel, Georg Wilhelm Friedrich: 181-82, 202, 236, 251 *n.16*; and description, 81; *Logic,* 76, 78; on the "negative," 78-79, 83; objective spirit, 151; *Phenomenology of Mind,* 76, 78, 106, 153, 170, 181; on religion, 220

Heidegger, Martin: 103, 145, 241, 254 *(Ch. 15) n.2*; *Being and Time,* 107; early work, 70; fundamental ontology, 82, 101; and hermeneutic circle, 104, 207, 222; on inauthenticity, 86

Hempel, Carl: 162-64

Hermeneutics: biblical, 92, 221-22; hermeneutic circle, 45-46, 90, 104, 134, 145, 207, 222; Jungian, 247 *n.1*; and phenomenology, 100; and philosophy, 232; and psychoanalysis, 105, 180, 247 *n.2*; and reflective thought, 87, 232; of suspicion, 214; and symbolism, 88, 101, 107, 236; task of, 215, 224, 234; and the text, 45, 135

Hirsch, E. D.: 142

Hjelmslev, Louis: 109-110, 118-19, 121, 176

Hobbes, Thomas: 230

Hope: 57

Humbolt, Wilhelm von: 111, 120-21, 123, 143, 230

Hume, David: 156

Husserl, Edmund: 12, 87; on the body, 80; *Cartesian Meditations,* 77, 101; on the *cogito,* 101; on the ego, 28; and existential phenomenology, 76-77; *Ideen I,* 101; on intentionality, 83; *Krisis,* 66; later work, 80; *Lebenswelt,* 66, 100; *Logical Investigations,* 77, 100, 101-102, 114; and the negative, 83; and phenomenology, 76; and phenomenology of will, 66, 70; and starting point for philosophy, 37

Hyppolite, Jean: 181

The Idea of History: 162

Ideen I: 101

Imagination: 11, 231; and psychoanalysis, 249 *n.5*; transcendental, 24-27, 30

Instincts and Their Vicissitudes: 189

Intention (Anscombe): 156

Intentionality: and action, 7; and consciousness, 9, 77; and evaluation, 12; in Husserl, 66, 83; intentional objects, 32; and volition, 67, 69

The Interpretation of Dreams: 172, 184, 189, 192, 193, 194, 250 *n.12*

Introductory Lectures on Psychoanalysis: 184, 188

260   Index

Jacobson, Roman: 129
Jaspers, Karl: 86-87
Jeremias, Joachim: 91
Jung, Carl Gustav: 247 *n.2*
Kant, Immanuel: 3, 31, 169, 171, 229–
30, 237; *Anthropology from a
Pragmatic Point of View*, 32;
antinomies, 63, 65, 70–71; and
Augustine, 55; *Critique of Practical
Reason*, 50; and duty, 73; "Essay
on Radical Evil," 21, 50, 54, 247
n.7-11; on freedom, 52; and imagination, 203; on morality, 48, 50–
51; and motivation, 65; regulative
ideas, 19, 236; *Religion Within the
Limits of Reason Alone*, 50; on
respect, 30; transcendental deduction, 234; transcendental imagination, 20, 24–27, 30; on will, 69; on
world, 78
*Karl Jaspers et la philosophie de l'exis-
tence:* 248 (*Ch. 6*) *n.2*
Kerygma: 91, 213, 220–21, 223, 229,
232, 235
Kierkegaard, Sören: 223, 237; on
anxiety, 83; *Concept of Dread*,
79, 236; on description, 81; on
existence, 79; and existential
phenomenology, 80; *Philosophical
Fragments*, 79; *Postscript*, 79;
Sickness Unto Death, 22–23
Knowledge and Human Interests: 196
Krafft-Ebing, Baron Richard von: 184
Krisis: 66

Lacan, Jacques: 191
Language: and action, 199; artificial,
129, 230; creative aspects of, 123,
233; and discourse, 123; games,
156–57, 164, 175; and hermeneutics, 91, 145; and history, 163, 234;
nature of, 112; ordinary, 87, 92,
127, 129; and polysemy, 120, 124–
28; and psychoanalysis, 185, 192–
93; and religion, 224, 230, 237;
scientific use of, 128, 233–34;
written and spoken, 143

*Language and Interpretation in Psycho-
analysis:* 251 *n.14*
Laporte, M.: 18
Lebenswelt: 66, 100
Leenhardt, Maurice: 98
Leeuw, G. van der: 98, 106
Leibniz: logic, 79; *Monadology*, 72,
105, 175, 177; on motivation, 64–
65, 72
Lévi-Strauss, Claude: 90, 118, 152
Libido: 172, 174, 189, 232, 249 *n.6*
Linguistics: 89, 113
Logic (Hegel): 76, 78
Logic of Explanation in Psychoanalysis:
200
Logical Investigations: 77, 100, 101–
102, 114
Logos: as discourse, 12; divine, 58; as
intention, 7; and *mythos*, 24; of
phainomena, 66; and speech, 82

Machiavelli: 230
Macquarrie, John: 92
Malebranche, Nicholas: 18
Marcel, Gabriel: 81–82, 87; on being
and having, 86; on freedom, 83; on
problems and mystery, 225
Marrou, Henri: 161
Marx, Karl: 89, 197, 218, 229, 234; on
anxiety, 83; early work, 217; and
eschatology, 217; on false consciousness, 102, 214; and interpretation, 232; phenomenology of
economic existence, 76, 214
Meditations (Descartes): 3
Merleau-Ponty, Maurice: 181; and existential phenomenology, 82; on
"owned body," 81, 84; on perception, 228; *Phenomenology of Perception*, 81
Metaphor: 242; in Aristotle, 146–47;
and discourse, 136–37; dynamics
of, 131; and explanation, 139; and
polysemy, 120–21, 129, 131, 138;
in psychoanalysis, 194
*Models and Metaphors: Studies in
Language and Philosophy:* 248
(*Ch. 10*) *n.2*

Monadology: 72, 105, 175, 177

Moses and Monotheism: 217

Motive, motivation: and action, 11, 61; and cause, 200; and choice, 18; confusion of, 19; and decision, 6; and desire, 64; language of, 87, 158–59; phenomonology of, 71; in Plato, 64; total field of, 74, 159

Mounier, Emmanuel: 84

Myth: Adamic, 43, 48, 51, 55; in Aristotle, 146; Babylonian, 56; in Bultmann, 220, 222; in Freud, 15; and hermeneutics, 88; and *mimesis,* 146–47; and *mythos* and *logos,* 24; Orphic, 48; philosophic assimilation of, 41; richness of, 44, 235; tragic, 48; and truth, 45

Nabert, Jean: 102, 177

Nagel, Ernest: 249 *n.2*

Neoplatonism: 50, 98; *see also* Plotinus

New Introductory Lectures on Psychoanalysis: 184

Newton, Sir Isaac: 63, 150

Nicomachean Ethics: 49–50, 61, 252 *n.17*

Nietzsche, Friedrich Wilhelm: 89, 218, 232; on description, 81; on false consciousness, 102, 234; *Genealogy of Morals,* 80; and religion, 213; on values, 97, 214–16, 252 *n.18*

Organon: 126

An Outline of Psychoanalysis: 184, 249 *n.3*

The Papers on Metapsychology: 173

Pascal, Blaise: 22–23

Paul, Saint: 219, 221; and allegory, 254 *(Ch. 14) n.1;* hermeneutics of, 221; on justification, 57

Pelagius: 48, 53

Perrin, Norman: 92

Phaedo: 3, 64

Phaedrus: 22

Phenomenology: existential, 76, 82, 85, 87; of freedom, 84; in Hegel, 76; Husserlian, 66, 70; in Kierke-

gaard, 79; and linguistic analysis, 93; in Marx, 76; meaning of, 75; transcendental, 76; of will, 69

Phenomenology of Perception: 81

Phenomenology of Mind: 76, 78, 106, 153, 170, 181

Philebus: 3, 21

Philosophical Fragments: 79

Philosophical Investigations: 100

Plato: 23, 169, 171, 177, 230; on motivation, 64; on non-being, 49; ontology of, 3, 77, 82; *Phaedo,* 3, 64, *Phaedrus,* 22; *Philebus,* 3, 21; *Republic,* 20, 247 *n.5;* on the soul, 29; *Symposium,* 22; *thumos,* 32; *Timaeus,* 3

Plotinus: 49

Poetics: 146–48, 161

Postscript: 79

Principia Mathematica: 129

Principles of Semantics: 124

Prolegomena to a Theory of Language: 109

Prometheus Bound: 42

Psychoanalysis: 15; and dream symbolism, 98, 189; and hermeneutics, 105, 193; and language, 71, 88, 185, 192; and phenomenology of will, 72; problem of verification in, 205ff.; proof in, 184ff., 250 *n.9;* and symbolism, 99, 190, 198; theory and therapy in, 184, 192, 195

Pythagoras: 23

Rapaport, David: 249 *n.3*

Ravaisson-Mollien, Felix: 14, 28

Religion Within the Limits of Reason Alone: 50

Republic: 20, 247 *n.5*

Richards, I. A.: 130, 138

Rilke, Rainer Maria: 19

Russell, Bertrand: 129

Sartre, Jean-Paul: *Being and Nothingness,* 83; and existential psychoanalysis, 80; on freedom, 83; on the negative, 83; on the Other, 84

Saussure, Ferdinand de: 109–111, 113, 121, 152, 176

Schelling, Friedrich Wilhelm von: 231

Schliermacher, Friedrich Daniel Ernst: 97, 103, 126, 134, 232

Semantics: 89, 97, 121; of action, 199; of desire, 174, 178, 186, 214; and hermeneutics, 100; and reflective analysis, 104

Semiology: 87, 114; and philosophy of language, 118

Shakespeare: 231

Sherwood, Michael: 200, 204–206, 253 n.24–25, 27, 254 n.29

Sickness Unto Death: 22–23

Skinner, B. F.: 249 n.3

Spinoza, Benedict: 175, 181, 217, 237; Ethics, 105

Stern, W.: 31

Stoics: 28, 78, 121

Strasser, Stephan: 29

The Structure of Psychoanalytic Theory: 249 n.3

Structuralism: 88, 90, 111, 116, 153–54; see also Lévi-Strauss

Studies on Hysteria: 190

Subjectivity: 10, 15

Symbol: 22; contrast with symbolic logic, 37, 230; definition of, 98; and hermeneutics, 88, 107; intentional structure of, 38; and myth, 41; and reflective thought, 47; and religion, 182; of the unconscious, 176, 198; as unique language, 38, 233

Symbolism of Evil: 86, 88, 177, 247 n.1

Symposium: 22

Tertullian: 229

Theodicy: 53

Three Essays on the Theory of Sexuality: 172, 189

Timaeus: 3

Totem and Taboo: 217

Treatise on the Passions: 3, 13, 17

Treatise to Simplician: 247 n.6

Tractatus: 129

Treatise of the History of Religions: 232

Turbayne, Colin: 130

Ullmann, Stephen: 124

Valéry, Paul: 228

Validity in Interpretation: 142

Vocabulary of Psychoanalysis: 191

Von Rad, Gerhard: 71

Von Wright, Georg Henrik: 155

Weber, Max: 161

Wittgenstein, Ludwig: 93, 145, 155; Philosophical Investigations, 100; Tractatus, 129